WORLD EXPLORER

EUROPE AND RUSSIA

PRENTICE HALL
Needham, Massachusetts
Upper Saddle River, New Jersey

Program Authors

Heidi Hayes Jacobs

Heidi Hayes Jacobs has served as an educational consultant to more than 500 schools across the nation. Dr. Jacobs is an adjunct professor in the Department of Curriculum on Teaching at Teachers College, Columbia University. She completed her undergraduate studies at the University of Utah in her hometown of Salt Lake City. She received an M.A. from the University of Massachusetts, Amherst, and completed her doctoral work at Columbia University's Teachers College in 1981.

The backbone of Dr. Jacobs's experience comes from her years as a teacher of high school, middle school, and elementary school students. As an educational consultant, she works with K–12 schools and districts on curriculum reform and strategic planning.

Brenda Randolph

Brenda Randolph is the former Director of the Outreach Resource Center at the African Studies Program at Howard University, Washington, D.C. She is the Founder and Director of Africa Access, a bibliographic service on Africa for schools. She received her B.A. in history with high honors from North Carolina Central University, Durham, and her M.A. in African studies with honors from Howard University. She completed further graduate studies at the University of Maryland, College Park, where she was awarded a Graduate Fellowship.

Brenda Randolph has published numerous articles in professional journals and bulletins. She currently serves as library media specialist in Montgomery County Public Schools, Maryland.

Michal L. LeVasseur

Michal LeVasseur is an educational consultant in the field of geography. She is an adjunct professor of geography at the University of Alabama, Birmingham, and serves with the Alabama Geographic Alliance. Her undergraduate and graduate work is in the fields of anthropology (B.A.), geography (M.A.), and science education (Ph.D.).

Dr. LeVasseur's specialization has moved increasingly into the area of geography education. In 1996, she served as Director of the National Geographic Society's Summer Geography Workshop. As an educational consultant, she has worked with the National Geographic Society as well as with schools to develop programs and curricula for geography.

Special Program Consultant
Yvonne S. Gentzler, Ph.D.
School of Education
University of Idaho
Moscow, Idaho

Content Consultant on Russia, Eastern Europe, Central Asia
Janet Valliant
Center for Russian, Eastern European, and Central Asian Studies
Harvard University
Cambridge, Massachusetts

Content Consultant on Western Europe
Ruth Mitchell-Pitts
Center for West European Studies
University of North Carolina
Chapel Hill, North Carolina

PRENTICE HALL
Simon & Schuster Education Group
A VIACOM COMPANY

Upper Saddle River, New Jersey
Needham, Massachusetts

ISBN 0-13-433693-3

6 7 8 9 10   01 00 99 98

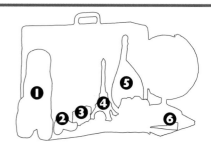

On the Cover

❶ Three Russian babushka nesting dolls

❷ Miniature wooden shoes from the Netherlands

❸ Model of an English double-decker bus

❹ Model of the Eiffel Tower

❺ Miniature Ukrainian bandura (a stringed instrument)

❻ Five-pound note from Great Britain

Content Consultants for the World Explorer Program

Africa
Barbara Brown
Africa Studies Center
Boston University
Boston, Massachusetts

Ancient World
Maud Gleason
Department of Classics
Stanford University
Stanford, California

East Asia
Leslie Swartz
Harvard University
    East Asian Outreach Program at
    the Children's Museum
    of Boston
Boston, Massachusetts

Latin America
Daniel Mugan
Center for Latin American Studies
University of Florida
Gainesville, Florida

Middle East
Elizabeth Barlow
Center for Middle Eastern and
    North African Studies
University of Michigan
Ann Arbor, Michigan

North Africa
Laurence Michalak
Center for Middle East Studies
University of California
Berkeley, California

Religion
Michael Sells
Department of Religion
Haverford College
Haverford, Pennsylvania

South Asia
Robert Young
South Asia Regional Studies
University of Pennsylvania
Philadelphia, Pennsylvania

Teacher Advisory Board

Jerome Balin
Lincoln Junior High
    School
Naperville, Illinois

Linda Boaen
Baird School
Fresno, California

Nikki L. Born
Harllee Middle School
Bradenton, Florida

Carla Bridges
Concord Middle School
Concord, North Carolina

Bruce L. Campbell
Walled Lake Middle
    School
Walled Lake, Michigan

**Barbara Coats
Grabowski**
Russell Middle School
Omaha, Nebraska

David Herman
North Carroll Middle
    School
Hampstead, Maryland

Fred Hitz
Wilson Middle School
Muncie, Indiana

William B. Johnson
La Mesa Junior High
    School
Canyon Country,
    California

Kristi Karis
West Ottawa Middle
    School
Holland, Michigan

Kristen Koch
Discovery Middle School
Orlando, Florida

Peggy McCarthy
Beulah School
Beulah, Colorado

Deborah J. Miller
Whitney Young Middle
    School
Detroit, Michigan

Lawrence Peglow
Greenway Middle School
Pittsburgh, Pennsylvania

Lyn Shiver
Northwestern Middle
    School
Alpharetta, Georgia

The World Explorer Team

*The editors, designers, marketer, market researcher, manager, production buyer, and manufacturing buyer
who made up the World Explorer team are listed below.*

Jackie Bedoya, Bruce Bond, Ellen Brown, David Lippman, Catherine Martin-Hetmansky,
Nancy Rogier, Olena Serbyn, Carol Signorino, John Springer, Susan Swan

TABLE OF CONTENTS

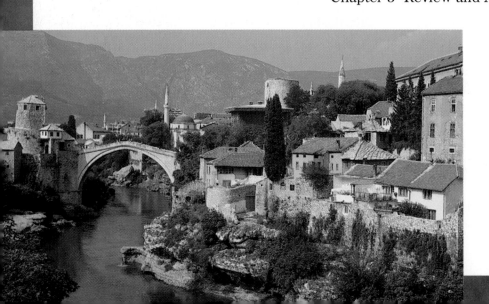

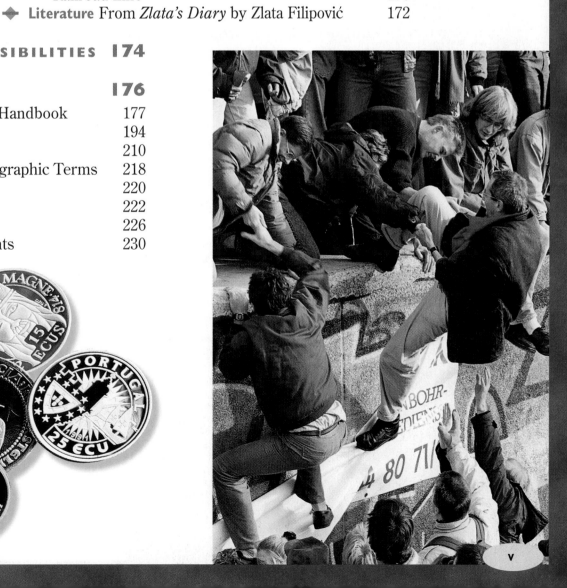

OF SPECIAL
INTEREST

A hands-on, active approach to practicing and applying key social studies skills

Engaging, step-by-step activities for exploring important topics in Europe and Russia

High-interest selections written by authors from Eastern and Western Europe tell about the lives of young people

HEROES

MAPS

CHARTS, GRAPHS, AND TABLES

READ ACTIVELY

How can I get the most out of my social studies book?

How does my reading relate to my world? Answering questions like these means that you are an active reader, an involved reader. As an active reader, you are in charge of the reading situation!

The following strategies tell how to think and read as an active reader. You don't need to use all of these strategies all the time. Feel free to choose the ones that work best in each reading situation. You might use several at a time, or you might go back and forth among them. They can be used in any order.

BEFORE YOU READ

Give yourself a purpose

The sections in this book begin with a list called "Questions to Explore." These questions focus on key ideas presented in the section. They give you a purpose for reading. You can create your own purpose by asking questions like these: How does the topic relate to my life? How might I use what I learn at school or at home?

Preview

To preview a reading selection, first read its title. Then look at the pictures and read the captions. Also read any headings in the selection. Then ask yourself: What is the reading selection about? What do the pictures and headings tell about the selection?

Reach into your background

What do you already know about the topic of the selection? How can you use what you know to help you understand what you are going to read?

Ask questions

Suppose you are reading about the continent of South America. Some questions you might ask are: Where is South America? What countries are found there? Why are some of the countries large and others small? Asking questions like these can help you gather evidence and gain knowledge.

Predict

As you read, make a prediction about what will happen and why. Or predict how one fact might affect another fact. Suppose you are reading about South America's climate. You might make a prediction about how the climate affects where people live. You can change your mind as you gain new information.

Connect

Connect your reading to your own life. Are the people discussed in the selection like you or someone you know? What would you do in similar situations? Connect your reading to something you have already read. Suppose you have already read about the ancient Greeks. Now you are reading about the ancient Romans. How are they alike? How are they different?

Visualize

What would places, people, and events look like in a movie or a picture? As you read about India, you could visualize the country's heavy rains. What do they look like? How do they sound? As you read about geography, you could visualize a volcanic eruption.

Assess yourself

What did you find out? Were your predictions on target? Did you find answers to your questions?

Respond

Talk about what you have read. What did you think? Share your ideas with your classmates.

Follow up

Show what you know. Use what you have learned to do a project. When you do projects, you continue to learn.

EUROPE AND RUSSIA

Europe is a continent filled with countries. Russia is one country that actually lies on two continents. Part of Russia is in Europe. The rest of Russia is in Asia. Together, Europe and Russia form a gigantic landmass. Together, they also form a rich pattern of different cultures, histories, and languages that stretch back hundreds of years. Deep roots in the past affect everyday life in this region, as you will learn in your study of Europe and Russia.

Guiding Questions

The readings and activities in this book will help you discover answers to these Guiding Questions.

- ☞ How has physical geography affected the environment and cultures of Europe and Russia?

- ☞ How have the people of Europe and Russia been shaped by historical experiences?

- ☞ What values and traditions do the people of Europe and Russia have in common?

- ☞ How have modern times changed the ways of life in the region?

- ☞ How do different people in Europe and Russia get along with each other?

Project Preview

You can also discover answers to the Guiding Questions by working on projects. Preview the following projects and choose one that you might like to do.

Changing Climates Make a survival guide for someone moving to a new climate.

Olympic Cities Plan a summer or winter Olympic season in a European city. Tell and show what advantages that city offers.

Tourism in Eastern Europe Choose one country in Eastern Europe. Create a travel ad for its land and culture.

Folklore Corner Set up a display of traditional European folktale books. Add visual aids and labels to reflect the countries' cultures.

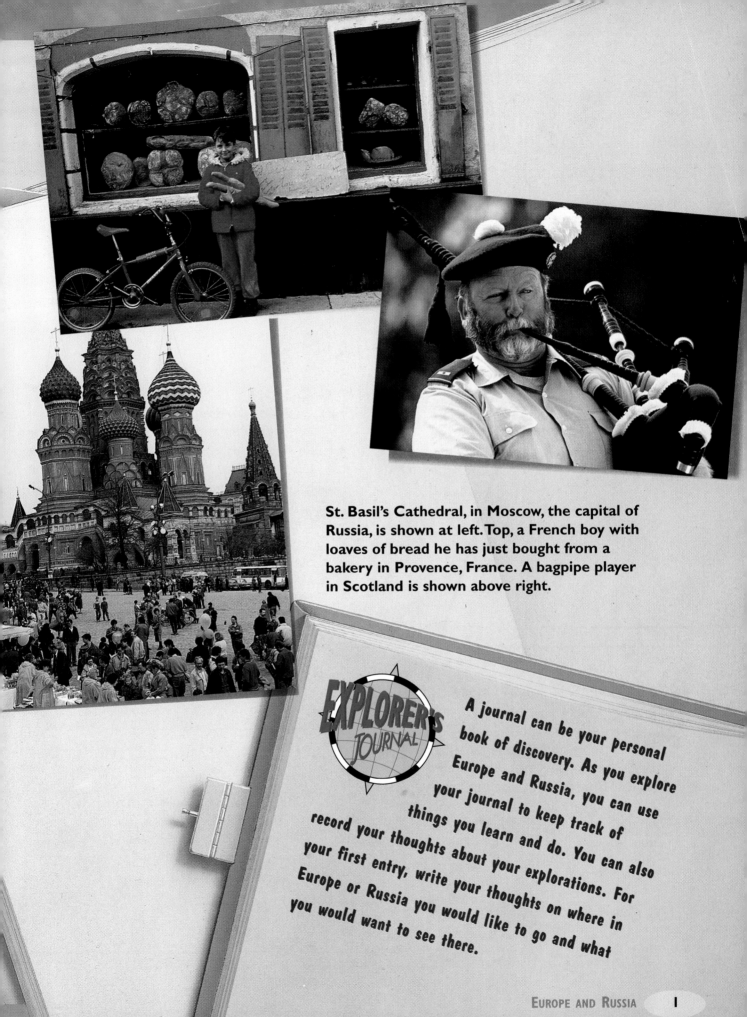

St. Basil's Cathedral, in Moscow, the capital of Russia, is shown at left. Top, a French boy with loaves of bread he has just bought from a bakery in Provence, France. A bagpipe player in Scotland is shown above right.

EXPLORER'S JOURNAL

A journal can be your personal book of discovery. As you explore Europe and Russia, you can use your journal to keep track of things you learn and do. You can also record your thoughts about your explorations. For your first entry, write your thoughts on where in Europe or Russia you would like to go and what you would want to see there.

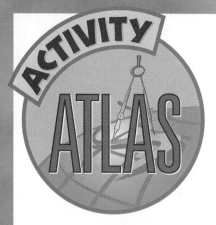

ACTIVITY ATLAS

Europe and Russia

Learning about Europe and Russia means being an explorer and a geographer. No explorer would start out without first checking some facts. Begin by exploring the maps of Europe and Russia on the following pages.

Relative Location

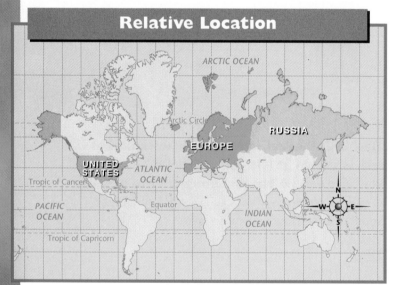

LOCATION

1. Explore Europe and Russia's Location

A geographer must know where a place is located in order to study it. Use the map at left to describe Europe and Russia's location relative to the United States. Which ocean separates Europe and Russia from the United States? Which is closer to the Equator, Europe and Russia or the United States? Which is closer to the Arctic Circle? Many people think the climates of Europe and the United States are similar. Look at the map. Then list three reasons why this might be so.

PLACE

2. Explore Europe and Russia's Size

Are Europe and Russia together larger or smaller than the United States? How does the size of Europe alone compare to that of the continental United States? Based on what you know, estimate the number of countries in Europe.

Relative Size

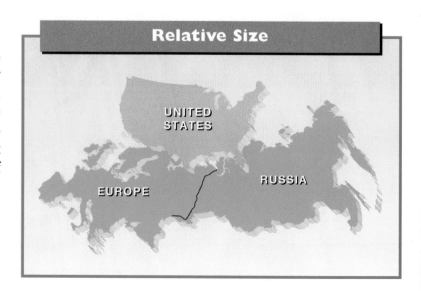

REGIONS

3. Compare Climates in Europe and Russia

As you can see from the map below, Europe and Russia have a wide variety of climates. Find Russia on the map. What are its three major climate regions? How does Russia's latitude, or distance from the Equator, affect its climate? Compare Russia's climate regions with those in Europe. Does Europe have a greater or lesser variety of climate regions than Russia? Generally speaking, does Europe have a warmer climate than Russia? Find Moscow and Rome on the map. Which city do you think has a warmer climate? Why?

INTERACTION

4. Discuss and Predict Ways of Living

The climate affects how people live. In warm countries such as Greece and Spain, many people live in houses with thick walls, which remain cool in the hot sun. In colder countries like Sweden, houses often have steep roofs to keep the snow from piling up on them. In what other ways do you think people have adapted to their climates? What kinds of foods do you think people in warmer climates are more likely to eat? What kinds of recreation might you find in cooler climates?

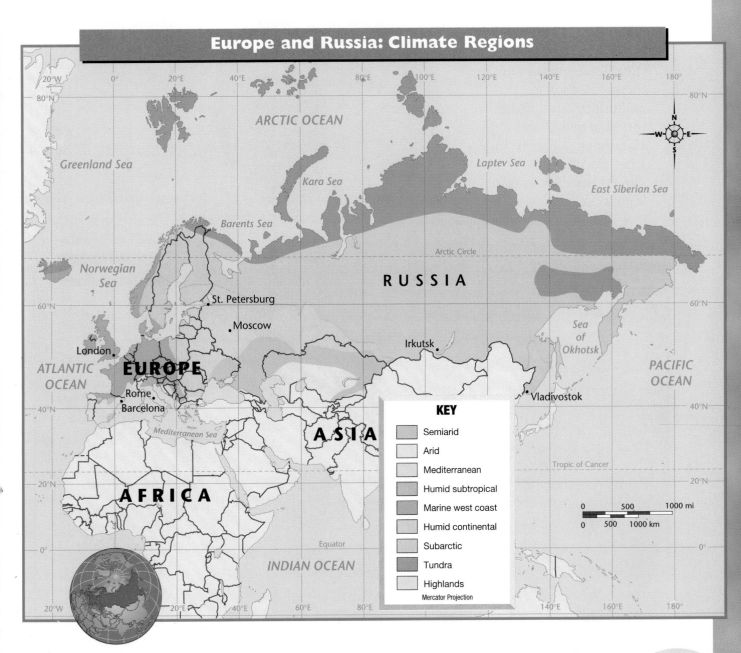

Europe and Russia: Climate Regions

KEY
- Semiarid
- Arid
- Mediterranean
- Humid subtropical
- Marine west coast
- Humid continental
- Subarctic
- Tundra
- Highlands

Mercator Projection

0   500   1000 mi
0   500   1000 km

5. Plan Geo Leo's Trip on the Rails Geo Leo wants to explore Europe and Russia by train. Read the goals he has set for his trip. Then, use the map below to help him plan generally which routes he should take. Estimate the distance of each route.

A. *"After my plane lands in Paris, I want to travel to Warsaw by the shortest route."*

B. *"From Warsaw, I want to go as far north as possible on my way to Moscow."*

C. *"From Moscow, I want to travel to Rome. I want to pass through as many major cities as I can on the way."*

D. *"From Rome, I will need to head straight back to Paris. What's the shortest route I can take?"*

BONUS

Geo Leo will be traveling in March. Using the climate map from the previous page and information from the Map and Globe Handbook, suggest what clothing he should pack for each leg of his journey.

GEO LEO

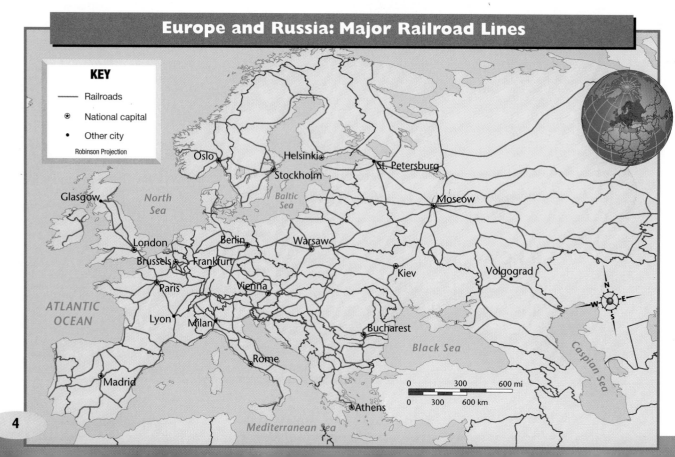

Europe and Russia: Major Railroad Lines

KEY

— Railroads
⊛ National capital
• Other city
Robinson Projection

PLACE

6. Compare Population Densities Population density is the number of people living within a certain area. Compare the parts of Europe that have many people to the parts that have only a few people. Do the same for Russia. How would you describe the population density of the two regions? What geographic features might explain the low population density of countries like Finland and Switzerland? What other factors might affect population?

MOVEMENT

7. Examine Population and Transportation Notice the population density in the northernmost part of Europe and Russia. Now look at the same region on the transportation map on the previous page. How many railroads do you see in this region compared to regions of the same size in central and southern Europe and Russia? Do regions with more people tend to have more or fewer rail routes? In what other ways might population and transportation affect each other?

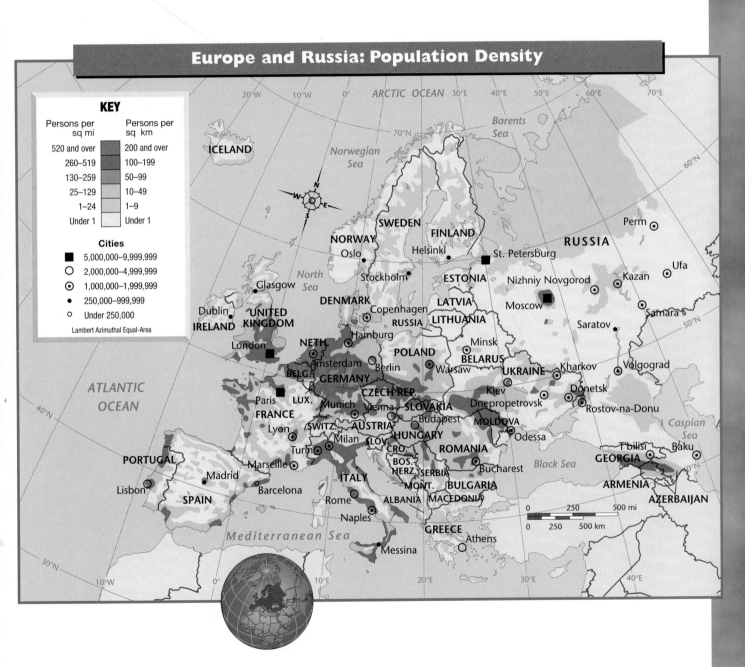

Europe and Russia: Population Density

KEY

Persons per sq mi	Persons per sq km
520 and over	200 and over
260–519	100–199
130–259	50–99
25–129	10–49
1–24	1–9
Under 1	Under 1

Cities
- ■ 5,000,000–9,999,999
- ○ 2,000,000–4,999,999
- ◎ 1,000,000–1,999,999
- • 250,000–999,999
- ○ Under 250,000

Lambert Azimuthal Equal-Area

8. Identify the Former Soviet Union From the 1920s until 1991, some of the countries in Eastern Europe were republics of the Soviet Union. Today, all of these countries are independent nations. The map below shows the former Soviet Union. The former republics are shown by color. Focus on Russia's western border. According to the map, how many countries in Eastern Europe are former Soviet republics? You can see that, in terms of size, Russia dominated the other Soviet republics.

9. Trace the Iron Curtain From the late 1940s to the late 1980s, the Soviet Union and other Eastern European countries were kept separate from Western Europe. The border between these two regions was called the Iron Curtain because Eastern European governments did not let people cross it freely. Look at the map on the next page. Find the countries on the eastern side of the Iron Curtain. Which ones were not part of the Soviet Union? Which country was divided by the Iron Curtain? How do you think this border affected life in that country?

Former Republics of the Soviet Union

The Iron Curtain

KEY

— Iron Curtain

— National boundary

• City

Lambert Azimuthal Equal-Area Projection

0 150 300 mi
0 150 300 km

SWEDEN

DENMARK

Baltic Sea

Potsdam • • Berlin Warsaw •

EAST GERMANY POLAND

WEST GERMANY CZECHOSLOVAKIA

SWITZ AUSTRIA HUNGARY

ITALY

YUGOSLAVIA

ALBANIA

GREECE TURKEY

ROMANIA

BULGARIA

Black Sea

SOVIET UNION

Tyrrhenian Sea

▼ In the picture below, people in Estonia gather in a town square to demonstrate their wish for independence for their country.

Gulf of Anadyr

Anadyr •

Bering Sea

Magadan •

Sea of Okhotsk

Vladivostok •

Sea of Japan

N. KOREA JAPAN

S. KOREA

EUROPE AND RUSSIA

Physical Geography

SECTION 1
Land and Water

SECTION 2
Climate and Vegetation

SECTION 3
Natural Resources

PICTURE ACTIVITIES

Water and land have affected where and how people live in Europe and Russia. The picture shows a freighter traveling the Rhine (ryn) River in Germany. To get yourself thinking about the ways in which geography affects people's lives, complete the following activities.

Study the picture
How do you think water is being used? What is the land used for? How can these uses of water and land help certain areas of Europe to grow?

Make a comparison
Compare the area shown in the picture to the area where you live. Consider the features of the land, the plant life, and what you can tell about the climate. How is the area similar to the area where you live? How is it different? Make a list of the similarities and differences.

Land and Water

Reach Into Your Background

How are land and water used where you live? Do you live near fertile plains, forested mountains, or an ocean coast? Do you live in a farming region or an industrial city? Think of the physical features of your area. Then list two ways in which these features have affected your way of life.

Questions to Explore

1. What are the main physical features of Europe and Russia?
2. How have the physical features of Europe and Russia affected where and how people live?

Key Terms

polder
population density
peninsula
plateau
tributary
navigable

Key Places

Europe
Russia
Eurasia
Ural Mountains
Alps
Siberia

If you cross a farm field in the Netherlands (NETH ur luhndz), you might well be walking where sea waves once roared. Water once covered more than two fifths of the country. Centuries ago, the people of the Netherlands began an endless battle to make land where there was water. They built long walls called dikes to hold back the water. They pumped the water into canals that empty into the North Sea. They also created patches of new land called **polders** (POHL durz).

The polders that lie below sea level are always filling with water. Netherlanders must continually pump them out. In early times, they set whirling windmills to do this work. Now they use pumps with powerful motors. Keeping the polders dry has always been important because the richest farmlands and the largest cities in the Netherlands are located on polders.

▼ Polders, like the ones shown on either side of this canal, make up about 3,000 square miles (7,770 sq km) of the Netherlands.

Why have the Netherlanders worked so hard to make new land? Consider the country's population density, or average number of people living in an area. The Netherlands has more than 1,175 people per square mile (453 people per sq km). By comparison, the world average is 99 people per square mile (38 people per sq km). The Netherlanders need all the land they can get.

Europe, in general, has a much higher population density than most of the world. By comparison, Russia has a much lower population density—only 23 people per square mile (9 people per sq km). Few people live in the vast plains and mountains of eastern Russia. The poor soil and cold climate make it a difficult place to live.

Size and Location

Europe and Russia are parts of Eurasia, the world's largest landmass. This landmass is made up of two continents, Europe and Asia. The country of Russia stretches over both continents. About one fourth of Russia is in Europe; the rest is in Asia. Find the Ural (YOOR ul) Mountains on the physical map of Asia in the Atlas at the back of the book. These mountains mark the dividing line between Europe and Asia.

A Small Continent and a Large Country   Europe is a small continent. Only Australia is smaller. While Europe lacks size, it has many different countries. Some 48 countries are located on the continent. As you might guess, most of the countries are small. Many are the size of an average state in the United States. Russia, on the other hand, is the largest country in the world. It is almost twice the size of Canada or the United States.

Farther North Than You Might Expect   How far north do you think Europe and Russia are? As far north as the United States? You can figure this out by comparing latitudes. First, find the World Political Map in the Atlas. Second, follow one of the lines of latitude across the map from the United States to Eurasia. You will see that a lot of Europe, and nearly all of Russia, is farther north than the United States. Berlin, the German capital, lies at about the same latitude as the southern tip of Canada's Hudson Bay.

Far to the North

This small church is located in the Highlands area of Scotland. Part of Europe's Northwestern Highlands region, the Scottish Highlands lie north of the 55°N line of latitude. In contrast, all of the United States, except for Alaska, is located south of 50°N.

Major Landforms of Europe and Russia

Look again at the physical map of Europe in the Atlas and study the shape of Europe. The continent of Europe forms a **peninsula** (puh NIN suh luh), a body of land nearly surrounded by water. The European peninsula juts out into the Atlantic Ocean. Look closely, and you will see that Europe has many smaller peninsulas with bays. These bays include many harbors, or sheltered bodies of water, where ships can dock. Good harbors have enabled Western European countries to become world leaders in the shipping industry.

Now find Russia on the political map of Asia in the Atlas. Notice that Russia lies on the Arctic Ocean. This body of water is frozen for most of the year and cannot be used for shipping. Between Russia and the countries of Europe, however, there are no physical features that form travel barriers. Movement between these two regions has always been easy.

Plains and Uplands of Europe Within the peninsula of Europe are four major land regions: the Northwestern Highlands, the North European Plain, the Central Uplands, and the Alpine Mountain System. Find these regions on the map on the next page.

The Northwestern Highlands stretch across the far north of Europe. These old mountains have been worn by wind and

READ ACTIVELY

Visualize If you flew in a plane over Europe and Russia, what physical features would you see?

▼ The Swiss Alps are popular with hikers and climbers in winter and summer.

weather. Because they have steep slopes and thin soil, they are not good for farming, and few people live here. Large parts of this region have fewer than 25 people per square mile (10 people per sq km). But the forests here support a successful timber industry.

Notice on the map below that more than half of Europe is covered by the North European Plain. Can you see where this plain begins and ends? It includes most of the European part of Russia and reaches all the way to France. This region has the most productive farmland and the largest cities in Europe.

In the center of southern Europe are the Central Uplands. What do you think uplands are? You probably guessed that this is a region of highlands. In fact, it is made up of mountains and **plateaus** (pla TOHZ), or large raised areas of mostly level land. Most of the land in this region is rocky and not good for farming. But the uplands have other uses. In Spain, people raise goats and sheep here. In Portugal, people mine the uplands for minerals.

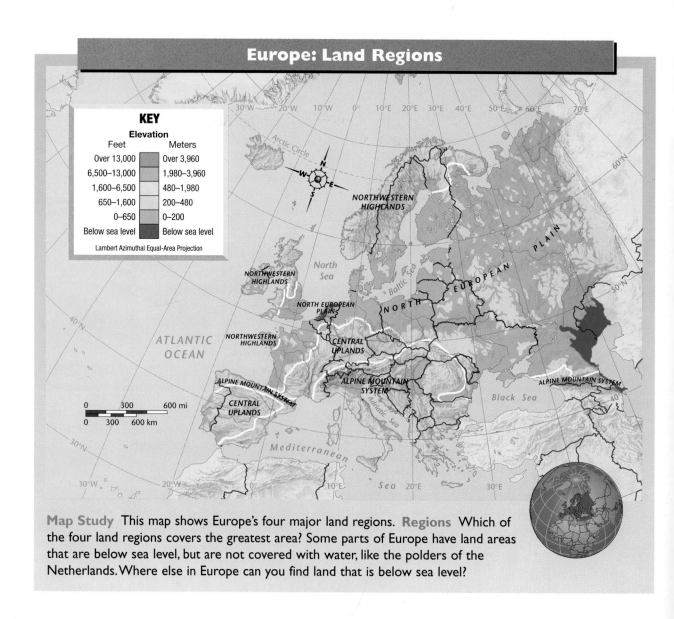

Europe: Land Regions

KEY

Elevation

Feet	Meters
Over 13,000	Over 3,960
6,500–13,000	1,980–3,960
1,600–6,500	480–1,980
650–1,600	200–480
0–650	0–200
Below sea level	Below sea level

Lambert Azimuthal Equal-Area Projection

0   300   600 mi
0   300   600 km

Map Study This map shows Europe's four major land regions. **Regions** Which of the four land regions covers the greatest area? Some parts of Europe have land areas that are below sea level, but are not covered with water, like the polders of the Netherlands. Where else in Europe can you find land that is below sea level?

These farm workers in Siberia are harvesting strawberries. The best farming country in Siberia lies in the region's southwestern section. Here, in addition to strawberries, farm workers harvest wheat, oats, and rye. **Critical Thinking** Based on this photograph, what do you think a job harvesting strawberries would be like?

Are you ready to see a spectacular landform? Look for the Alpine Mountain System. These mountains stretch from Spain to the Balkan Peninsula. The Alps are the highest and most beautiful mountains in this system. They are also a popular vacation place. Some families make a living from small-scale farming in the mountain valleys and meadows of the Alps.

Russian Plains and Uplands   Europe and the western part of Russia share the North European Plain. Russia's largest cities, Moscow (MAHS kow) and St. Petersburg, are in this region. Most of Russia's industries are here, too. There are more people living in this region than in any other part of Russia.

Where the plains end, the uplands begin. On the eastern border of the European Plain you will find the Ural Mountains. To the east of the Urals is the Asian part of Russia—a region known as Siberia (sy BIHR ee uh). This region makes up about 75 percent of Russian territory, but it has only about 20 percent of Russia's people. The region's harsh climate has limited settlement there.

If you continue east into Siberia from the Ural Mountains, you will cross the largest plain in the world—the West Siberian Plain. This low, marshy plain covers more than one million square miles (2.58 million sq km), but it rises only 328 feet (100 m) above sea level. Farther east is the Central Siberian Plateau, which slopes upward from the West Siberian Plain. If you travel still farther east, you will need to watch your step. The East Siberian Uplands include more than 20 active volcanoes among the rugged mountains and plateaus.

READ ACTIVELY

Ask Questions What questions would you like to ask a person who lives in a cold, harsh climate?

The Rivers of Europe and Russia

The highlands of Europe and Russia are the source for many important rivers. High in the Alps in Switzerland (SWIT sur lund), melting glaciers create two streams that combine to form the Rhine River. Winding through forests and plains, the Rhine makes a journey of 865 miles (1,391 km), from Switzerland to the Netherlands and the North Sea. Along its course through Germany, the river flows past old castles on cliffs and smoky mills and factories.

The Rhine River serves as a major highway. Canals and tributaries (TRIB yoo tehr eez) connect it to the furthest reaches of Western Europe. A **tributary** is a river or stream that flows into a larger river.

The longest river on the continent of Europe is Russia's Volga (VAHL guh) River. It flows 2,193 miles (3,528 km) through western Russia and empties into the Caspian (KAS pih un) Sea. The Volga has many tributaries and canals. They link the Volga to the Arctic Ocean and the Baltic

The Deepest Lake on Earth

Lake Baikal, Russia, holds about one fifth of Earth's fresh water. More than 300 rivers and streams flow into Lake Baikal from the surrounding mountains. Because Lake Baikal holds so much water, it affects the weather in the area around it. The land near the lake is cooler in the summer and warmer in the winter than land that lies farther away. **Critical Thinking** What other bodies of water can change the weather?

The Danube River

The Danube River flows from the mountains of Germany through eight countries before it empties into the Black Sea in Romania. It is the second longest river in Europe—only Russia's Volga River is longer. Because it is both navigable and long, the Danube is an important trade route. Ships from the Mediterranean can travel as far as this port in Braila, Romania, before their cargo is transferred to smaller vessels. **Critical Thinking** At one time, composers wrote music celebrating the beauty of the Danube River. Today, that beauty has been dimmed by air and water pollution from factories. What parts of this photograph are hard to see because of smog?

Sea. Unfortunately, the Volga freezes for most of its length for three months of each year. During the winter months, it is not **navigable** (NAV ih guh bul), or clear enough for ships to travel.

Other Russian rivers freeze, too. Some of them are frozen for five or more months of the year. And many flow north to the frozen Arctic Ocean, which is also not navigable. These rivers do not serve as dependable trade routes.

SECTION 1 REVIEW

1. **Define** (a) polder, (b) population density, (c) peninsula, (d) plateau, (e) tributary, (f) navigable.

2. **Identify** (a) Europe, (b) Russia, (c) Eurasia, (d) Ural Mountains, (e) Alps, (f) Siberia.

3. What are the major physical features of Europe and Russia?

4. Give two examples of ways in which physical features have affected life in Europe and Russia.

Critical Thinking

5. **Drawing Conclusions** Think about the areas of Europe and Russia that are the most densely populated. What physical features attract people to settle in those areas?

Activity

6. **Writing to Learn** Which physical feature described in this section are you most interested in learning more about? Why? In your journal, make a list of the things you would like to learn about this physical feature.

Climate and Vegetation

BEFORE YOU READ

Reach Into Your Background

Do you live where it is warm year round? Or do you live in an area with warm summers and cold winters? Think of the climate in your area. Identify three ways in which it affects your way of life.

Questions to Explore

1. How do oceans and mountains affect climate in Europe and Russia?
2. What different climates and kinds of vegetation do Europe and Russia have?

Key Terms

rain shadow
prairie
tundra
permafrost
taiga
steppe

Key Places

Barcelona
Irkutsk

I t is February in Barcelona (bar suh LOH nuh), Spain. Twelve-year-old Nicholas wakes up to the sun streaming through his bedroom window. It's another warm day, and the temperature is already 65°F (18°C). Nicholas dresses quickly in shorts and a T-shirt and eats a breakfast of thick hot chocolate and *churros,* twisted loops of fried dough. He wants to get out and play soccer with his friends on this sunny Saturday morning.

At the very same moment, it is late afternoon in Irkutsk (ihr KOOTSK), a city in southern Siberia. Vasily (VAS uh lee) returns home from a day of cross-country skiing. He takes off his fur hat, gloves, boots, ski pants, and coat. The day has been sunny but cold, with an average temperature of −15°F (−11°C). Now Vasily warms up with a dinner of *pelmeny* (PEL muh nee), chicken broth with meat-filled dumplings.

▼ In the snowy Siberian winter, skiing is a good way to get from place to place.

A Wide Range of Climates

Nicholas and Vasily live in vastly different climates. Barcelona, where Nicholas lives, lies on the Mediterranean Sea. Here, the summers are hot and dry, and the winters are mild and rainy. In Irkutsk, Vasily's home in Siberia, summers are short, and the winters are long and very cold. Temperatures in winter can drop to −50°F (−45°C). Snow covers the ground for about six months of the year.

Two Cities, Two Climates

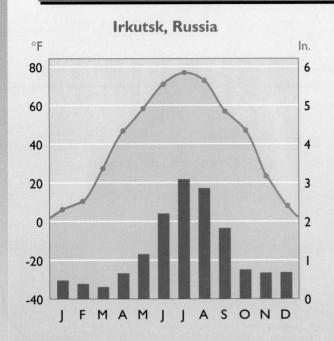

Irkutsk, Russia

°F | In.
80 — 6
60 — 5
40 — 4
20 — 3
0 — 2
-20 — 1
-40 — 0

J F M A M J J A S O N D

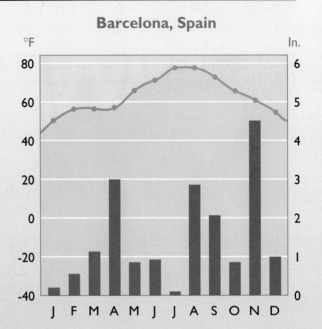

Barcelona, Spain

°F | In.
80 — 6
60 — 5
40 — 4
20 — 3
0 — 2
-20 — 1
-40 — 0

J F M A M J J A S O N D

Curved lines show temperatures in Fahrenheit degrees. **Bars** show precipitation in inches.

Graph Study Siberia, where the city of Irkutsk is located, endures the coldest winters of any place in the world except Antarctica. In contrast, Spain, where Barcelona is located, enjoys mild weather throughout the year. **Critical Thinking** Find Irkutsk and Barcelona on the climate regions map in the Activity Atlas. How do you think location influences the climates of these two cities?

Oceans Affect Climate You can partly explain the difference between the climates of Barcelona and Irkutsk by looking at the two cities' distances from an ocean or a sea. Areas that are near an ocean or a sea have fairly mild weather year round. Areas that are far from the ocean often have extreme weather.

Look at the map on the next page and find the Gulf Stream. Notice how it becomes the North Atlantic Current as it crosses the Atlantic Ocean. This ocean current carries warm water from the tropical waters of the Gulf of Mexico to northwestern Europe. Also, winds blowing from the west across the Atlantic Ocean are warmed by this powerful ocean current. The warm waters and winds bring mild weather to much of northwestern Europe.

London is farther north than any city in the continental United States, but it has mild weather. How is this possible? The North Atlantic Current is the reason. But the most dramatic effect of the North Atlantic Current can be seen in northern Norway. Snow and ice cover most of this area in winter. Yet Norway's western coast is free of ice and snow all year. Snow melts almost as soon as it falls. Norway's ice-free ports have helped to make it a great fishing country.

The ocean affects climate in other ways. Winds blowing across the ocean pick up a great deal of moisture. When these winds blow over land,

READ ACTIVELY

Predict How do you think the ocean affects the climate in some parts of Europe?

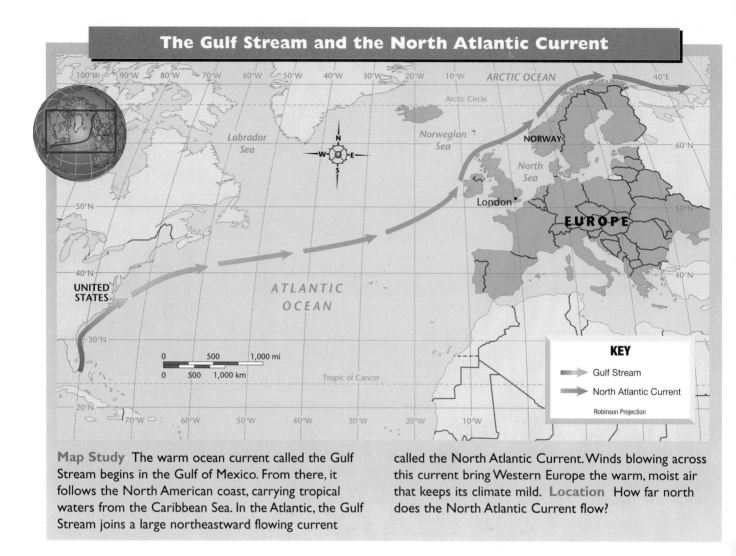

The Gulf Stream and the North Atlantic Current

Map Study The warm ocean current called the Gulf Stream begins in the Gulf of Mexico. From there, it follows the North American coast, carrying tropical waters from the Caribbean Sea. In the Atlantic, the Gulf Stream joins a large northeastward flowing current called the North Atlantic Current. Winds blowing across this current bring Western Europe the warm, moist air that keeps its climate mild. **Location** How far north does the North Atlantic Current flow?

they drop the moisture in the form of rain. Winds blowing from the west across the Atlantic bring a fairly wet climate to much of Western Europe.

Mountains Affect Rainfall   Mountains also affect the amount of rainfall in an area. In Europe, areas west of mountains receive heavy rainfall. These areas include parts of Great Britain, France, Germany, and Norway. Areas east of mountains have much lighter rainfall.

Why is this so? As winds rise up a mountain, they cool and drop their moisture. The air is dry by the time it reaches the other side of the mountain. Areas on the leeward side of a mountain, or away from the wind, are in a rain shadow. A **rain shadow** is an area on the dry, sheltered side of a mountain that receives little rainfall.

Major Climate Zones of Europe and Russia

Earlier, you read that oceans affect climate. Look at the climate regions map in the Activity Atlas to see a good illustration of this. Notice that much of northwestern Europe has a marine west coast climate. The

North Atlantic Current helps make the climate mild all year. Moisture-carrying winds from the Atlantic Ocean make these areas rainy through all the seasons. In London, the capital of Great Britain, rain is a part of life. Many people who live here are in the habit of carrying an umbrella every day.

Look again at the map. Notice the climate region that surrounds the Mediterranean Sea. It is easy to remember the name of this type of climate—Mediterranean, just like the sea. Remember that Barcelona, where Nicholas lives, is on the Mediterranean. In this kind of climate, summers are hot and dry. Winters are mild and rainy. Look at the climate graph earlier in the section to see the average monthly temperatures and rainfall for Barcelona.

Some inland areas far away from the ocean have a humid continental climate. In these areas, winters are long and cold. But summers can be blazing hot!

Now find Irkutsk, Russia, on the map. Notice that it is located in a huge subarctic climate zone. Here summers are short, and winters are long and cold. You can see how cold it is all year by looking at the climate graph for Irkutsk. The northernmost areas of Europe and Russia have a tundra climate. In these areas it is just plain cold! On the warmest days, temperatures rarely get above 40°F (5°C).

LINKS TO SCIENCE

Hot and Cold Iceland's Loki volcano lies beneath Vatnjokul, Europe's largest glacier. In the fall of 1996, Loki erupted. This created a deep crack in the glacier some 6 miles (10 km) long. Melting ice and eruptions of water from a huge "underground lake" beneath the glacier flooded the surrounding area.

My Family in Winter

STUDENT ART

Helin Tikerpuu
13 years old
Estonia

This student has painted her family on a skiing trip. **Critical Thinking** Based on this picture, do you think Helin's family skis just for fun? Or do you think their ski trip has a more practical purpose? Explain your answer.

The Vegetation of Europe and Russia

The natural vegetation, or plant life, of Europe and Russia is as varied as the climate. And vegetation regions are related to climate regions. Compare the climate map with the natural vegetation maps below and on the next page to see how the climate and vegetation bands overlap.

Forests and Grasslands of Europe The natural vegetation of much of Europe is forest. However, most of these forests have been cleared to make way for farms, factories, and cities. In northern Europe, you can still find large coniferous (koh NIF ur us) forests, which have trees with cones that carry and protect the seeds.

The central and southern parts of the North European Plain were once covered by grasslands, called **prairies.** Like the forests, most of the prairies have also been cleared. Today, the land is used for farming.

The Russian Tundra, Forests, and Grasslands Russia has three great vegetation zones: the tundra, the forests, and the grasslands. The tundra and forest zones extend across Siberia. Grasslands cover southwestern Russia.

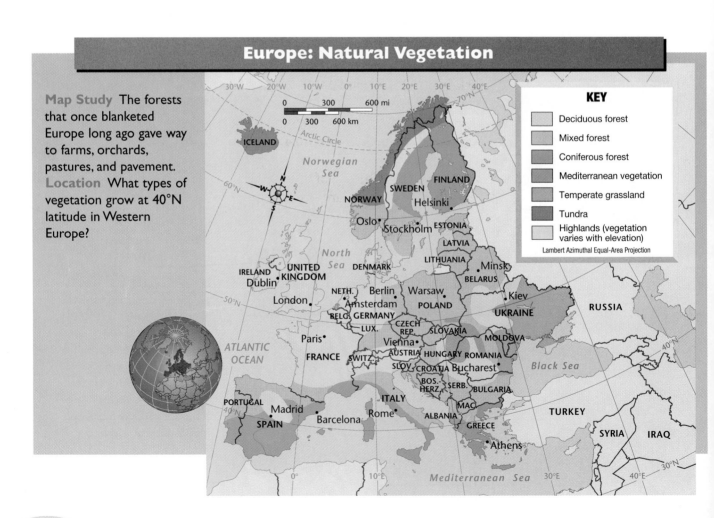

Europe: Natural Vegetation

Map Study The forests that once blanketed Europe long ago gave way to farms, orchards, pastures, and pavement. **Location** What types of vegetation grow at 40°N latitude in Western Europe?

KEY
- Deciduous forest
- Mixed forest
- Coniferous forest
- Mediterranean vegetation
- Temperate grassland
- Tundra
- Highlands (vegetation varies with elevation)

Lambert Azimuthal Equal-Area Projection

Russia: Natural Vegetation

KEY

- Deciduous forest
- Mixed forest
- Coniferous forest
- Temperate grassland
- Desert scrub
- Tundra
- Ice cap

Two-Point Equidistant Projection

Map Study Far from the Equator and from warm ocean currents, Russia's cool climate supports three types of vegetation. **Regions** Which type of vegetation covers the largest area? In the far north, what type of vegetation grows? Which region provides Russia's rich farmland?

The **tundra** is a treeless plain where grasses and mosses grow. Here, winters last up to nine months and the ground is **permafrost,** or permanently frozen soil. When the top surface of the permafrost thaws, fantastic growth spurts take place.

Russia also has more than its share of forests. One, called the **taiga** (TY guh), covers more than 4 million square miles (6.4 million sq km). It is the largest forest in the world.

The Russian grasslands are called **steppes.** The soil of this region is fertile and black and good for farming. The steppes are similar to the Great Plains of the United States.

SECTION 2 REVIEW

1. **Define** (a) rain shadow, (b) prairie, (c) tundra, (d) permafrost, (e) taiga, (f) steppe.

2. **Identify** (a) Barcelona, (b) Irkutsk.

3. How does the North Atlantic Current affect the climate of northwestern Europe?

4. What are the major climate and vegetation regions of Europe and Russia?

Critical Thinking

5. **Recognizing Cause and Effect** How do oceans and mountains affect climate?

Activity

6. **Writing to Learn** Plan a trip to one of the cities mentioned in this section. Decide what time of year you want to go. Based on the climate of the city you have chosen, make a list of the clothes you will pack.

Using Regional Maps

Do you dream of someday traveling around the world? Just by crossing Russia, you can travel halfway around the world.

Russia is the largest country on the planet. It reaches across Europe and Asia. When it is noon at one end of the country, it is close to midnight at the other. How can this be?

Get Ready

There is such a big time difference because Russia stretches across 10 of the world's 24 time zones. Why do we have time zones?

Suppose every clock in the world showed the same time at once. At noon, the sun would be rising in some places and setting in others. It would be very confusing.

The Earth has 24 time zones—one for each hour of the day. Noon everywhere is always about when the sun is at its highest point.

You may someday be talking on the phone with people in Russia. If you understand time zones, you can avoid calling someone at 3:00 A.M. The best way to understand time zones is by learning how to read a time zone map.

Try It Out

The map on the next page shows time zones across the globe. Compare the number of time zones in the United States and in Russia. Use the time zone map to complete the following steps:

A. Find the time zone boundaries. The boundaries are shown by solid lines. Notice that they are mostly straight, but sometimes bend to follow political boundaries. Why do you think this is so?

B. Understand the difference between time zones. The difference in time between one time zone and the next is one hour. (Each time zone represents the distance the Earth rotates in one hour.) As you travel west of the Prime Meridian, the time becomes one hour earlier for every time zone you cross. As you travel east of the Prime Meridian, it becomes one hour later for every time zone you cross. Note the two sets of labels on the map on the next page. At the top are hours labeled A.M. and P.M.

The Prime Meridian is labeled 12 noon. The numbers below the map show the time difference in hours from 12 noon.

C. Follow a three-step process to use the map.

Step 1. The United States covers 6 of the 24 time zones. Find your location on the map. Check what time it is now.

Step 2. Locate the place for which you wish to know the time. Notice its time zone.

Step 3. If the place is in the same time zone as your location, the time is the same as your time. If it is in a different time zone, look at the times in the key below the map to see how many hours away it is. Then add or subtract the hours from your current time. Remember, if the place is east of where you are, add to your time. If it is west of where you are, subtract from your time.

Write down your current time. Now calculate the current time for the five United States cities shown on the time zone map.

Apply the Skill

Russia is the widest country on the Earth. In other words, it stretches across more time zones than any other country does.

1 Consider the differences in time. Study the map. In Russia, how many hours' difference is there between the time zone farthest east and the time zone farthest west? When it is 3 P.M. in Moscow, what time is it in Perm? What time is it in Novosibirsk? What time is it in Vladivostok? When it is lunch time in St. Petersburg, what part of the day is it in Anadyr?

2 Think about the challenges posed by these great differences. Write a paragraph to answer this question: What challenges might the Russian government and businesses face by having to work with so many different time zones?

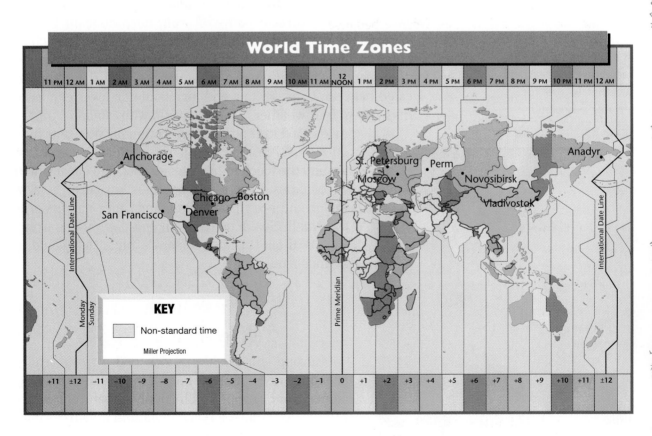

World Time Zones

KEY

Non-standard time

Miller Projection

SECTION 3

Natural Resources

BEFORE YOU READ

Reach Into Your Background

The United States has many natural resources. Which resources do you think are most important? Why?

Consider these questions as you read about the natural resources of Europe and Russia.

Questions to Explore

1. What are the major natural resources of Europe and Russia?
2. How do Europe and Russia differ in their use of natural resources?

Key Terms

loess
hydroelectric power
fossil fuel
reserves

Key Places

North Sea
Ruhr
Silesia

▼ On a North Sea oil rig, workers brave icy seas and foul weather to drill for underwater petroleum deposits.

How would you like to live and work on an ocean? Oil workers on the North Sea work to pump oil from deep beneath the ocean floor. They anchor a tower called an oil rig over an oil field. In such a rig, oil workers live and work as if they were on a ship. But oil workers cannot sail for the safety of a harbor when a big storm is stirring. And the North Sea, located between Great Britain and mainland northwestern Europe, sometimes has violent weather. Severe storms with winds of up to 100 miles (160 km) an hour are common. Waves as high as 90 feet (27 m) batter oil rig platforms. Crews work around the clock to operate, inspect, and repair the rigs.

Making sure a rig operates properly is a very important job. Great Britain and other nations around the North Sea depend on oil and natural gas from the rigs. Without this fuel, Europe's industries would be in serious trouble.

Resources of Western Europe

Europe is a wealthy region and a world leader in economic development. Part of this wealth and success comes from Europe's rich supply of natural resources. This region's most important natural resources include fertile soil, water, and fuels.

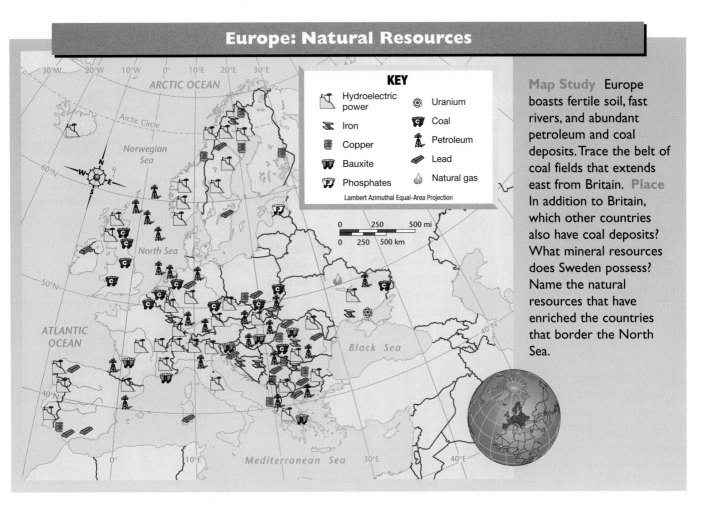

KEY

- ⚒ Hydroelectric power
- 🐟 Iron
- 🛢 Copper
- ⬛ Bauxite
- ⬛ Phosphates
- ⊚ Uranium
- C Coal
- ⛏ Petroleum
- ▬ Lead
- 🔥 Natural gas

Lambert Azimuthal Equal-Area Projection

0   250   500 mi
0   250   500 km

Map Study Europe boasts fertile soil, fast rivers, and abundant petroleum and coal deposits. Trace the belt of coal fields that extends east from Britain. **Place** In addition to Britain, which other countries also have coal deposits? What mineral resources does Sweden possess? Name the natural resources that have enriched the countries that border the North Sea.

Fertile Soil Why do you think soil is one of the most important natural resources? You have probably guessed that it is important because it is needed to grow food. Much of Western Europe is covered with rich, fertile soil, especially the region's broad river valleys.

Wind helps create the fertile soil of the North European Plain. Over thousands of years, winds have deposited a type of rich, dustlike soil known as **loess** (LOH es). This soil, combined with plentiful rain and a long growing season, enables European farmers to produce abundant crops.

An Excellent Supply of Water Western Europe's water is another important resource. People need water to drink. Water nourishes crops. Water can also be used to produce electricity, an important source of energy for industries. To be used as a source of energy, water must flow very quickly. The force of water from a waterfall or a dam can be used to spin machines called turbines (TUR bynz). Spinning turbines generate, or create, electric power. Power generated by water-driven turbines is called **hydroelectric** (hy droh ee LEK trik) **power.**

Many countries in Europe have good locations for the development of hydroelectric power. Some rivers that flow down through the mountains have been dammed to create hydroelectric power. Norway

LINKS ACROSS THE WORLD

Loess in China Winds blowing from Mongolia and the Gobi carry loess to the Huang He valley. The river carries the soil downstream and, during floods, deposits it across the North China Plain. This fertile soil makes the plain one of China's most important farming areas.

From Fossils to Fuel

From Plankton to Oil

1. Drifting throughout the oceans and fresh water of the Earth are tiny marine plants and animals called **plankton**. Plankton that died millions of years ago settled on the ocean floor.

2. Over the years, the plankton was covered with mud and sand. The weight of this material gradually changed the plankton into oil. The oil remained trapped inside **porous rock** that also formed.

3. With huge machinery people dig through the rock and remove the trapped oil, called **crude oil**.

4. Crude oil must then be cleaned, or refined. **Refined oil** is used to make many important products, including home heating oil.

From Plants to Coal

1. **Peat** is made of decayed plant material.

2. Over millions of years, material built up over ancient peat deposits. The pressure of this material gradually changed the peat into **brown coal**.

3. Continuing pressure gradually turned brown coal into soft coal. **Soft coal** is the most common coal found on the Earth. It is often used in industry.

Chart Study The fossil fuels coal and oil formed over millions of years. Oil formed when plankton died and was covered with mud. The plankton decayed and the mud turned to rock, filled with pockets of oil. Coal started with swamp-growing plants whose decayed remains formed a substance called peat. **Critical Thinking** What is the difference between crude oil and refined oil?

Connect What kinds of natural resources have you used so far today?

gets almost all of its electric power from water. Hydroelectric power also keeps factories in Sweden, Switzerland, Austria, Spain, and Portugal humming.

Fuels Like flowing water, fossil fuels provide a source of energy for industries. **Fossil fuels** include coal, oil, and natural gas. They are so named because they developed from fossils, or the remains of ancient plants and animals.

You already know that Great Britain has large deposits of oil and natural gas. Norway does as well. Great Britain also has large coal fields, as does Germany. The largest coal deposits in Germany are located in the Ruhr (roor), a region named for the Ruhr River. Because of its fuel resources, the Ruhr has long been one of Western Europe's most important industrial regions.

An abundance of coal, along with another mineral, iron ore, gave Western Europe a head start in the 1800s, when industries grew rapidly. Today, Europe remains a leading world industrial power.

Resources of Eastern Europe

Now, shift your view from Western to Eastern Europe. Turn back to the map showing Europe's natural resources. Notice that Eastern Europe has similar resources to those of Western Europe. Place a finger on the area around 50°N and 20°E. This is where Poland, the Czech (chek) Republic, and Germany come together. This area is called Silesia (sy LEE shuh). Large deposits of coal here have made Silesia a major industrial center.

Ukraine (yoo KRAYN), a large country in Eastern Europe, has coal deposits, too. It also has several other fuel resources—oil and natural gas. However, its most important resource is probably its soil. This black earth, or *chernozem* (CHEHR nuh zem), is very fertile. Not surprisingly, farming is an extremely important activity in Ukraine.

Resources of Russia

Russia has developed its natural resources far less than Western Europe. Russia has a huge variety of resources—even more than the United States. Our country has used its resources to become the richest nation on earth. You might wonder why Russia has not done the same. The answer is that Russia's harsh climate, huge size, and few navigable rivers have made it difficult to turn resources into wealth.

A Slovakian Steel Factory

Slovakia has large deposits of iron ore. However, it does not have enough iron to supply all its factories, so it imports some. This photograph shows steel being made out of iron at the steelworks in the Slovakian town of Podbrezova. **Critical Thinking** Steel is very strong and can be molded into many different shapes. What products do you know of that are made out of steel?

Russia: Natural Resources

KEY

⛏ Hydroelectric power   🖲 Copper   💰 Gold   P Phosphates   🗜 Coal   🪙 Lead   ◻ Tungsten   🔥 Natural gas

⚒ Iron   🝛 Bauxite   🪙 Silver   ⊙ Uranium   🗼 Petroleum   △ Nickel   ● Tin   ♦ Diamonds

Two-Point Equidistant Projection

Map Study Under Russia's permafrost lie coal, oil, natural gas, diamonds, and gold. **Regions** Name five other Russian resources. **Movement** How might the rivers of Siberia be used to transport resources from remote regions when they are frozen in the winter?

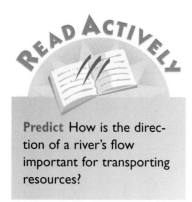

Predict How is the direction of a river's flow important for transporting resources?

Russia's Fossil Fuels and Iron Ore Russia can proudly claim the title of the world's largest oil producer. It also has the largest **reserves,** or available supply, of natural gas in the world. And scientists estimate that the country has about one third of the world's coal reserves.

In addition, Russia has the world's greatest reserves of iron ore, which is used to make steel. Many of these deposits are in the part of Russia that is on the continent of Europe. That is one reason why most of Russia's industry is west of the Ural Mountains.

The Special Case of Siberia Look at the map above. Notice that most of Russia's deposits of oil, natural gas, and coal are located in Siberia. Three fourths of the Russian forest lies here, too. This forest holds half of the world's reserves of softwood timber. Siberia is far from the population and industrial centers of the country, however. Retrieving these resources is not easy.

Russia's huge size presents a major challenge. Transporting Siberian resources to areas where they are needed can be a struggle.

Except for the Volga, Russia's rivers are not as useful for transportation as those in Western Europe. Siberia's rivers do not flow toward Russia's most important cities. Instead, they flow north into the Arctic Ocean. In spite of these problems and the very cold weather, Russia is continually finding ways to move the resources from Siberia. Pipelines carry oil and natural gas, and railroads transport coal to European Russia.

The efforts to get to the resources and use them have created a new challenge—protecting the environment. Some of the world's worst cases of pollution are found in Siberia. Nuclear waste has been dumped into rivers for 40 years. Air pollution from factories is very high. Scientists not only have to find ways to develop Russia's valuable resources, they must also consider how to restore polluted areas.

▲ Siberia's forests (above left) are one of Russia's most important resources. Loggers transport wood from these forests to other parts of Russia by train (above). Unlike coal and oil, forests are a renewable resource if they are managed carefully.

SECTION 3 REVIEW

1. **Define** (a) loess, (b) hydro-electric power, (c) fossil fuel, (d) reserves.

2. **Identify** (a) North Sea, (b) Ruhr, (c) Silesia.

3. Describe the main natural resources of Western Europe, Eastern Europe, and Russia.

4. Explain how Western Europe and Russia differ in their development of natural resources.

Critical Thinking

5. **Drawing Conclusions** Russia is richer in natural resources than Western Europe. Yet Russians are generally not as wealthy as Western Europeans. How does geography help explain this?

Activity

6. **Writing to Learn** What do you think is Europe and Russia's most important natural resource? What makes that resource so important? Write a paragraph explaining your choice.

Review and Activities

Reviewing Main Ideas

1. Describe the land and rivers of Europe and Russia.
2. How have physical features aided Europe's growth and hurt Russia's growth?
3. Describe the climates of Europe and Russia.
4. Describe the vegetation of Europe and Russia.
5. What effect do large bodies of water have on climate in Europe and Russia?
6. Identify the main natural resources of Western Europe, Eastern Europe, and Russia.
7. Compare the development of natural resources in Western Europe and Russia.

Reviewing Key Terms

Use each key term below in a sentence that shows the meaning of the term.

1. polder
2. peninsula
3. plateau
4. tributary
5. rain shadow
6. prairie
7. tundra
8. permafrost
9. steppe
10. hydroelectric power
11. fossil fuel
12. reserves

Critical Thinking

1. **Making Comparisons** Choose one of the land regions of Europe or Russia. Compare it with the area where you live. Consider the landscape, climate, and vegetation.
2. **Recognizing Cause and Effect** Think about what you have learned about the rivers of Europe and Russia. Explain why the direction in which rivers flow is important.

Graphic Organizer

Copy the chart onto a separate sheet of paper. Then, using information from the chapter, fill in the empty boxes.

	Physical Features	Climate	Vegetation	Natural Resources
Europe				
Russia				

Map Activity

Europe and Russia
For each place listed below, write the letter from the map that shows its location. Use the maps in the Atlas at the back of the book to help you.

1. Europe

2. Ural Mountains

3. Alps

4. Siberia

5. Rhine River

6. Volga River

7. North Sea

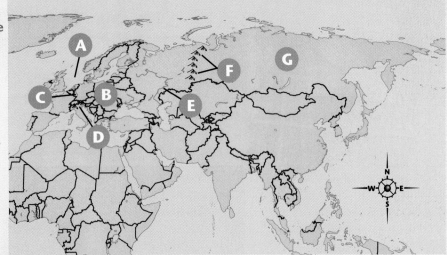

Writing Activity

Writing a Travel Brochure
Write a travel brochure for Americans who want to visit Siberia. Provide descriptions of the land, climate, and plant life. Suggest clothing for the trip.

Internet Activity

Use a search engine to find the **CIA World Factbook 1995.** Choose Russia or a country in Europe. Read about the terrain and climate of your selected country. Draw a map to show the country's landforms or climates. Make symbols to represent the different landforms or types of climates and glue them on your map.

Skills Review

Turn to the Skills Activity.
Review the steps for using a time zone map. Then, use the U.S. time zone map to find the current time for the following places:

a) where you are

b) Boston, Massachusetts

c) Anchorage, Alaska

How Am I Doing?

Answer these questions to help you check your progress.

1. Can I identify and describe the main physical features of Europe and Russia?

2. Can I give some examples of how physical features, climate, and vegetation affect life in Europe and Russia?

3. Can I identify important natural resources of Europe and Russia?

4. What information from this chapter can I use in my book project?

Shaped by History

PICTURE ACTIVITIES

This is the Colosseum in Rome. It is an example of the ancient Romans' great skill in building. To help you understand the importance of this building, complete the following activities.

Write a caption
Identify the main features of this building. Then write a caption describing these features.

Sketch an American landmark
Sketch a building you think is a symbol of the United States. You might choose the United States Capitol or the Empire State Building in New York City. How is this building important to Americans? What do you think of when you see a picture of it?

From Ancient Greece to Feudal Europe

BEFORE YOU READ

Reach Into Your Background

The accomplishments of ancient Europe still have an impact on our world. What U.S. accomplishments do you know about? Think of some great things Americans have done. Explain why people remember these achievements today.

Questions to Explore

1. What were the main accomplishments of the ancient Greeks and Romans?

2. What was the impact of Christianity and feudalism on life during the Middle Ages?

Key Terms

Middle Ages   Pax Romana
democracy   feudalism
city-state   manor
policy   serf
empire

Key People and Places

Alexander the Great
Augustus
Constantine
Athens
Rome

For many years now, on a special morning in April, thousands of people from around the world have come together in a small Massachusetts town. At noon, they begin a marathon race that requires great strength and willpower. The race ends in the city of Boston, some 26 miles (42 km) away.

But what does the Boston Marathon have to do with European history? To find out, you need to go back 2,500 years to a story about the ancient Greek city of Athens. In 490 B.C., the people of Athens were at war with the Persians. The Athenians finally won at the Battle of Marathon. To announce their victory, an Athenian soldier named Pheidippides (fuh DIP uh deez) ran all the way to Athens, about 25 miles (40 km) away. Pheidippides reached Athens and shouted, "Rejoice, we conquer!" as he entered the city. Then he died.

The story of Pheidippides may or may not be true. But the Greeks loved the story, and people all over the world still run long races called marathons. In repeating this race, people show how history lives on. This

▼ The glory of ancient Greece inspires each running of the Boston Marathon. Shown here is Moses Tanui of Kenya, the winner in the 1996 men's race.

Chart Study Greece, whose ideas influence us to this day, borrowed ideas from older civilizations in Mesopotamia and Egypt. But the Greeks sometimes failed to give much credit to these other societies. In fact, the famous Greek thinker Plato bragged, "Whatever the Greeks have acquired from foreigners, they have, in the end, turned into something finer." **Critical Thinking** Which of Greece's achievements do you think has had the most important influence on our lives today? Why?

Area of Achievement	Influence on Modern Society
Drama	Aristotle created the rules for drama known as *The Poetics*. These rules are still used in plays and movie scripts.
Architecture	Many modern building designs reflect the common Greek styles known as Ionic, Doric, and Corinthian.
Science	The ancient Greeks introduced many principles of modern medicine, physics, biology, and mathematics.
Politics	The democratic ideals of government by the people, trial by jury, and equality under the law were formed in Athens around 500 B.C.
History	Herodotus collected information from people who remembered the events of the Persian wars. This method of research set the standard for the way history is recorded today.

chapter discusses three periods in the history of Europe and Russia—ancient times; recent times; and the time between the two, called the **Middle Ages.** We will see how the past affects the present in Europe and Russia.

The Greek Heritage

The Athenians and other ancient Greeks were Europe's first great philosophers, historians, poets, and writers. They did not accept old ways and old thinking. Instead, they observed plants, animals, and the human body. In the process, they invented today's scientific way of gathering knowledge. The Greeks also invented ideas about how people should live. One idea was **democracy** (dih MAHK ruh see), a kind of government that citizens run themselves.

The Power of Democracy In ancient times, there were over a hundred **city-states** in Greece. Each was both a city and an independent nation. This gave the Greeks plenty of chances to try different kinds of government. Many of their city-states were democracies.

The most famous Greek city-state was Athens. In this city-state, every male citizen voted on laws and government **policies,** or the

READ ACTIVELY

Connect How was democracy in Athens different from today's democracy in the United States?

methods and plans a government uses to do its work. Citizens were either elected or chosen at random for government positions.

Democracy was a fresh idea for the Greeks, but it was not the same as what we call democracy today. Citizens in Greece owned slaves. Non-Greeks, women, and slaves were not citizens. They could not vote. Still, the Greek idea that citizens should have a voice in their own government had a strong impact on people in later times.

Greek Ideas Spread Greek ideas might have stayed within their city-states if not for a young man named Alexander, later called Alexander the Great. At age 20, he became king of Macedonia (mas uh DOH nee uh), in northern Greece. But he was not satisfied with this small kingdom. In 334 B.C., Alexander set out to conquer the world. In only 10 years, he conquered an empire almost as big as the United States. An **empire** is a collection of lands ruled by a single government.

In all his new lands, Alexander established Greek cities, the Greek language, and Greek ideas. At the time of his death, in 323 B.C., Greek culture linked the entire Mediterranean world. The people who next ruled the region, the Romans, borrowed much from the Greeks.

▲ The Greek thinker Aristotle, shown here in this marble sculpture, was Alexander the Great's teacher. Later, Alexander spread Aristotle's ideas across an empire.

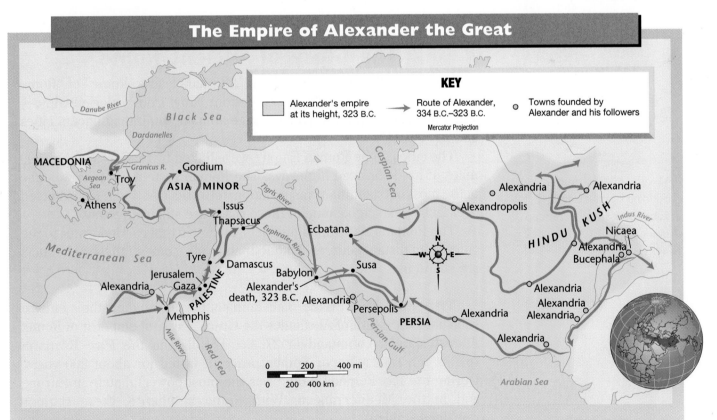

The Empire of Alexander the Great

KEY

Alexander's empire at its height, 323 B.C.

Route of Alexander, 334 B.C.–323 B.C.

Towns founded by Alexander and his followers

Mercator Projection

Danube River
Black Sea
Dardanelles
MACEDONIA
Granicus R.
Gordium
Aegean Sea
Troy
ASIA MINOR
Athens
Issus
Thapsacus
Tigris River
Euphrates River
Ecbatana
Caspian Sea
Alexandria
Alexandropolis
HINDU KUSH
Indus River
Nicaea
Alexandria
Bucephala
Mediterranean Sea
Tyre
Damascus
Susa
Jerusalem
PALESTINE
Babylon
Alexandria
Gaza
Alexander's death, 323 B.C.
Alexandria
Alexandria
Alexandria
Alexandria
Alexandria
Memphis
Persepolis
PERSIA
Nile River
Red Sea
Persian Gulf
Arabian Sea

0   200   400 mi
0   200   400 km

Map Study Alexander moved from one military victory to the next without losing a single battle.
Movement How many towns did Alexander and his followers establish?

Critical Thinking After Alexander's death, his empire split into pieces. Why do you think Alexander's empire was difficult to keep united?

Even during the Pax Romana, Roman citizens continued to serve in the military. They kept the peace by stopping revolts in Egypt, Germany, and Britain. This carving showing Roman soldiers is on a column honoring Antoninus Pius, the emperor of Rome from A.D. 138-161. Antoninus Pius ruled Rome during the calmest period of the Pax Romana.

READ ACTIVELY

Visualize Visualize the building of roads and aqueducts without modern equipment.

The Glory of Ancient Rome

Have you ever heard the saying "All roads lead to Rome" or "Rome was not built in a day"? These expressions come from a glorious time—when the Roman Empire ruled a huge area and built magnificent cities and structures.

The cities of the Roman Empire were linked by roads—about 50,000 miles of hard-surfaced highways. The Roman system of roads was one of the most outstanding transportation networks ever built. Constructed over 2,000 years ago, some of these roads are still used today.

The Romans also built aqueducts, or canals that carried water to the cities from distant sources. Like Roman roads, some of these aqueducts are still in use.

The Pax Romana The Romans began building their empire soon after the death of Alexander the Great. The first emperor of Rome, Augustus, took command in 27 B.C. This began the **Pax Romana** (pahks roh MAH nah), or Roman peace. It lasted for about 200 years. During the Pax Romana, Rome was the most powerful state in Europe and in the Mediterranean. With Rome in charge, these regions remained stable.

Roman Law One of Rome's greatest gifts to the world was a system of laws. Roman lawmakers were careful and organized. They did not pass their laws on by word of mouth. Instead, they wrote them down. When a judge made a decision, he based it on written law. His decision was also put in writing to guide other judges. After a while, the law became so complex that the Romans organized it. Today, the legal system of almost every European country reflects the organization of ancient Roman law.

Roman laws protected all citizens. At first, citizens included only people who lived in Rome, except slaves. In time, however, the term came to include people all over the empire. The idea thus protected the rights of all citizens, not just the powerful and wealthy. Modern ideas about law and citizenship are based on this idea.

The Decline of Rome Hundreds of years of warfare followed the Pax Romana. People outside the empire grew strong and broke through Roman lines of defense. Sometimes they even entered Rome itself. There they terrorized, looted, and destroyed. The empire needed more and more soldiers. To pay for the wars, the government raised taxes. This hurt the empire's economy. The empire had grown too big for one person to govern, so it was divided into two empires, one in the eastern Mediterranean and one in the west. The eastern empire remained healthy. But the western one continued to weaken.

LINKS TO SCIENCE

The Volcano and the City of Pompeii The city of Pompeii stood at the foot of a volcano called Mt. Vesuvius. In A.D. 79, the volcano erupted. Smoke, ash, and cinders rained on the city. In two days, the eruption covered the city with about 20 feet (6.6 m) of ash. It sealed the city like a volcanic "time capsule." Archaeologists have uncovered Pompeii's buildings, almost perfectly intact. They have even found loaves of bread in ovens!

◀This statue shows Augustus, who ruled Rome from 27 B.C. to A.D. 14. He declared that he had "found Rome brick and left it marble." Indeed, during the reign of Augustus, Rome's first emperor, the Romans constructed many buildings and built roads, bridges, and aqueducts.

The weakening of the Roman Empire in Western Europe led to a time of uncertainty. The powerful laws of the great Roman government no longer protected people. People had to look elsewhere for something to protect them.

Europe in the Middle Ages

Picture a building like a hollow mountain of stones. Each stone has been cut and set in place by careful workers. The building's graceful arches sweep to the sky. This building is a cathedral—a great church. Many cathedrals were built in Europe during the Middle Ages.

Today, a building can be raised in a few months. But in the Middle Ages, it took as long as 100 years to build a cathedral. People devoted so much time and energy to building cathedrals because they believed that the work was God's wish. Such strong religious faith was a key part of life in Europe during the Middle Ages.

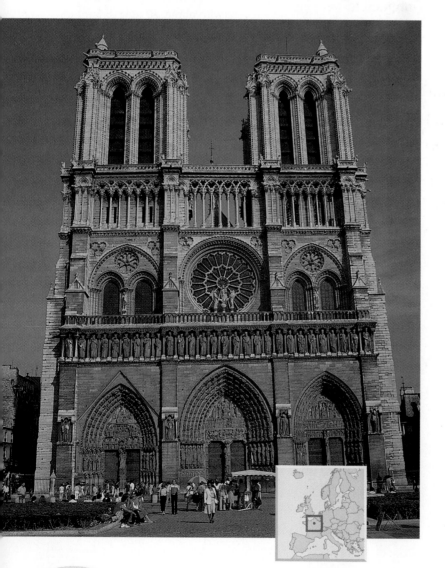

▼ Paris's Notre Dame Cathedral took about 150 years to complete. It was one of the first buildings constructed with flying buttresses, which are supporting arches on the outside of the building.

Christian Faith The religion of Christianity arose from the life and teachings of Jesus, who lived in a region called Palestine. After Jesus' death, his followers began spreading his teachings. These followers taught that Jesus was the Son of God.

One person who became a Christian, or follower of Jesus Christ, was a Roman emperor named Constantine. Christianity spread quickly throughout the Roman Empire. Later, the empire collapsed. Government, law and order, and trade broke down. But Christianity remained. The people of Europe, living in a period of difficulty and danger, drew strength from Christianity. In such dark times, faith was like a welcoming light.

Feudalism Christianity was one important part of people's lives during the Middle Ages. Another was **feudalism** (FYOOD ul iz um), which is a way to organize society when there is no central government. In feudalism, leaders called lords ruled the local areas. Lords swore oaths of loyalty to a more powerful leader, such as a king. In return, the king allowed the lord to own a piece of land called a **manor.** The lord owned all the crops and received all income from the land. He collected taxes, maintained order, enforced laws, and protected the **serfs,**

Feudal Society

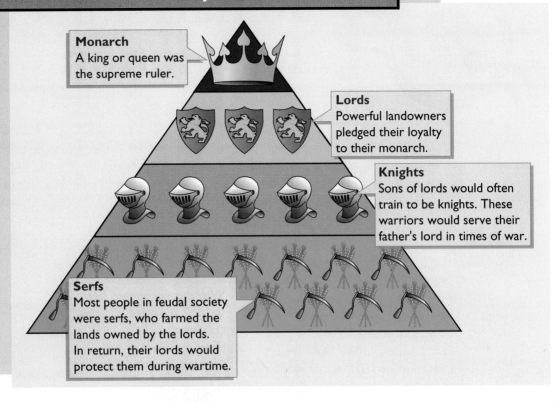

Monarch
A king or queen was the supreme ruler.

Lords
Powerful landowners pledged their loyalty to their monarch.

Knights
Sons of lords would often train to be knights. These warriors would serve their father's lord in times of war.

Serfs
Most people in feudal society were serfs, who farmed the lands owned by the lords. In return, their lords would protect them during wartime.

Chart Study
European society in the Middle Ages was shaped like a pyramid. At the bottom were peasants, who made up 90 percent of the population. Above the peasants were the nobles, made up of knights, lords, and the king. Though there were many fewer nobles than peasants, the nobles had nearly all the wealth and power.

Critical Thinking
How did the feudal system tie different social groups together?

the people who lived on the land and farmed it. Serfs were not slaves, but they could not leave without the lord's permission. They owned no land and depended on the lord for protection in times of war.

As centuries passed, life in Europe changed. Trade increased. Many serfs bought their freedom from the lords and moved to towns, which offered excitement and opportunity. Towns grew into cities. By the 1400s, a new way of life had begun to develop in Europe.

SECTION 1 REVIEW

1. **Define** (a) Middle Ages, (b) democracy, (c) city-state, (d) policy, (e) empire, (f) Pax Romana, (g) feudalism, (h) manor, (i) serf.

2. **Identify** (a) Alexander the Great, (b) Augustus, (c) Constantine, (d) Athens, (e) Rome.

3. What were the most important ideas given to us by (a) the ancient Greeks and (b) the ancient Romans?

4. What role did Christianity play during the Middle Ages?

5. What did feudalism provide during the Middle Ages?

Critical Thinking

6. **Making Comparisons** Describe some ways in which Europe under the Pax Romana was different from Europe in the Middle Ages.

Activity

7. **Writing to Learn** You are a Roman governor in Britain, far from your home and family in Rome. Write a journal entry describing the things you miss about Rome. Be as specific as you can.

Renaissance and Revolution

BEFORE YOU READ

Reach Into Your Background

Tales of rich and wondrous lands to the east inspired European explorers. Have you ever read or seen stories that made you want to travel to distant lands? Think of a list of places that you would like to visit. Write a few sentences telling how you learned about them and why you want to visit them.

Questions to Explore

1. Why did Europeans begin to look outward to other continents?

2. How did the Age of Revolution change science and government?

Key Terms

Renaissance
humanism
monarch
middle class
absolute monarch
revolution
colony
Scientific Revolution

Key People

Marco Polo
Michelangelo
Louis XIV

▼ More than 100 years after Marco Polo's departure from Venice in 1271, illustrations like this celebrated his adventures.

The time is about A.D. 1295. The place is a prison in an Italian city called Genoa (JEN uh wuh). An explorer named Marco Polo lies on a cot, telling stories to a fellow prisoner. The tales are amazing because Marco Polo has had quite a life! For a time, he was a messenger of the great Mongol (MAHN gul) emperor Kublai Khan (KOO bly kahn), ruler of China. Polo also traveled across burning deserts and sailed south of the Equator. He visited the Spice Islands, sources of cinnamon, nutmeg, and cloves—spices that Europeans loved. He earned great riches, only to be robbed on his way home to Italy.

These stories were published in a book we know today as *The Travels of Marco Polo*. From the very beginning, the book was a great success. Two hundred years later, Marco Polo's book inspired Christopher Columbus, another explorer. When Columbus sailed west from Europe, he was searching for a new route to the rich lands Marco Polo had described: China, Japan, and India.

Leonardo da Vinci (above), one of the best-known artists of the Renaissance, is famous for his painting, *Mona Lisa* (left). But he also excelled as a scientist, an engineer, and an inventor.

Glories of the Renaissance

Columbus's search for a new route to wealth was only one example of the energy sweeping Europe. The changes began in Italy in the 1300s and spread over the continent. Traders were busy buying and selling again. The rich were becoming even richer. They had the time to enjoy art and learning—and the money to support artists and scholars. This period is called the **Renaissance** (REN uh sahns), which refers to a "rebirth" of interest in learning and art. The Renaissance reached its peak in the 1500s.

Renaissance scholars and artists rediscovered the ancient world. Once again, people learned about its great poetry, plays, ideas, buildings, and sculpture. What they learned changed them. They began writing fresh, powerful poetry. They built glorious new buildings and filled them with breathtaking paintings. People began to focus on improving this world rather than hoping for a better life after death. In trying to understand the world around them, they looked at the ideas of Greek and Roman thinkers. This new approach to knowledge was called **humanism.**

Humanism affected every part of the Renaissance. For example, in the early Middle Ages, statues had been carved as stiff symbols. But during the Renaissance period, statues carved by artists such as Michelangelo (my kul AN juh loh), an Italian sculptor, were lifelike. In fact, some people say that no better sculptor than Michelangelo has ever lived.

READ ACTIVELY

Ask Questions What would you like to ask a Renaissance artist about the influence of humanism?

More Trade, Stronger Rulers

In the Renaissance, people also began to travel outside of Europe more often. In the 1400s, Portuguese explorers traveled along the western coast of Africa. There they traded in gold, ivory, and slaves. This trade was very profitable. Finally, the Portuguese reached the Indian Ocean. They set up new trade routes for the most profitable goods of all—spices. Rulers of other European countries envied the Portuguese. Spain, France, England, and the Netherlands all wanted a share of the trading wealth. Then, in 1492, Christopher Columbus found even more possibilities for wealth. Far to the west were two vast continents: the Americas.

The Effects of Trade Europeans raced to the Americas in search of wealth. Precious minerals, such as gold and silver, and trade goods, such as fur and tobacco, poured into Europe. Most of the wealth went to European **monarchs** (MAHN urks), rulers such as kings and queens. Some of it went to traders and merchants. These people formed a group between the poor and the very rich. They became the **middle class.** The taxes paid by the middle class made monarchs even wealthier. Soon, kings no longer needed the support of feudal lords. Feudalism declined, local lords grew weaker, and kings gained power.

More Gold, More Knowledge

After the great voyages of exploration, gold began to pour into Europe. A good part of it was turned into coins. These gold coins (below) were minted in London in 1566. The voyages also increased Europeans' understanding of the world. Geographers displayed this new knowledge on accurate globes (right).

The Age of Monarchs

From 1643 to 1715, the king of France was Louis XIV. One of Europe's most powerful kings, Louis XIV ruled at a time when France was a leading world power. Like other kings of his time, Louis was an **absolute monarch;** that is, he exercised complete power over his subjects. As he said, "I am the state." His wishes were law, and no one dared to disagree with him. Like other European monarchs, Louis believed that his power to rule came from God. To oppose him was the same as opposing God.

Louis used his power to make people pay heavy taxes. These taxes, in part, paid for his very expensive lifestyle. But Louis also wanted to make France strong. Other rulers wanted the same thing for their countries. Over time, these monarchs made their countries stronger and more unified. As these changes took place, people began thinking again about government. What should it be? What should it do for them?

Twelve miles from Paris, the palace at Versailles with its glittering Hall of Mirrors advertised the French king's wealth. Paintings on the ceiling illustrate the royal family's accomplishments.

Revolutions in Government and Science

The 1600s and 1700s are often called the Age of Revolution. A **revolution** is a far-reaching change. European thought, beliefs, and ways of life all changed. This period was the beginning of the modern age of science and democracy that we know today.

Revolutions in Government One sign of revolution was that people began questioning their governments. For instance, people wondered if kings should have all the power. In the 1600s, when England's king refused to share power with Parliament (PAHR luh munt), the elected legislature, he was overthrown. England had no monarch for several years. This change in power failed, and the monarchy returned. But this event showed that the people, not the monarch, should decide which type of government is best for them.

This idea of government spread to North America, where Great Britain had 13 colonies. A **colony** is a territory ruled by another nation,

ACROSS THE WORLD

A Share in Two Revolutions In 1776, Thomas Paine wrote *Common Sense,* a pamphlet urging the American colonies to fight for independence. The pamphlet sold more than 500,000 copies and greatly influenced the American Revolution. Later, Paine wrote *The Rights of Man,* which influenced the French Revolution of 1789.

On July 14, 1789, an angry French mob seized control of the Bastille, a prison (below). The people were angry at King Louis XVI and the queen, Marie Antoinette (right), because the monarchs were spending money on clothes and building projects at a time when the poor in Paris were starving. Eventually, the king and queen were both executed.

Predict How might humanism have affected science?

usually one far away. In 1776, the colonies rebelled against the British king. The colonists defeated the British and formed the independent nation of the United States. And in 1789, 13 years after the Americans declared their independence, there was a revolution in France. The French Revolution overthrew the French monarchy once and for all.

The Scientific Revolution There was also a revolution in science. For centuries, European scientists had studied nature to explain how the world fit with their religious beliefs. During the Age of Revolution, that approach changed. Scientists began to watch carefully to see what really happened in the world. They would base their theories on facts. They would not try to make the facts fit their religious beliefs. This change is called the Scientific Revolution.

The Scientific Revolution required new procedures. These procedures make up what is called the scientific method, in which ideas are tested with experiments and observations. Scientists do not accept an idea as correct unless several tests prove that it is.

Using the scientific method, scientists made dramatic advances. For example, in the Middle Ages, Europeans believed that the Earth was at the center of the universe. Later, Renaissance scientists challenged this belief. Then, during the Scientific Revolution, scientists used a new form

The Scientific Method

Chart Study A revolution in thinking paved the way for the scientific method, which today's scientists still use. Employing this method, scientists began to record what they could actually observe instead of what they merely believed to be true. Followers of the scientific method usually repeat their work many times, in order to make sure that their conclusions are accurate. **Critical Thinking** Why do you think scientists should repeat their work before coming to a conclusion?

STEP ONE

State the problem.

STEP TWO

Gather information about the problem.

STEP THREE

Form a hypothesis, or educated guess.

STEP FOUR

Experiment to test the hypothesis.

STEP FIVE

Record and analyze data.

STEP SIX

State a conclusion.

of mathematics called calculus (KAL kyoo lus). It helped them learn how the moon and planets move. Their work led to better ideas about such things as gravity.

By the end of the Age of Revolution, Europe was a continent of powerful nations. They were bustling with trade and bursting with new scientific ideas. Europe was about to begin a new kind of revolution. This time it would be an economic one—the rise of industry.

SECTION 2 REVIEW

1. **Define** (a) Renaissance, (b) humanism, (c) monarch, (d) middle class, (e) absolute monarch, (f) revolution, (g) colony, (h) Scientific Revolution.

2. **Identify** (a) Marco Polo, (b) Michelangelo, (c) Louis XIV.

3. How did Europeans' desire for wealth lead to voyages of exploration?

4. How did the art of the Renaissance differ from the art of the Middle Ages?

5. How did government and science in Europe change during the Age of Revolution?

Critical Thinking

6. **Identifying Central Issues** Explain how trade affected the power of kings during the 1500s and 1600s.

Activity

7. **Writing to Learn** Marco Polo's writings excited readers and made them want to explore the world just like he had. Think about a place that you have visited. What makes it special? What details make you like it—or dislike it? Then write about the place in a way that would make a reader want to go there, too.

SKILLS ACTIVITY

Interpreting Diagrams and Illustrations

Sandra bolted through the front door of her grandmother's house.

"Hey, Grandma! Dad just told me that you went to France once, before I was born."

"Yes, I did," said her grandmother. "I went to visit my mother's family. But I was much younger then."

"What was it like? What did you do there?" Sandra wanted to know all about it.

"Well, that little town looked a lot different than it does now—that was 40 years ago."

"Did they have knights and castles then?" Sandra asked eagerly.

Her grandmother laughed. "Oh, no, it wasn't *that* long ago. But you can see for yourself. I think I still have my pictures from that trip. Shall we get them out?"

Sandra nodded.

"There's just one problem," her grandmother warned. "You'll understand the pictures, but all the writing is in French!"

Get Ready

There are many kinds of illustrations—maps, photographs, paintings, drawings, and diagrams, to name a few. Often, diagrams and illustrations are explained by captions and annotations. Annotations are labels that include extra information. They help you understand diagrams and illustrations.

To get the most out of any illustration, you need to study carefully both the illustration itself and all of the annotations. You may find this even more useful when you look at illustrations of life long ago. These illustrations can bring history alive for you. They can help you picture life in other times and other places.

◀ You can learn how to interpret diagrams and illustrations by making one of your own. In addition to the labels shown on this mailbox, the student might have added a caption such as "The post office collects the mail and delivers it to the recipients."

Try It Out

Of course, the world today is much different than the world young people lived in hundreds of years ago. Far in the future, the world will be much different than it is now. Students many years from now will read in their history books about the way *you* live. You can help them out by creating an illustration to help them picture "life long ago"—your life today.

A. Choose your subject. Draw an illustration of something that is common today but might not be common in the future. Perhaps chalkboards will be replaced by computers, or automobiles by personal jets. Be sure to draw something you know well.

B. Illustrate your subject. Using a pencil and unlined paper, draw your subject. Try to be as accurate as possible. Imagine that the students of the future will never have seen the real thing.

C. Add annotations to your illustration. Write brief notes explaining the main features of what you have drawn. Try to have your annotations explain the object's parts. Tell how they are used or how they relate to each other.

Apply the Skill

Now that you have made your own illustration and annotations, you can read one by someone else. Complete the following steps.

1 **Study the illustration.** Look it over in a general way. What is the subject of this illustration? From what time period is it? Does it show something as it really looked, or does it show how something might have looked?

2 **Read the annotations.** The annotations provide key information about the illustration. What are the main parts of a manor? Who lived in the manor house? How were the fields divided? What was the demesne (dih MAYN)? How were the meadows used? Where did the peasants live?

3 **Think about the illustration.** After you have studied the illustration and read the annotations, take another look. This time, imagine yourself as the lord of the manor, or as a peasant who worked there. What was life like for you? Write a journal entry from this point of view. Try to capture the sights, sounds, and smells of life on the manor.

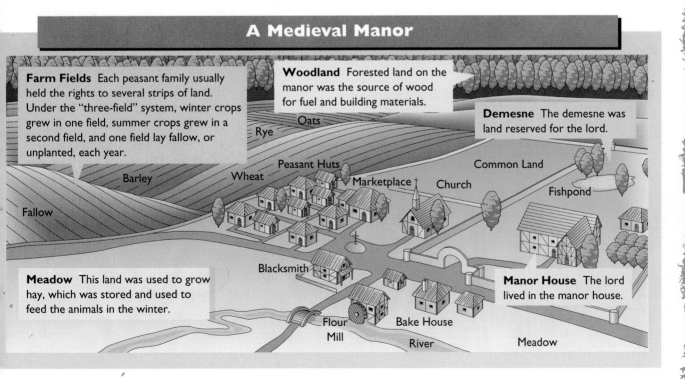

A Medieval Manor

Farm Fields Each peasant family usually held the rights to several strips of land. Under the "three-field" system, winter crops grew in one field, summer crops grew in a second field, and one field lay fallow, or unplanted, each year.

Woodland Forested land on the manor was the source of wood for fuel and building materials.

Demesne The demesne was land reserved for the lord.

Meadow This land was used to grow hay, which was stored and used to feed the animals in the winter.

Manor House The lord lived in the manor house.

Oats
Rye
Barley
Wheat
Fallow
Peasant Huts
Marketplace
Church
Common Land
Fishpond
Blacksmith
Flour Mill
Bake House
River
Meadow

Industrial Revolution and Nationalism

BEFORE YOU READ

Reach Into Your Background

Have you ever spent a whole day working very hard? Perhaps you helped with spring housecleaning or took part in a car wash. Do you remember how tired you were at the end of the day? During the Industrial Revolution, many people your age worked in factories 12 hours a day, 6 days a week.

Questions to Explore

1. How did the Industrial Revolution change life in Europe?

2. How did nationalism change Europe?

Key Terms

Industrial Revolution
textile
imperialism
nationalism
alliance

▼ This late 1800s picture shows smoke belching from factories beside the Don River in Sheffield, an industrial city in northern England.

It was dawn. Thick, black smoke rose from the tall smokestack of the factory. Dust blew through the air and settled over the crowded rows of houses. The smoke and the roar of machines showed that the factory workday had begun.

Inside, women and children worked at rows of machines that wove cotton thread into cloth. Their work was dirty, noisy, and dangerous. The day before, a worker had caught his hand in a machine and was severely injured. Today, another worker stood in his place. Both were only 13 years old. No matter what, the machines kept going. Workers fed them thread for 12 hours every day—6 days out of every 7. Vacations did not exist.

You could see scenes like this all across Europe in the early 1800s. The great age of factories had begun. Products that once had been made by people in homes or in small shops were now made by machines in huge factories. This change is called the **Industrial Revolution.** The new factories caused great suffering. But as time went by, the rise of industry brought an easier way of life to people all over the world.

During the Industrial Revolution, spinning wheels (below) were replaced by spinning mules (left) that could spin up to 1,300 times as much thread in the same amount of time. Special buildings, called factories, were built to house the spinning mules. **Critical Thinking** How do you think the shift from spinning wheel to spinning mule affected the average worker?

The Industrial Revolution

Did you ever wonder what life would be like without factories? You would have to make everything you need at home or buy it from a small shop nearby. People produced goods this way until about the late 1700s. Then, inventors began to create machines that could make goods quickly and cheaply. Huge factories housed the machines. People left their homes to work in the factories and keep the machines running. This was a revolution in the way goods were made. It was also a revolution in the ways people lived and worked.

Changes in Production The Industrial Revolution began in Great Britain. The first machines were invented to speed up the spinning of thread and the weaving of textiles, or cloth products. The new factories made their owners very wealthy. Businesspeople in other countries saw this and decided to try the same thing. Factories sprouted up all over Europe and in the United States. By 1900, factories produced almost all goods made in the United States and most of Western Europe.

Changes in Society The Industrial Revolution changed life across Europe. For hundreds of years, families had farmed the land. Now they moved to industrial centers to work in factories. Cities grew rapidly. People were packed into cramped, dirty housing. Because of unclean and crowded conditions, diseases spread rapidly.

LINKS ACROSS TIME

Urbanization When industrialization took hold in Europe, people moved from the country to the cities in huge numbers. In 100 years, the population of London grew from 831,000 to 4.5 million. The population of Paris grew from 547,000 to 2.9 million.

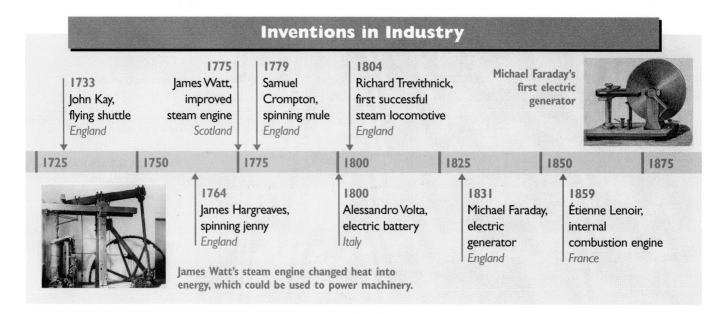

Inventions in Industry

1733 John Kay, flying shuttle *England*

1775 James Watt, improved steam engine *Scotland*

1779 Samuel Crompton, spinning mule *England*

1804 Richard Trevithnick, first successful steam locomotive *England*

Michael Faraday's first electric generator

1725	1750	1775	1800	1825	1850	1875

1764 James Hargreaves, spinning jenny *England*

1800 Alessandro Volta, electric battery *Italy*

1831 Michael Faraday, electric generator *England*

1859 Étienne Lenoir, internal combustion engine *France*

James Watt's steam engine changed heat into energy, which could be used to power machinery.

▲ As you read the time line, find the inventions that could be used to produce power. These inventions paved the way for machines that required more energy than humans or animals could provide.

READ ACTIVELY

Predict How did the Industrial Revolution promote democracy?

The changes were difficult for many people. For a long time, factory owners took advantage of workers. Wages were low. Factory conditions were not safe. However, workers slowly began to form labor unions and to demand better working conditions. In the early 1900s, governments began passing laws to protect workers. Conditions improved and wages rose.

Changes in Government

Government had to respond to workers' complaints. Making and selling goods was a big part of a country's economy. This meant that workers had become very important. As a result, the Industrial Revolution helped give working people a bigger voice in government. Many European nations became more democratic.

At the same time, though, European governments were becoming more aggressive abroad. During the 1800s, many European nations took over other countries and turned them into colonies. This is called **imperialism.** European nations were making more goods than their people could buy. They needed more customers. Colonies could supply those buyers. Colonies also provided raw materials, such things as cotton, wood, and metals, that industry needed.

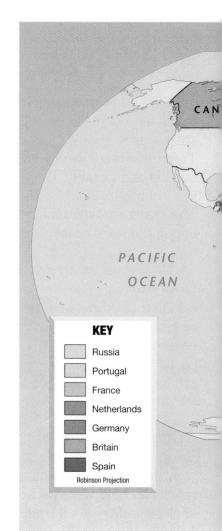

CAN

PACIFIC OCEAN

KEY

Russia
Portugal
France
Netherlands
Germany
Britain
Spain

Robinson Projection

The late 1800s are called the Age of Imperialism. Most of Africa was divided up by the European nations of Belgium, France, Italy, Spain, Portugal, Germany, and Great Britain. These countries also took over much of Southeast Asia and many South Pacific islands. In time, struggles among the colonial powers would bring disaster to Europe.

A Century of War and Nationalism

At the start of the 1900s, the people of Europe were filled with **nationalism,** or pride in one's country. Nationalism can either be a destructive or creative force, depending on how people express it.

Destructive Nationalism   Nationalism can be very destructive. It can make one nation harm another in an effort to get ahead. It can also prevent nations from working with one another. Then anger and hatred can erupt between countries. Between 1900 and 1950, destructive nationalism played a part in causing two world wars and the deaths of millions of people.

Ask Questions What would you like to know about the impact of nationalism on world history?

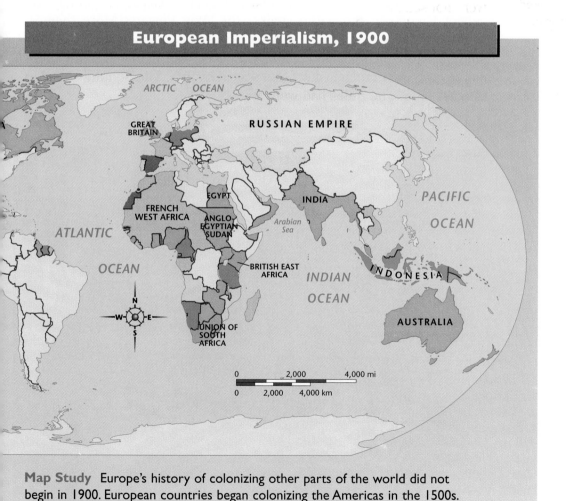

European Imperialism, 1900

Map Study Europe's history of colonizing other parts of the world did not begin in 1900. European countries began colonizing the Americas in the 1500s. Most of the Americas had become independent by 1900. **Regions** What three European countries had the largest empires in 1900?

HEROES

Working Together
Jeannine Picabia was 18 in 1941. She worked with a French medical group that traveled to places where prisoners were questioned by German soldiers. She listened carefully to the conversations. One day she decided to go to an American government building in France to tell what she had heard. Secretly, for the rest of World War II, she gathered information for the forces that were trying to defeat Germany.

▼ One of the most frightening weapons of World War I was poison gas. These Russian soldiers are caught in a German gas attack.

During the early 1900s, European nations feared one another. Each nation was afraid another would invade or try to take over its territory. To protect themselves, nations made **alliances** (uh LY un sez), or agreements with one another. In such alliances, a nation promises to protect its friends if someone attacks them. Soon, Europe was divided into two alliances. On one side were Germany, Austria-Hungary, and Italy. On the other side were Great Britain, France, and Russia.

In 1914, fighting between the alliances broke out into what is now called World War I. By the end of the war, in 1918, over 9 million soldiers had been killed. About 13 million civilians, or nonsoldiers, had also died. Europe had lost almost a whole generation of young men.

But nationalism still burned like a flame. In 1939, another war broke out. This war was called World War II. Again there were two alliances. On one side were the Axis Powers—Germany and Italy, which were joined by Japan. These countries wanted to increase their national wealth and power. Therefore, they took control of other countries. They quickly captured most of Europe and parts of China and the South Pacific. Germany also attacked the Soviet Union, a nation made up of Russia and several smaller regions.

In time, the United States joined the Allies—Great Britain and the Soviet Union—in the battle against the Axis Powers. More than 50 nations took part in this war, which was the most destructive ever fought. More people died, more property was damaged, and more money was spent than in any other war in history. The fighting ended in August 1945. The Allies had won.

A Tunnel Connecting Britain to France

During the Ice Age, France and Great Britain were connected by a low plain. Later, the English Channel separated Britain and France—but not forever. In 1987, France and Great Britain began working together to dig a tunnel under the English Channel. In 1994, these men dug the breakthrough hole linking Britain and France. They exchanged flags and shook hands. Today trains carry passengers and freight through the Channel Tunnel, which many people call the Chunnel. **Critical Thinking** What do you think kept Great Britain and France from building the Chunnel earlier?

Creative Nationalism After the war, all of Europe was in ruins. It was time to rebuild. The European nations were sick of imperialism and war. After hundreds of years, they were no longer world leaders. Now the world looked on the United States and the Soviet Union as leading nations.

Europeans began learning to work together. They became trading partners, not competitors. A new type of nationalism began, a European nationalism. People have not forgotten that they are French, or British, or German. At the end of the 1900s, Europeans were working hard to build a common European community. It may carry them into the new century in peace.

SECTION 3 REVIEW

1. **Define** (a) Industrial Revolution, (b) textile, (c) imperialism, (d) nationalism, (e) alliance.

2. What changes occurred in the lives of ordinary people during the Industrial Revolution?

3. What changes in government occurred in industrialized nations during the Industrial Revolution?

4. Give an example of creative nationalism.

Critical Thinking

5. **Identifying Central Issues** The Industrial Revolution caused many changes. Name two changes that helped bring about imperialism.

Activity

6. **Writing to Learn** After World War II, colonies in Africa and Asia demanded their freedom from the European colonial powers. Suppose you were a citizen of a colony. Write a paragraph explaining why you would want to be free from European rulers.

Imperial Russia

BEFORE YOU READ

Reach Into Your Background

The rulers of Russia could do almost anything they wanted. They could make any laws and carry out any plans they chose. Imagine being able to make any changes you wanted in the United States. What would you change? What would you keep the same?

Questions to Explore

1. How did Russia develop into a huge empire by 1900?

2. How did the serfs' living conditions lead to opposition to the czars?

Key Terms
westernization
czar

Key People
Catherine the Great
Golden Horde
Peter the Great
Nicholas II

▼ This picture shows Catherine the Great wearing the crown of the empress of Russia.

At dawn on June 28, 1762, a maid awakened Catherine in her rooms at a small palace outside St. Petersburg, Russia. Catherine's supporter, Aleksei Orlov (ul yik SEEAY ur LAHF), was waiting for her. "Time to rise," he told her. "Everything is prepared." Catherine hurried to a coach waiting to whisk her to St. Petersburg.

As the coach hurried along, Catherine may have remembered how she had first come to Russia, 17 years before. At age 16, she had been brought here from Germany to marry Peter, who later became emperor. Peter was a weak and foolish ruler. Now Catherine was hoping to remove him from the throne and become empress herself. Would the Russian people support her?

As Catherine's coach rattled down St. Petersburg's main street toward the Winter Palace, crowds streamed out to cheer her on. When she arrived at the palace, she was greeted by government, military, and church leaders. Their support helped make Catherine the new Empress of Russia.

Catherine was witty and charming. She loved the arts, literature, philosophy, and French culture. Under her rule, the court at St. Petersburg glittered with French actors and dancers, German teachers and craftspeople, and artistic treasures from foreign lands. Her court attracted the greatest minds of Europe. She dreamed of creating a great nation, as glorious as France under Louis XIV. Little wonder that she was called Catherine the Great.

Catherine cared about the Russian people. She built schools and hospitals and gave people more religious freedom. Early in her rule, she became interested in ideas about liberty. She even thought about freeing the serfs, the peasant farmers who worked on the estates of wealthy landowners. Then there was a violent serf revolt, and Catherine changed her mind. She strengthened control over the serfs and crushed their attempts to gain freedom.

Though Catherine did not make Russia a land of freedom, she did make Russia a grand empire. By her death in 1796, she had expanded her nation's borders southward to the edge of the Black Sea. She had also taken over parts of Poland in the west. Her expansion followed a pattern of empire-building that had been taking place in Russia for many centuries.

As Catherine's rule shows, the history of Russia is a story with three themes: (1) expansion; (2) harsh treatment of the common people; and (3) slow **westernization,** a process of becoming more like Western Europe. As you read Russia's story, notice how these three themes show up again and again.

Predict What changes do you think took place because of Mongol rule?

Building a Vast Empire

Russia began as a small country called Muscovy (MUHS kuh vee), or Moscow. In the early 1100s, Kiev (KEE ev) was the most important city in the region. It was home to the grand prince. Other, lesser princes ruled their own lands. They continually fought among themselves. Each hoped to gain enough power to become the grand prince. In 1238, Mongol conquerors, who were called the Golden Horde, swept into the region from Asia. Weakened by the struggles among themselves, the princes were defeated quickly. In 1240, the Mongols conquered Kiev and the whole territory became part of the Mongol empire.

Life Under the Golden Horde
The Golden Horde dominated Russia for almost 250 years. The Mongols mostly wanted two things: to collect heavy taxes and to force the Russians to serve in the Mongol army. The conquerors appointed a Russian prince to handle the day-to-day

A Mongol Archer

Russians called Mongol warriors like this archer the Golden Horde after the color of their tents. The Mongols plundered and burned Kiev and other Russian towns. They killed so many Russians that a historian claimed "no eye remained to weep for the dead."

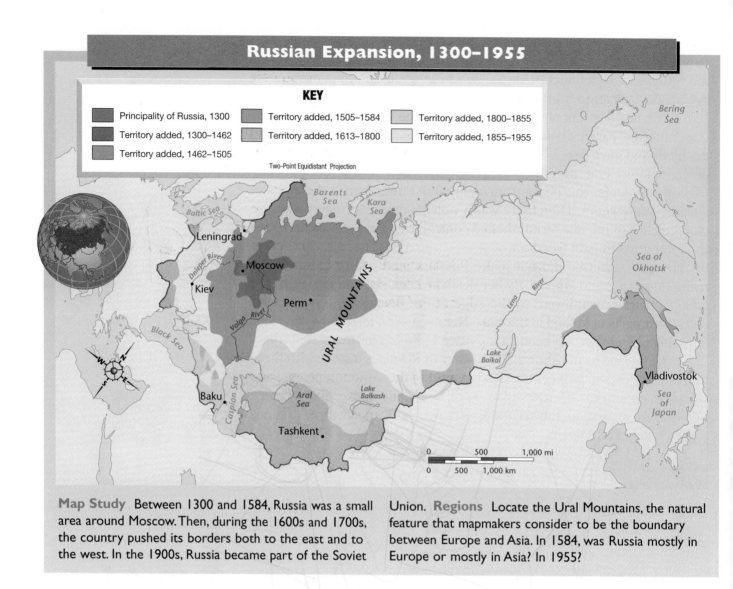

Russian Expansion, 1300–1955

KEY

- Principality of Russia, 1300
- Territory added, 1300–1462
- Territory added, 1462–1505
- Territory added, 1505–1584
- Territory added, 1613–1800
- Territory added, 1800–1855
- Territory added, 1855–1955

Two-Point Equidistant Projection

Map Study Between 1300 and 1584, Russia was a small area around Moscow. Then, during the 1600s and 1700s, the country pushed its borders both to the east and to the west. In the 1900s, Russia became part of the Soviet Union. **Regions** Locate the Ural Mountains, the natural feature that mapmakers consider to be the boundary between Europe and Asia. In 1584, was Russia mostly in Europe or mostly in Asia? In 1955?

affairs of the country. To make sure that the people did not rebel, the Mongols attacked the country from time to time. Because Russia was cut off from the West by the Mongols, Russia did not take part in the Renaissance of art and learning that was changing Western Europe.

The Rise of Moscow During the early 1330s, the Mongols selected Ivan I of Muscovy to be grand prince. Ivan collected taxes for the Mongols. In return, they let him keep some of the money. Ivan the Moneybag, as he was soon called, began to buy land and expand the size of Muscovy.

As Muscovy grew stronger, the Mongol empire began to fall apart. In 1480, Ivan III, Grand Prince of Muscovy, challenged Mongol control by refusing to pay taxes. The Golden Horde was too weak to force its wishes on Ivan and take back control of Russia.

Rise of the Czars As Muscovy became more powerful and spread its control over Russia, its grand prince became known as a **czar** (zar), or emperor. The first czar, Ivan IV, was crowned in 1547. He was also known as Ivan the Terrible. He was cruel and distrusted others. But he increased Russia's size by conquering Mongol lands in the southeast and by conquering western Siberia.

After Ivan IV's death, Russia lived through nearly 30 years of war. Finally, in 1613, Michael Romanov (ROH muh nawf) became czar. He was the first in a long line of Romanovs who ruled Russia until 1917. The Romanovs expanded Russian territory through the 1600s.

In 1689, Peter the Great came to power. A strong leader, Peter started to bring Western European ideas and culture to Russia. In 1697, he sent a Russian official to visit Western Europe. His goals were to find out about western culture and methods and to meet with European officials. Peter went along, dressed as a minor official. On his return to Russia, he started new schools and reorganized his government and the army. He hired foreign professors, scientists, and advisors. He encouraged Russians to adopt western customs.

Visualize Visualize Peter the Great in disguise in meetings with European officials.

◄ The Winter Palace at St. Petersburg, completed in 1762, was the world's largest royal palace. It was the winter home of the czars until 1917.

Peter also enlarged Russia. He believed that Russia must have good seaports to become a world power, so he conquered land on the Baltic (BAWL tik) and Black seas. Czars who followed Peter, including Catherine the Great, continued to expand Russia's borders, gaining territories in Poland, Turkey, China, and Sweden. With many lands under its rule, Russia truly became an empire.

The Fall of the Czars

Russia was becoming powerful, but the lives of its serfs had not improved. For hundreds of years, Russia had been divided into two groups—the very rich and the very poor. Tension between the two groups began to rise.

In 1855, a new czar, Alexander II, came to the throne. He, too, wanted Russia to be more like European nations. One way to do that, he believed, was to have the czars and the wealthy give up some of their powers. In 1861, a few years before Abraham Lincoln ended slavery in the United States, Alexander freed the serfs and gave them their own land. Towns were given more control over their own affairs. However, Alexander's son, Czar Alexander III, reversed many of his father's reforms. The country again came under harsh rule.

In 1894, Nicholas II became czar. He would be the last. After Russia was badly beaten in a war with Japan in 1904 and 1905, unrest grew among serfs and workers. On January 22, 1905, thousands of workers in

LINKS ACROSS THE WORLD

Peace Between Russia and Japan Between 1904 and 1905, Japan and Russia fought over control of Manchuria, in northeastern Asia, and Korea, a peninsula in East Asia. Finally, U.S. President Theodore Roosevelt arranged a peace conference in Portsmouth, New Hampshire. For his role in the settlement, Roosevelt was awarded the Nobel Peace Prize in 1906.

The Russian Famine of 1892

Even after Alexander II freed them from serfdom, the lives of Russian peasants did not improve much. In the 1890s, there were several bad harvests, and many peasants starved to death. This etching shows peasants begging in the streets of Kazan, Russia. The famine was one of many problems that eventually helped to incite the people of Russia to revolution. **Critical Thinking** How can you tell that the people in the sleigh were wealthy?

The Czar and the Czarevitch

Czar Nicholas (right) and his son Alexis posed for a photograph shortly before the Russian Revolution of 1917. Alexis was the czarevitch, which means that he was the next in line to the throne. If the Russian Revolution had not taken place, he would have become the next czar. **Critical Thinking** Czars, like all monarchs, must learn to be strong leaders. What skills do you think the young czarevitch needed to learn in order to become czar?

St. Petersburg marched on the Winter Palace to ask the czar for reforms. They were met by troops, who fired into the crowd, killing hundreds.

After this mass killing, known as Bloody Sunday, Czar Nicholas was forced to agree to establish the Duma (DOO mah), a kind of congress. Members were elected by the people. The Duma held power, along with the czar, until 1917. Progress toward reform had been made. Some people wanted more, however, as you will read in the next section.

SECTION 4 REVIEW

1. **Define** (a) westernization, (b) czar.

2. **Identify** (a) Catherine the Great, (b) Golden Horde, (c) Peter the Great, (d) Nicholas II.

3. What territories did the princes of Muscovy and the czars take to expand Russian territory?

4. How did Russian czars treat the serfs?

5. Which rulers did the most to westernize Russia?

Critical Thinking

6. **Identifying Central Issues** At the beginning of the section, you learned about three themes in Russian history. How do the reigns of Ivan I, Ivan IV, and Peter the Great express those themes?

Activity

7. **Writing to Learn** You are Peter the Great. Write a journal entry about the ways in which you would like to make Russia a better and stronger country.

The Rise and Fall of the Soviet Union

BEFORE YOU READ

Reach Into Your Background

Imagine going shopping and finding only one style of shoes or one type of shirt. What if the grocery store had row after row of empty shelves? How would your life be different?

Questions to Explore

1. What is communism and why did it fail in the Soviet Union?
2. What happened in the Soviet Union under Lenin and Stalin?

Key Terms

revolutionary
communism
civil war
dictator
Cold War
consumer goods

Key People

Vladimir Lenin
Josef Stalin
Mikhail Gorbachev

▼ A rival said that the fiery Lenin—shown here making a speech in Red Square, Moscow—was so determined that "even when he sleeps, he dreams of nothing but the revolution."

On the afternoon of April 16, 1917, a small group of Russians gathered at a railroad station in a German town. Among them was a man named Vladimir Lenin. Earlier, the Russian government had thrown Lenin out of Russia and told him not to return. He had been spreading ideas that the government thought were **revolutionary**—ideas that could cause a revolution, or the overthrow of a government.

Now the Germans were supplying a train to take Lenin back to Russia. The Germans made two rules. No member of Lenin's group could leave the train or talk to any Germans during their journey. The Germans, too, knew that ideas can be more powerful than any army. Germany was at war with Russia and hoped that Lenin would cause changes in Russia. And he did. Lenin led one of the most important revolutions in history.

Grigori Rasputin, an adviser to the czar's family, is often accused of having helped to bring about the Russian Revolution. Rasputin had some success treating the czar's son, Alexis, who suffered from a serious illness. As a result, Rasputin had a great deal of influence with the czar and the czarina, the czar's wife. Some people think Rasputin convinced the czar and czarina to make bad decisions in the years leading up to the revolution. Supporters of the czar feared Rasputin's growing power. A group of them murdered him in 1916.

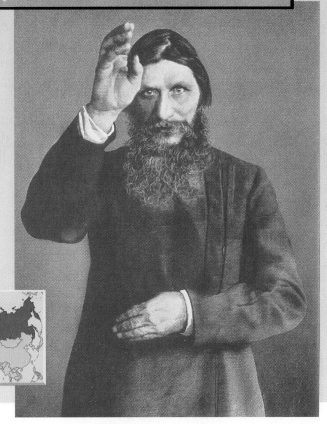

The Russian Revolution

To understand why the Germans helped Lenin, you need to go back to 1914. That year, Russia entered World War I, fighting against Germany. It was a harsh war. Millions of Russian soldiers were killed or wounded. At home, people suffered severe food and fuel shortages. By March 1917, the Russian people began rioting. Troops were sent to put down the uprising. However, they joined the people instead. The czar was forced to give up his throne. A weak government took over.

In November 1917, Lenin and his supporters pushed the weak government aside. Lenin knew the Russians wanted peace more than anything else. In March 1918, Russia signed an agreement with Germany and withdrew from World War I. This was just what the Germans had hoped for.

As the new leader of Russia, Lenin wanted a communist government. **Communism** (KAHM yoo nizum) is a theory that says all the people should own the farms and factories. Everyone should share the work equally and receive an equal share of the rewards.

In theory, communism appealed greatly to many of the Russian people. Remember the deep split between Russia's rich and poor? For hundreds of years, Russia's poor had suffered terrible hardships while the rich lived in luxury. In a communist nation, everyone is supposed to be equal. Lenin told the workers and serfs that communism would bring fairness and equality to all Russians.

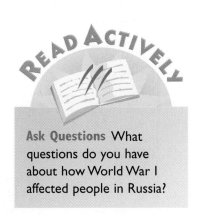

READ ACTIVELY

Ask Questions What questions do you have about how World War I affected people in Russia?

Building a Communist State

The treaty with the Germans ended the war, but peace did not come. After the Communists came to power, there was a terrible **civil war,** a war between groups inside a country. On one side were the Communists. On the other were many groups opposed to them.

The Russian civil war lasted three years and cost millions of lives. Finally, the Communists won. In 1922, Lenin created the Union of Soviet Socialist Republics (U.S.S.R.), also called the Soviet Union. The Soviet Union was made up of Russia and smaller areas, or republics, under Russian control.

Lenin began taking steps to turn the Soviet Union into a communist country. He jailed and even killed people who opposed him. Such people were enemies of the revolution, he said. Lenin died in 1924. He was followed by Josef Stalin, whose rule would be even more harsh.

Stalin's Dictatorship

Josef Stalin was a **dictator** (DIK tayt ur), a leader who has absolute power. Stalin did not care about the suffering his decisions caused. For example, he wanted to build industry in the Soviet Union. He knew that factory workers would need plenty of food. Therefore, Stalin forced serfs to give their farm products to the government. When the serfs opposed the plan, Stalin sent millions of them to prison camps in Siberia. Most died there. And when people questioned him about other actions, Stalin simply got rid of them. He sent them to the camps, or had them executed. All of the Soviet Union lived in terror of Stalin.

▼ This World War II Soviet poster shows a worker holding up a red flag bearing the portraits of Lenin and Stalin. The slogan encourages the Soviet people to produce more for the war effort.

СОРЕВНУЙТЕСЬ НА ЛУЧШУЮ ПОМОЩЬ ФРОНТУ!

When the Germans invaded the Soviet Union during World War II, they had to contend with the combined forces of bad weather and the Soviet army. First, rain caused German tanks to get stuck in the mud. Then, bitterly cold temperatures gave soldiers frostbite and caused machinery to break down. Finally, they had to fight determined Soviet soldiers who were ready to defend their country regardless of the cost. This picture shows Soviet soldiers in their victorious battle for the city of Stalingrad, which is now known as Volgograd. **Critical Thinking** How do you think the weather helped the Soviet soldiers to win victory over the Germans?

World War II   In 1939, Stalin signed an agreement with the Germans. It stated that the two countries would not fight each other. But the Germans invaded anyway. In 1941, three million German soldiers, with tanks and airplanes, drove deep into the Soviet Union.

For a time, a German victory appeared likely. Soviet cities were destroyed, and millions of soldiers died or were captured. But the Soviet people, helped by the harsh Russian winter, fought bravely. In 1943, the Soviets began pushing the Germans back toward their own borders. By 1945, Soviet troops had captured Berlin, the capital of Germany.

The Cold War

After World War II, the United States and the Soviet Union were the world's two strongest countries. They were so much stronger than other countries that people called them "superpowers." Relations between the superpowers were very tense, though the two sides never fought each other. This time of tension without actual war, which lasted roughly from 1945 until 1991, is called the **Cold War.**

Causes of the Cold War   Two things caused the tension. First was the problem of Eastern Europe. During World War II, the Soviet army moved westward all the way to Berlin. As the army advanced, it freed Eastern European countries the Germans had conquered. But after the war, Soviet troops did not leave. The Soviets forced these countries

LINKS TO LANGUAGE ARTS

Worried About War Many people during the Cold War feared that the United States and the U.S.S.R. would attack each other and destroy the world. Grace Paley's "Anxiety" is a story about people living with this fear. In the story, an old woman tells a young father to treat his daughter well because her future "is like a film which suddenly cuts to white."

A Voice of Protest By the age of 32, Andrei Sakharov was one of the Soviet Union's best scientists. In 1961, Sakharov began speaking out against the testing of nuclear bombs. As a result, he lost his job and was exiled to Siberia. He quickly became a hero to many Russians and in 1975 was awarded the Nobel Peace Prize.

to become communist. Most contact with the West was cut off. British leader Winston Churchill said that it was as if an "iron curtain" had fallen across Eastern Europe, dividing East and West.

Second, the Soviets tried to expand their power beyond Eastern Europe. They encouraged rebels in other nations to turn to communism. The United States was determined to stop this. The superpowers often backed opposing sides in conflicts in Asia and Africa. The superpowers also built powerful weapons to use against one another. By the 1960s, they had enough nuclear (NOO klee ur) bombs to destroy the entire world.

Collapse of an Empire During the Cold War, the Soviet Union's economy did not grow fast enough. The government invested most of its money in heavy industries, such as steel. It paid little attention to **consumer goods,** such as cars or blue jeans, that the common person might enjoy.

By the early 1980s, almost all of the Soviet people had lost faith in the communist system. They did not want the government to control almost every part of their lives. In the mid-1980s, one Soviet leader responded. Mikhail Gorbachev (mee khah EEL GOR buh chawf), who took power in 1985, made many changes in the Soviet system. He allowed more personal freedom. He also reduced government control of the economy.

▼ Under communism, food shortages and long lines became a daily fact of life for unhappy Soviet shoppers.

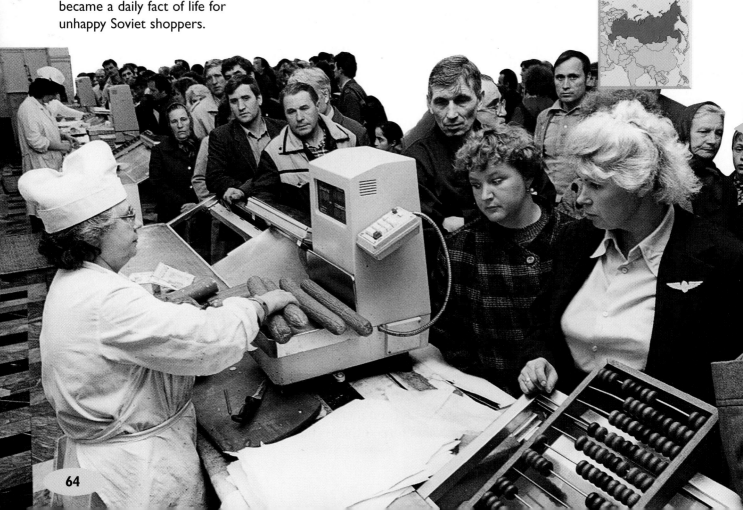

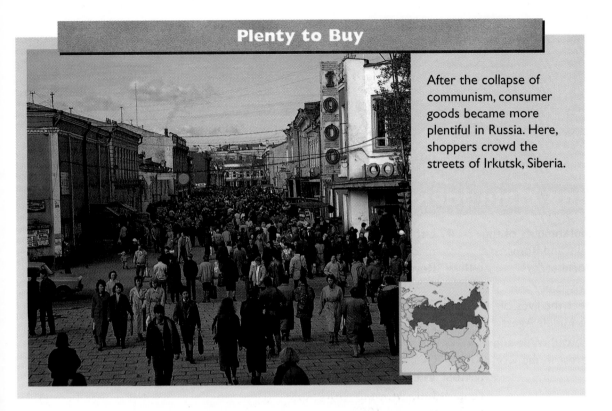

Plenty to Buy

After the collapse of communism, consumer goods became more plentiful in Russia. Here, shoppers crowd the streets of Irkutsk, Siberia.

Often, when people have a taste of freedom, it makes them want more. By the late 1980s, this happened across Eastern Europe and the Soviet Union. Eastern European countries abandoned communism. And the Soviet republics demanded their independence. They wanted to decide their own futures. Finally, at the end of 1991, the Soviet Union broke apart. Russia and most of the former Soviet republics became independent nations.

Today, Russia faces a huge challenge. For hundreds of years, the Russian people have suffered hardships, under the czars and under communism. Now Russians control their own fate. It is up to them to build a new way of life.

SECTION 5 REVIEW

1. **Define** (a) revolutionary, (b) communism, (c) civil war, (d) dictator, (e) Cold War, (f) consumer goods.

2. **Identify** (a) Vladimir Lenin, (b) Josef Stalin, (c) Mikhail Gorbachev.

3. How did Lenin become leader of the Soviet Union?

4. Why was Josef Stalin feared?

5. Why were the people of the Soviet Union unhappy with the communist government?

Critical Thinking

6. **Recognizing Cause and Effect** Why did the Germans send Lenin back to Russia?

Activity

7. **Writing to Learn** Some people in Russia want to go back to the old communist way of life. Write a paragraph arguing against returning to communism.

Review and Activities

Reviewing Main Ideas

1. What accomplishments of the ancient Greeks and Romans affect our world today?

2. How did Christianity and feudalism affect the lives of people in the Middle Ages?

3. How did renewed trade affect Europe's interest in the world?

4. List two important changes made during the Age of Revolution.

5. How did the Industrial Revolution change life for people in Europe?

6. How did nationalism help to cause World War I and World War II?

7. Explain how Russia gained territory and became an empire.

8. Why did the Russian people come to oppose the czars?

9. What changes did Lenin and Stalin make in the Soviet Union?

10. Why did the Soviet Union collapse?

Reviewing Key Terms

Use each key term below in a sentence that shows the meaning of the term.

1. democracy
2. empire
3. feudalism
4. Renaissance
5. humanism
6. monarch
7. colony
8. Scientific Revolution
9. Industrial Revolution
10. imperialism
11. nationalism
12. alliance
13. communism
14. civil war
15. dictator
16. Cold War

Critical Thinking

1. **Recognizing Cause and Effect** Describe causes that led to the fall of the Roman Empire.

2. **Making Conclusions** How were the main ideas of the Renaissance different from common ideas of the Middle Ages?

3. **Identifying Central Issues** How was Russia under the czars different from the Soviet Union under communism?

Graphic Organizer

Copy the chart on a sheet of paper. Fill in the empty boxes with important events that happened in Western Europe and in Russia for each century listed.

	Western Europe	Russia
1300s		
1500s		
1700s		
1900s		

Map Activity

Europe and Russia

For each place listed below, write the letter from the map that shows its location. Use the maps in the **Activity Atlas** to help you.

1. Athens

2. Rome

3. Italy

4. Great Britain

5. St. Petersburg

Place Location

Writing Activity

Writing an Interview
Choose a historical figure from this chapter. Write a "personal interview" with that person. First, think of questions that you would like to ask. Do research to learn how that person might have answered the questions. Then write the "interview" as if you were asking that person the questions and he or she were answering them.

Internet Activity

Use a search engine to find **Treasures of the Czars.** Take the **Museum Tour** and explore the **Czar Timeline.** Choose **Playground of the Czars** to play the **Name Game,** to learn some Russian in **Alphabet Borscht,** and to learn some fun facts about the czars.

Skills Review

Turn to the **Skills Activity.**
Review the steps for interpreting diagrams and illustrations. Then, find a diagram or illustration somewhere else in this book. Following the steps, write a brief paragraph detailing your interpretation.

How Am I Doing?

Answer these questions to help you check your progress.

1. Can I list the major accomplishments of the Greeks and the Romans?

2. Do I understand how people's views of the world changed during the Renaissance?

3. Do I understand how the Industrial Revolution changed European life?

4. Can I identify Russia's important rulers and their accomplishments?

5. Do I understand what communism is and why it did not work in the Soviet Union?

6. What information from this chapter can I use in my book project?

FROM

Pearl in the Egg

BY DOROTHY VAN WOERKOM

BEFORE YOU READ

Reach Into Your Background

In Europe in the Middle Ages, an average day for a person your age looked quite different than an average day today. For one thing, a twelve-year-old at that time was seen as much closer to being an adult.

People in those days did not live as long as they do today. A 20-year-old person was considered middle-aged!

Pearl in the Egg was the name of a real girl who lived in the 1200s. Historians know little about her except her name. Dorothy Van Woerkom has written a book of historical fiction about Pearl. Her descriptions of Pearl's life are based on what historians know about life in the 1200s. At that time, people in Europe were just beginning to use family names. Usually they gave themselves names that described their work or their families in some way.

In this part of Pearl's story, you will see something of a typical day in her life.

Questions to Explore

1. What does this story tell you about the life of a serf?
2. What can you learn from this story about work on a feudal manor?

rushlight *n.:* a lamp made with grease and part of a rush, or swamp plant

dripping *n.:* fat and juices drawn from cooking meat

serf *n.:* peasant farmers who worked the land as slaves of wealthy landowners

Pearl set the bowl of cabbage soup down on the floor near the rushlight. She knelt beside the box of straw that was her father's bed. She wiped his forehead, listening to his heavy breathing.

"Please, Fa," she coaxed. She broke off a piece from a loaf of black bread and dipped it into the soup. She placed it on his lips, letting the soup trickle into his mouth. She ate the chunk of bread, and dipped another.

"I will be in the fields until the nooning," she said, "so you must try to eat a little now. See, I have put a bit of dripping in the soup."

She forced the warm, mild liquid down his throat until the bowl was half empty. She drank the rest herself, chewing hungrily on the lump of fat that the sick man had not been able to swallow.

Again she wiped his face, and then she blew out the light. She crossed the smooth dirt floor, and pulled a sack from a peg on the wall near the door as she left the hut. Outside, the sky was gray with the dawn. Ground fog swirled around her feet. The air smelled of ripening grain and moist earth.

From other huts of mud and timber, serfs hurried out into the early morning mist. Some, like Pearl, would spend the day in their own small holdings in the fields. It was the time for harvesting their crops, which would feed their families through the winter. Others, like Pearl's older brother, Gavin, had already left for work in the manor fields to bring in Sir Geoffrey's crops.

Sir Geoffrey was lord of the manor, which included his great stone house and all the land surrounding it. He owned this tiny village. He even owned most of the people in it. A few, like the baker, the miller, and the soapmaker, were freemen and free women. They worked for themselves and paid the lord taxes. For tax, Sir Geoffrey collected a portion of everything they produced. No one in the village had money.

But the serfs were not free. They could never leave the manor, or marry without the lord's permission. They could not fish in the streams or hunt in the forest. They owned only their mud huts and small gardens, called holdings, and an ox or cow, or a few geese or sheep. The serfs also paid taxes. Each year they gave Sir Geoffrey a portion of their crops. He took a share of their eggs; if a flock of sheep or geese increased, he took a share; and if a cow had a calf, he took that also. On certain days of the week each family had to send a man—and an ox if they had one—to help plow the lord's fields, harvest his crops, and do their work. Each woman had to weave one garment a year for the lord and his family.

The sun was up when Pearl reached the long furrows of her field, where the flat green bean pods weighed down their low bushes. She bent to see if the leaves were dry. Wet leaves would wither when she touched them.

The sun had dried them. Pearl began filling her sack, wondering how she could finish the harvest all by herself before the first frost. She had other plots to work as well.

Now that their father was ill, twelve-year-old Gavin was taking his place for three days each week in the manor fields. Sir Geoffrey would get *his* crops safely in! But if the frost came early, or if the only one left at home to work was an eleven-year-old like Pearl, that was of small matter to Sir Geoffrey.

Pearl stood up to rub her back. A serf's life was a hard life. Her father's was, and his father's before him. She sighed. Who could hope to change it?

Old Clotilde came swaying up the narrow path between her field and Pearl's. She waved her empty sack by way of greeting and squatted down among her plants.

"How be your Fa this morning?" she asked Pearl.

"He took some soup. But he wanders in his head. He thinks I am my mother, though she's been dead three summers now."

furrows *n.*: rows in the earth made by a plow
Clotilde (kluh TILD)

▼ This painting from the Middle Ages shows peasants working in a field.

▶ This wall painting from the 1300s shows the kind of hunt Pearl saw.

bowmen *n.:* men with bows and arrows; archers
defiant *adj.:* bold or resistant

Connect Why does Pearl shed tears of anger?

"Ah, and he'll join her soon, Big Rollin will." Clotilde's wrinkled face was nearly the same dirty gray as her cap. "They all do, soon as they take a mite of sickness. For the likes of us to stay alive, we must stay well! Get the priest for him! He won't plow these fields again."

Before Pearl could reply, the shrill blare of a hunting horn sounded across the meadow, followed by the baying of hounds on the trail of a wild boar. Startled to their feet, the serfs watched the terrified boar running in and out among the rows of crops.

"Run, lest you get trampled!" Clotilde screamed, dashing down the path toward the forest. The others followed her. Someone pulled Pearl along as she stumbled forward, blinded by angry tears, her fingers tightly gripping her sack.

The hounds came running in pursuit of the boar. Behind the hounds rode the hunting party of twenty horsemen, led by Sir Geoffrey. At the rear was another man Pearl recognized. Jack, one of Sir Geoffrey's bowmen, had come upon her one day as she scrounged for dead branches near the edge of the forest. He had baited her with cruel words, rudely ruffling her hair with the shaft end of an arrow.

"Jack's my name. What's yours?" he had demanded, taking pleasure in her discomfort. For answer she had spat at him, and he had pressed the arrow's metal tip against her wrist until she'd dropped her bundle. Laughing, he had scattered the branches with his foot and grabbed her hair.

"Spit at me again, girl, and that will be the end of you!" Though his mouth had turned up in a grin, his eyes had been bright with anger. His fingers had tightened on the nape of her neck, bending her head back. She stared up at him, frightened, but defiant.

"Perhaps you need a lesson in manners right now," he'd said, raising his other hand. He probably would have struck her, but for the rattle of a wagon and the tuneless whistle signaling someone's approach. He had let her go with a suddenness that had left her off balance, and had stalked away.

Shaken, Pearl had turned to see Sir Geoffrey's woodcutter driving out of the forest with a wagonload of wood for the manor house.

Now Pearl shuddered at the memory; but Jack was taking no notice of her. His eyes were on the boar and on his master. If the boar became maddened during the chase and turned on one of the hunters, Jack was ready with his arrows to put an end to the beast.

Over the meadow they galloped, and onto the fields. They churned up the soft earth, trampled down the precious bean plants, crushed the near-ripe ears of the barley and oats, tore up the tender pea vines. They chased the boar across the fields and back again, laughing at the sport.

When they had gone, Pearl ran back to her field. She crawled in the turned-up earth, searching for unbroken bean pods. The other serfs were doing the same.

"What is the matter with us?" she demanded of Clotilde, "Why do we stay silent, with spoiled crops all around us, just so Sir Geoffrey will have his sport?"

"Shish!" Clotilde warned, looking quickly around to see who might have heard. "Do you want a flogging for such bold words? Hold your tongue, as you see your elders do."

For the rest of the morning they worked in silence. At midday, Pearl picked up her half-filled sack. It should have been full by now. She glared fiercely across the meadow at the manor house, but she held her tongue.

Pearl returned home to find that her father had worsened. When she could not rouse him, she went for the priest.

flogging *n.:* beating or whipping

EXPLORING YOUR READING

Look Back

1. Why does Pearl work alone in her family's holdings?

Think It Over

2. Why did the serfs give Sir Geoffrey a portion of their crops every year?

3. What did the serfs use instead of money?

4. What did Clotilde mean when she said, "Do you want a flogging for such bold words?"

Go Beyond

5. The feudal system existed for more than 400 years. Why do you think it did not change for such a long time?

6. Based on what you know about Pearl, how do you think she might act the next time she sees the lord or one of his men?

Ideas for Writing: Story

7. Write an addition to Pearl's story that tells how she got the name Pearl in the Egg.

Cultures of Europe and Russia

PICTURE ACTIVITIES

In many cities and towns in Europe and Russia, people live and work among things that remind them of their cultural backgrounds. This is a picture of Cologne (kuh LOHN), Germany. To learn more about Cologne's culture, complete the following activities.

Study the picture
Find a modern building and a historic one. For what use do you think each building was constructed?

Draw conclusions
From looking at the picture, what conclusions can you draw about the people of Cologne? Do they have a modern way of life? Do they value their cultural background? How do you know?

The Cultures of Western Europe

BEFORE YOU READ

Reach Into Your Background

Think about your community and your way of life. Now think of another community that you have visited or heard about from relatives or friends. How are the ways of life in each community different? How are they the same? List some differences and similarities.

Questions to Explore

1. What makes the cities of Western Europe great cultural centers?
2. How do people of the many countries of Western Europe interact with one another?

Key Terms
urbanization
immigrant
multicultural
tariff

Key Places
Paris
London
Madrid
Berlin

The train speeds down the track with hardly a whisper. As the passengers sit in their comfortable seats, they can look out the window at the highway next to the railroad. They know that the cars are traveling at 60 miles (96 km) per hour, but the cars seem to be moving backward. That's because the train is traveling *three times faster* than the cars—about 180 miles (289 km) per hour.

Would you like to take a trip like that? You can if you go to France, which has the world's fastest trains. Great Britain, too, has speedy rail travel. Some British trains reach speeds of 140 miles (225 km) per hour. In Western Europe, high-speed trains have made travel between countries easy and fast. Europeans can be in another country in a matter of hours. You will soon see how such easy movement through Western Europe affects the culture of the region.

▼ France's high-speed trains travel about 47 times faster than a person can walk.

Cultural Centers

READ ACTIVELY

Visualize Visualize a European city street with modern and old buildings.

When people travel in Europe, they are usually heading for a city. People travel from small towns and villages to cities to find jobs. Some people go to cities to go to school. People also travel to cities to enjoy the cultural attractions. These include museums, concerts, restaurants, nightclubs, and stores.

Most Western European cities are a mix of the old and the new. Public buildings and houses from the Middle Ages are a common sight. They stand next to modern apartments and office buildings. Cars and buses drive along cobblestone streets once used by horse-drawn carriages. Monuments stand for leaders who lived hundreds of years ago.

Each city in Western Europe is different from the other. Paris, the capital of France, attracts scholars, writers, and artists from all over the world. England's capital, London, is known for its grand historic buildings and lovely parks. The Spanish capital city of Madrid (muh DRID) is known as a friendly place where people meet in cafes to relax after work. The German city of Berlin is always full of activity.

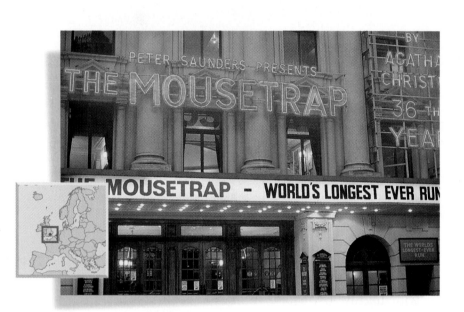

▲ "The Mousetrap," a play by mystery writer Agatha Christie, has been playing continuously in London since its opening in November 1952.

▼ This glass pyramid houses the entrance to the Louvre, a famous art museum in Paris.

Let's focus on life in Germany for a moment. Most visitors to Germany think that the Germans are efficient. In other words, Germans do their work without waste or extra effort. Visitors get this idea from what they see. In Germany, cities, streets, and buses are clean. Hotels are well run. German cars are well designed and long-lasting. Travel is swift on an excellent system of four-lane highways. Travel is equally fast on high-speed trains.

But life in Germany is not all hard work and fast-paced activity. Many workers enjoy up to six weeks of vacation each year. Outdoor recreation is popular. Mountains and highlands allow skiing, hiking, and camping. The country's many rivers, as well as the North and Baltic seas, are good for swimming and boating. Those who prefer city life enjoy the museums, concerts, and plays.

Growing Cities, Growing Wealth

People in most Western European countries enjoy a similar lifestyle. That's because these countries are prosperous, or wealthy. This prosperity is based on industry. Factories in Western Europe make consumer goods that are in great demand around the world. Western European workers also make steel, cars, machines, and many other vital products.

Oktoberfest in Munich, Germany

In the fall, tourists jam the streets of Munich to observe Oktoberfest. They have a wonderful time eating and listening to music. The festival was first held in the early 1800s to mark a royal wedding. Today, however, it is a joyful celebration of German culture.

Industry and the Growth of Cities   Industry has been developing in Western Europe since the late 1700s. It has not always been so important to the economy, however. In the past, farming played a bigger role.

About 200 years ago, there were few machines to help do farmwork. To meet basic food needs, most of the people worked on farms. Gradually, things changed. New and better farm machines were invented. These machines could do tasks that once required many workers. Farmers also learned ways to improve soil quality and fight insects. With these advances, farms could produce more and better crops with fewer workers.

This revolution in farming came at the same time as the Industrial Revolution. Thus, as the need for farmworkers fell, the need for industrial workers grew. Many people began moving to cities, where

The Labor Force in Selected Western European Countries

Chart Study Today, most people in the Netherlands, Norway, Spain, and Austria make a living as service workers. A service is any task that one person does for another—like selling groceries, typing a letter, or teaching a class. Workers in industry make products, such as clothing, automobiles, and video games. Agricultural workers grow crops and raise livestock. **Critical Thinking** Of the four countries shown here, which two have the most service workers? Which two have the most industrial workers? Would you expect to find service and industrial workers in cities or rural areas? Why?

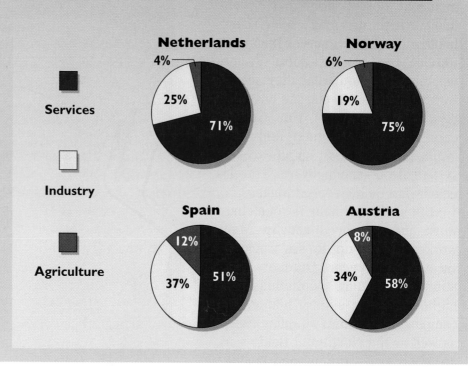

Services

Industry

Agriculture

Devoted to Nature
Writers of the English Romantic Age (1798–1832) reacted strongly to the events of their time. They disliked the way the Industrial Revolution changed the ways people lived. In "My Heart Leaps Up When I Behold," William Wordsworth describes the beauty of a rainbow and wishes every day was bound "each to each by natural piety," which means living each day in devotion to nature.

the factories were. This growth of cities, known as **urbanization** (ur bun ih ZAY shun), sped up after World War II. The United States provided billions of dollars to help Western Europe recover from the war. With this help, the region's industries came back stronger than ever. And even more people left rural areas to work in cities.

Today most Western Europeans work in factories or in service industries such as banking and food service. And most Western European workers earn good wages and have a comfortable life.

A Home for Immigrants Life in Western Europe was not always so good. In the 1800s and early 1900s, millions of Western Europeans left Europe. Most went to the United States, Canada, and the countries of South America. They left in search of a better life.

Since World War II, the direction of human movement has changed. No longer are large numbers of people leaving Western Europe. As industry developed in the postwar years, more workers were needed. As a result, people began moving to Western Europe. Today, **immigrants** (IM uh grunts), or people who move to one country from another, make up about 6 percent of the workers in Western Europe. Most are from Eastern Europe, North Africa, South Asia, and the Middle East.

Yang-Mee Tang is an example. She moved to London to start a career in business. Her homeland was Mauritius (maw RISH ee us), an island in the Indian Ocean, off the eastern coast of Africa. Yang-Mee is learning to get around London on the "tube," or subway. She is learning a much different lifestyle from her lifestyle in Mauritius. "There is so much to do here!"

says Yang-Mee. "In my hometown in Mauritius, everything shuts down at around 10:00 P.M. But every night in central London, the streets are still crowded with people at 1:00 A.M."

Immigrants do not simply leave their cultures when they leave their homelands. They bring their languages, religious beliefs, values, and customs. But most immigrants make changes in their ways of life. They may change the way they dress. They may try new foods and discover new ways of cooking. Most of them learn the language of their new country.

In many ways, immigration has changed the cultures of Western Europe. In countries like Britain and France, people from many different backgrounds live and work together. They learn about one another's way of life. In the process, the cultures blend and change. In this way, many Western European countries have become multicultural. A **multicultural** (mul tih KUHL chur ul) country's way of life is influenced by many different cultures.

L·I·N·K·S
ACROSS THE WORLD

Staying in the Neighborhood Have you ever been to Chinatown or Little Italy? New immigrants feel most comfortable with people from their own country—and often form their own little cities within a city. For example, early Italian and Russian immigrants in New York would combine their money to build a church or synagogue. They also formed social clubs where they could meet and talk in their first language.

◄These British children are on a school field trip to the West End, London's shopping and entertainment district.

Open Borders

Predict How do you think open borders help Western Europe grow and succeed?

Turn to the political map of Europe in the Activity Atlas in the front of your book. Notice that most European countries are small and close together. Picture a high-speed train traveling across Europe. It's little wonder that travelers can get from one country to another in a matter of hours. Ideas, goods, and raw materials can travel quickly as well. The open exchange of ideas and goods has helped make Western Europe prosperous.

It was not always so easy for people, goods, and ideas to move throughout Western Europe. Changes began around 1950, when France and Germany agreed to work together to help rebuild after World War II. Other nations soon joined them. Now there is an organization called

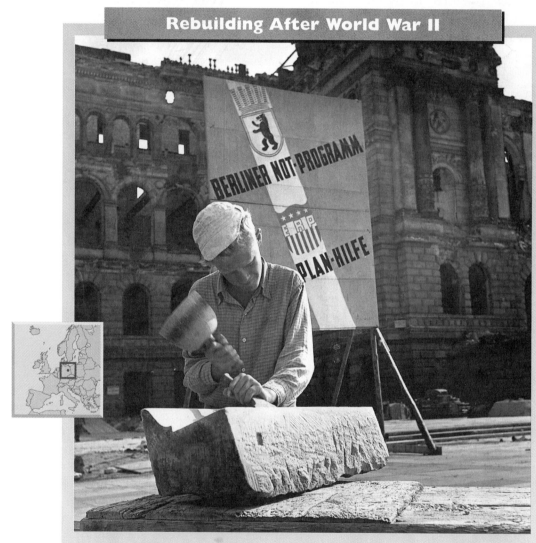

Rebuilding After World War II

After World War II, Germany lay in ruins. The Allied countries worked together to rebuild West Germany and make it a democracy. This man is helping to repair and repaint the Titiana Palace, West Berlin's largest concert hall. The Allies also helped to rebuild homes and factories. **Critical Thinking** Why do you think it was important to the Allies to rebuild Germany as a democracy?

Europe's New Money—the Euro

To make it easier for member countries to trade among themselves, the European Union decided to adopt a single currency. Initially, the EU named the new money the European Currency Unit, or ECU. Later, the ECU was renamed the Euro. By 2002, the national currencies of EU members will be replaced by Euro notes and coins. **Critical Thinking** How might the Euro make travel and trade among the European countries easier?

the European Union (EU), which has 15 member nations. The EU works to expand trade in Europe. One way to do this is to end **tariffs,** or fees that a government charges for goods entering the country. The EU hopes to create a "united states" of Europe, where people, money, goods, and services move freely among member countries.

SECTION 1 REVIEW

1. **Define** (a) urbanization, (b) immigrant, (c) multicultural, (d) tariff.

2. **Identify** (a) Paris, (b) London, (c) Madrid, (d) Berlin.

3. How did the growth of industry affect cities in Western Europe?

4. Why is there ease of movement among the countries in Western Europe?

Critical Thinking

5. **Drawing Comparisons** This section describes how the lives of many immigrants to Western Europe change when they settle in their new country. What effect do you think the immigrants have on the way of life in their new home?

Activity

6. **Writing to Learn** Write down two facts about Western Europe that you were surprised to learn. How has this new information changed the way you think about Western Europe?

Summarizing Information

How many words are in this sentence? You should count seven words. How many words do you think are in this paragraph? When you finish reading it, count them.

You can easily count the words in a sentence or a paragraph. But how many ideas do you think are on this page? What about in this entire book?

Think of all the books, magazines, and newspapers you read at school and at home. They all give you a mind-boggling amount of information. No one person could remember them all. You are not expected to. But you can summarize the basic ideas to help yourself remember them.

Get Ready

Summarizing information is a good skill to have. It will help you pick out the main points of what you read. It will also help you study for tests. Most important, it will help you make sense of all the ideas you read or hear about.

You may not know it, but you have already done a lot of summarizing. How can that be? People summarize without even knowing it. For example, suppose someone asked you, "How was math class?" You would not answer with every detail. You would tell the main things that happened, along with a just a few important details. That is just what a summary is: a description of the main points along with a few important details.

Try It Out

To see how easy summarizing is, try this exercise. Write a summary of yesterday. Your goal will be to describe the main points of your day from when you woke up to when you went to sleep. Follow these steps to write your summary.

A. Work from start to finish. When you summarize, you will do best to start at the beginning and work through to the end. When summarizing your day, start with when you woke up.

B. List the main points. Remember that a summary describes the main points, not every little detail. List only the main things that you did yesterday.

C. Add some details to the list. Although you do not want to list too many details, it helps to list a few that will later jog your memory. For example, you might write "ate breakfast" as a main point. You can add the details of what you ate if the meal was special in some way. As you make your list, add details after some of the main points.

D. Turn your list into a summary. Summaries are often in paragraph form. Once you have made your list, you can add transitions to make it into a paragraph. Transitions are words that connect one idea

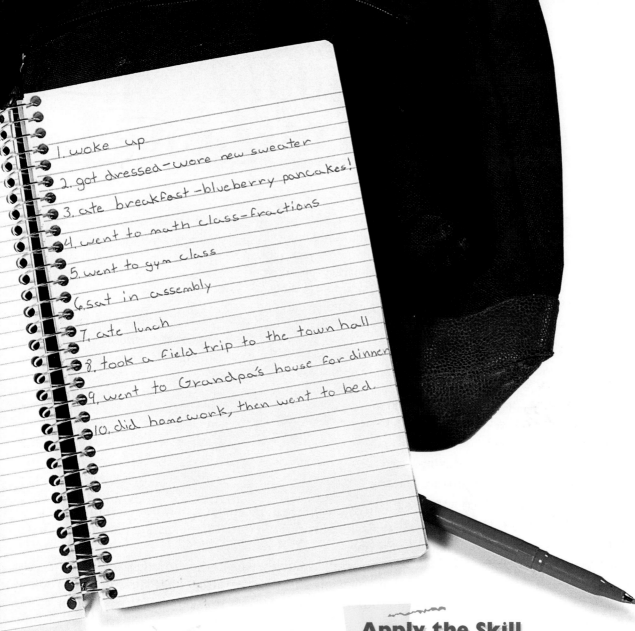

1. woke up
2. got dressed — wore new sweater
3. ate breakfast — blueberry pancakes!
4. went to math class — fractions
5. went to gym class
6. sat in assembly
7. ate lunch
8. took a field trip to the town hall
9. went to Grandpa's house for dinner
10. did homework, then went to bed.

Apply the Skill

to the next by showing how the ideas are related to each other. For example, if your list reads "1) woke up, 2) got dressed, 3) ate breakfast," you might write, "First, I woke up. Then, after I got dressed, I ate breakfast."

Congratulations! You have just summarized an entire morning in a single paragraph.

Summarizing a day is good for diary writing, but not much help in your schoolwork. However, the steps you just took will help you in school when you apply them to what you read or hear.

Practice by writing a summary of this chapter. Follow the four steps you took when summarizing your day. The headings in the chapter will help you pick the main points to list. Topic sentences in paragraphs will also help you find main points and interesting details. Remember to turn your list into a written summary. When you have finished, reread your summary. How can your summary help you remember what was in the chapter and help you prepare for a test?

The Cultures of Eastern Europe

Reach Into Your Background

Are the people of your community a blend of several cultures? Or do most people come from the same cultural group? How do you think the cultural background of your community affects the way people get along with one another?

Questions to Explore

1. How have the Slavs shaped life in Eastern Europe?
2. How do the peoples of Eastern Europe get along?

Key Terms

migration
ethnic group
dialect

Key People and Places

Czech Republic
Slovakia

ook at a map of Europe in 1900 and you may notice something odd. Poland is missing. From 1795 to 1918, this nation disappeared from the maps of Europe.

A geographer could quickly solve this mystery of the missing country. Poland lies on the North European Plain. There are few mountains or other natural barriers to keep invaders out. In 1795, Russia, Prussia, and Austria moved into Poland and divided it among themselves. Poland did not become independent again until the end of World War I.

Movement throughout much of Eastern Europe is easy. For thousands of years, groups have entered or crossed this region. This movement from place to place, called **migration** (my GRAY shun), is still happening today.

There are many reasons for migration in Eastern Europe. Long ago, people moved to find places with a good supply of natural resources. Sometimes people moved to escape enemies. In more recent times, people have fled places where their religious or political beliefs put them in danger. And they have often moved to find a better life.

▼ Poland is not shown on this map of Europe, which was drawn in 1870.

Map Study Two out of three people in Eastern Europe speak languages that developed in this region. These include Slavic languages, like Czech, Polish, and Russian, and Baltic languages, which come from northern European countries like Latvia and Lithuania. Romance languages come from France, Italy, Portugal, Romania, and Spain. Thraco-Illyrian languages are believed to have originated in ancient Italy and Albania. **Place** In what countries do people speak Baltic languages? Non-Indo-European languages are languages that originate outside of Europe. In what countries do people speak a non-Indo-European language?

KEY

- Slavic languages
- Romance languages
- Thraco-Illyrian languages
- Baltic languages
- Non-Indo-European languages

Lambert Azimuthal Equal-Area Projection

Ethnic Groups in Eastern Europe

Among the groups that long ago migrated to Eastern Europe were the Slavs (slahvz). These people first lived in the mountains of modern Slovakia (sloh VAH kee uh) and Ukraine. By the 700s, they had spread south to Greece, east to the Alps, and north to the coast of the Baltic Sea.

Slavic Cultures Today, the Slavs are one of the major ethnic groups in Eastern Europe. People of the same **ethnic group** share things, such as a culture, a language, and a religion, that set them apart from their neighbors. Two thousand years ago, there was a single Slavic language. But as the Slavs separated, different Slavic languages were born. Today, some 10 Slavic languages are spoken in Eastern Europe. These include Czech, Polish, and Russian.

Also, even two Slavs who speak the same language may not speak the same dialect. A **dialect** (DY uh lekt) is a different version of a language that can be found only in a certain region.

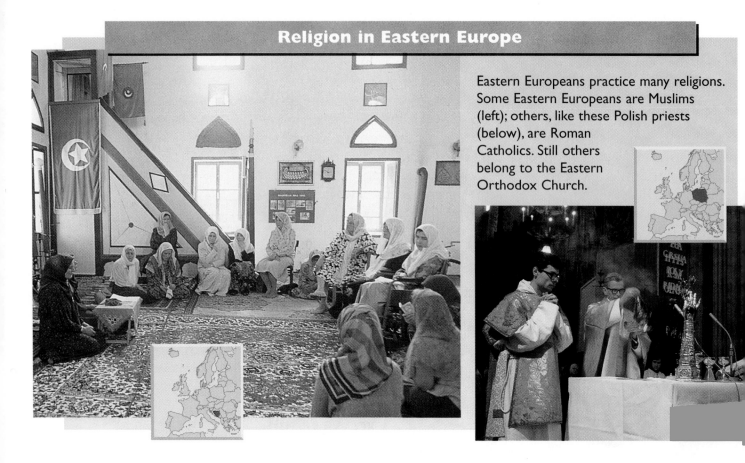

Eastern Europeans practice many religions. Some Eastern Europeans are Muslims (left); others, like these Polish priests (below), are Roman Catholics. Still others belong to the Eastern Orthodox Church.

There are also major religious differences among Slavs. Some follow the Eastern Orthodox faith, while others may be Protestant, Roman Catholic, or Muslim.

Though the Slavs now have different languages and live in different nations, they still have many of the same customs. This is partly because Eastern Europe has fewer factories and factory workers than Western Europe. Large numbers of Eastern Europeans still live in rural areas and work as farmers. Customs change more slowly in rural areas than in cities.

READ ACTIVELY

Predict What happens when different groups cannot solve their differences?

Other Ethnic Groups Such countries as Poland, Croatia (kroh AY shuh), Slovenia (sloh VEE nee uh), and the Czech Republic are almost entirely Slavic. But many other ethnic groups live in Eastern Europe. About 95 percent of the people of Hungary belong to an ethnic group called the Magyars (MAG yarz). In the country of Romania, most people belong to yet another ethnic group, the Romanians. Similarly, the Bulgars of Bulgaria and the Albanians of Albania are separate ethnic groups. And people belonging to the German ethnic group live in several of the countries of Eastern Europe.

Ethnic Conflict

In some Eastern European countries, people of different ethnic groups live together in harmony. But in other places, there have been ethnic conflicts.

Czechs and Slovaks: A Peaceful Division For most of the 1900s, Czechoslovakia (check uh sloh VAH kee uh) was a single country. The two main ethnic groups were the Czechs and the Slovaks. The Czechs lived mostly in a western region called Bohemia. Czechs and Slovaks lived in the central region of Moravia. The Slovaks lived mostly in the eastern region of Slovakia. Hungarians, Ukranians, Germans, and Polish people also lived in these areas.

Czechoslovakia was a parliamentary democracy from 1918 to 1935. After World War II, the Soviet Union controlled Czechoslovakia. Almost overnight, the Communist party took over the country. Many people were not happy with the Communist government. For example, writers and scientists could not gain work unless they were members of the Communist party. From the 1960s to the 1980s, students and writers formed groups promoting a return to democracy. Vaclav Havel, a playwright, was a major voice of protest. He spoke out against the government for more than 20 years and was repeatedly put in jail. The government urged him to move out of the country, but he always refused. In 1988, he explained his reasons for staying in Czechoslovakia.

LINKS TO ART

Glassware The people of northern Bohemia, in the Czech Republic, have been making glass since the 1200s. In the 1700s, glass factories made Bohemia one of the wealthiest parts of Europe. The glassware from this region is often decorated with castles, people, and animals. One artist, Caspar Lehmann, engraved glass and copper and bronze tools shaped like wheels.

Prague Castle

STUDENT ART

Darina Vassova
10 years old
Czech Republic

Prague Castle was a symbol of unified Czechoslovakia for many years. It was the home of the president of the country, and before that, it was the home of kings. Prague Castle still houses many valuable works of art. It stands high on a hill above the Vlatva River. **Critical Thinking** Why do you think Czechs built Prague Castle on a hill above a river? What are the benefits of such a location?

❝I am Czech. This was not my choice, it was fate. . . . This is my language, this is my home. I live here like everyone else. I don't feel myself to be patriotic, because I don't feel that to be Czech is to be something more than French, English, or European, or anybody else. . . . I try to do something for my country because I live here.**❞**

Mass protests forced the communist government to consider changes. In 1989, the Communist party gave up its power and worked in cooperation with the democratic groups. This generally nonviolent change in power from a communist government to a democratic system is called the Velvet Revolution. Havel later was elected president of Czechoslovakia.

The Czechs and the Slovaks had strong ideas about the future of their groups. Both sides disagreed about how to carry out the goals of the newly democratic country. In 1993, they agreed to separate, and the countries of the Czech Republic and Slovakia were born. Perhaps because most Czechs and Slovaks already lived in separate parts of the country, the split was peaceful.

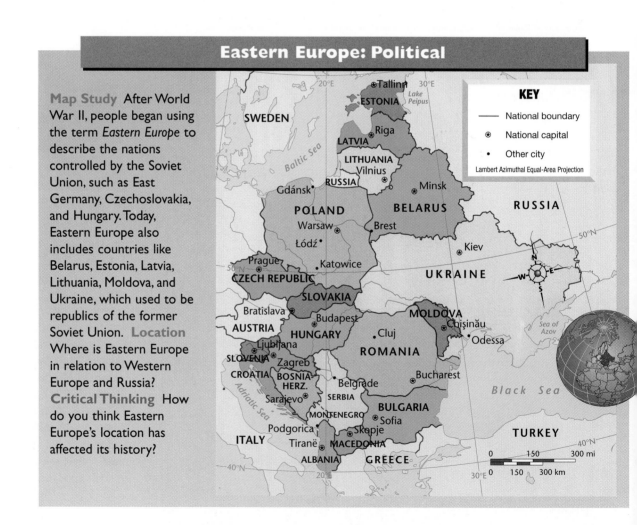

Eastern Europe: Political

Map Study After World War II, people began using the term *Eastern Europe* to describe the nations controlled by the Soviet Union, such as East Germany, Czechoslovakia, and Hungary. Today, Eastern Europe also includes countries like Belarus, Estonia, Latvia, Lithuania, Moldova, and Ukraine, which used to be republics of the former Soviet Union. **Location** Where is Eastern Europe in relation to Western Europe and Russia? **Critical Thinking** How do you think Eastern Europe's location has affected its history?

KEY

— National boundary

⊛ National capital

• Other city

Lambert Azimuthal Equal-Area Projection

◀ In the war-torn country of Bosnia-Herzegovina, United Nations troops struggle to keep a fragile peace among the warring parties.

When Ethnic Groups Clash   But not all ethnic conflicts in Eastern Europe have ended peacefully. Yugoslavia (yoo goh SLAH vee uh) was sometimes called one country with two alphabets, three religions, four languages, and five nationalities. Most Yugoslavs were part of the same ethnic group—the Slavs. However, various groups within the country had distinct religions and cultures. These differences led to the breakup of Yugoslavia in 1991. The new countries of Bosnia-Herzegovina (BAHZ nee uh hert suh goh VEE nuh), Croatia, Slovenia, Serbia and Montenegro, and Macedonia were formed. The breakup of Yugoslavia caused a war that killed thousands of people, most of them Bosnians. Deep ethnic conflicts still exist, and violence in the region continues today.

SECTION 2 REVIEW

1. **Define**   (a) migration, (b) ethnic group, (c) dialect.

2. **Identify**   (a) Czech Republic, (b) Slovakia.

3. Why are the Slavs important in Eastern Europe?

4. Give an example of Eastern Europeans (a) getting along with one another and (b) being in conflict with one another.

Critical Thinking

5. **Recognizing Cause and Effect**   This section explains that Slavs in rural areas follow customs that have lasted for centuries. Why do you think customs change more slowly in rural areas than in urban areas?

Activity

6. **Writing to Learn**   Write a paragraph about how you think ethnic conflicts affect the ways in which people think of other ethnic groups. How can people's attitudes make it harder to solve these conflicts?

1-5

#7 list countries
in west Eourpe
&
East Eourpe

The Cultures of Russia

BEFORE YOU READ

Reach Into Your Background

Do you and your family celebrate certain holidays each year? Why are these holidays important? Do other people in your community observe these holidays, or do they observe different ones?

Questions to Explore

1. How have ethnic groups in and around Russia affected Russian history?

2. How are the people of Russia reconnecting with their traditions?

Key Terms
heritage
repress
propaganda

Key People and Places
Leo Tolstoy
Peter Tchaikovsky
St. Petersburg

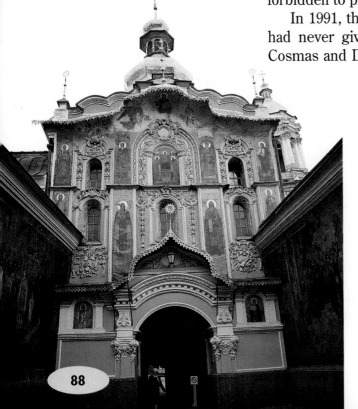

▼ Under communism, worship in Soviet churches was forbidden. Now, the doors of churches all over the former Soviet Union are open again for worshippers.

For many years, Russians passing the Church of Saints Cosmas and Damian in Moscow never heard a choir. They never saw a bride and groom leave the church. They never heard religious services. The only sound they heard was the hum of machines printing government documents. The communist government of the Soviet Union owned the church and used it as a printing shop. In the Soviet Union, people were forbidden to practice religion.

In 1991, the Soviet Union collapsed. Two years later, Russians who had never given up their faith took back their church. Now Saints Cosmas and Damian is filled with people singing songs of worship. In recent years, hundreds of other churches in Moscow have reopened their doors. The same return to religion can be seen in places of worship across all of Russia.

Russia's Ethnic Mix

The Russian Orthodox religion, a branch of Christianity, has been a powerful bond among Russians for hundreds of years. It is part of the Russian **heritage** (HEHR ut ij), or the customs and practices that are passed from one generation to the next. Another part of the Russian heritage is ethnic. More than 80 percent of the Russian people belong to the ethnic group of Russian Slavs. These people generally speak the Russian language and live in western parts of the country.

Other Ethnic Groups   Besides the Slavs, more than 75 different ethnic groups live in Russia. Most of the minority groups live far from the heavily populated western areas. The Finns and Turks live in regions of the Ural and Caucasus (KAW kuh sus) mountains. Armenians and Mongolians live along Russia's southern edges. The Yakuts (yah KOOTS) live in small areas of Siberia. These groups speak languages other than Russian. They also follow different religions. Muslims make up Russia's second-largest religious group, after Russian Orthodox believers. Many followers of Buddhism (BOOD izum) live near Russia's border with China.

United or Divided?   When the Soviet Union came apart, some non-Russian ethnic groups broke away from Russia and formed their own countries. Since that time, other ethnic groups have tried to break ties with Russia.

The new Russian government has tried to keep the country unified by giving ethnic groups the right to rule themselves. At times, however, groups have called for complete independence from Russia. In response, the Russian government has sent the army to **repress**, or put down, the independence movements.

LINKS ACROSS THE WORLD

The East-West Split In 1054, it was official. The Christian Church was split into the Eastern Orthodox Church (which included the Russian Orthodox Church) and the Roman Catholic Church. The leaders of each church excommunicated each other; each man said that the other man could not belong to his church. It was not until 1965 that the two sides officially removed the excommunications.

Families in Siberia

Many ethnic groups live in Siberia, Russia's largest region. The father and child (left) are Nentsy, an ethnic group that lives in northwest Siberia. The Russian family (above) lives in the city of Yakutsk.

Socialist realism was the only acceptable style of art in the Soviet Union. Socialist realist paintings and sculptures showed idealized—or perfect—views of heroic workers and farmers, often struggling against great odds. The only purpose of socialist realist art was to further the aims of the Soviet government. **Critical Thinking** This sculpture in Moscow is a monument to Soviet workers. The two workers are holding aloft a hammer and sickle, the symbols of the Soviet Union. What aspects of socialist realist art does this sculpture illustrate?

Russian Ballet Sergei Diaghilev created the Ballets Russes—a Russian ballet company—in 1909. He had a flair for using unusual dance and music in his shows. In one ballet, the music was so strange that the audience complained—and the dancers were unable to hear the music from the nearby orchestra pit.

Russian Culture and Education

Russia has produced many great artists, thinkers, and writers. Russia's artistic heritage includes outstanding architecture, fine religious paintings, great plays, and intricate art objects like the Fabergé (fah ber ZHAY) egg on the opposite page. Novelist Leo Tolstoy (TOHL stoy) wrote powerful stories of life in Russia in the 1800s. Peter Tchaikovsky (chy KAWF skee) composed moving classical music. Russian painters, such as Vasily Kandinsky (kan DIN skee), were leaders in the modern art movement in the early 1900s. In a way, creating works of art is a tradition among Russians.

Under communism, the creation of great new works of art nearly came to a halt. The Soviet government believed that the purpose of art was to glorify communism. The government banned any art it did not like and jailed countless artists. The only art that the government did like was **propaganda**—the spread of ideas designed to support some cause, such as communism. With the collapse of communism, the Russian people eagerly returned to their artistic traditions. Creating new works was once again possible.

Elegant St. Petersburg An important center of Russian culture is the city of St. Petersburg. Visitors to the city can clearly see the Russian mixture of European and Slavic cultures. This city has many Western influences. Peter the Great founded it in 1703. His goal was to create a Russian city as beautiful as any Western European city.

Elegant is the best word for St. Petersburg. The Neva (NEE vuh) River winds gracefully through the city. Along the river's banks are palaces, and public buildings hundreds of years old. St. Petersburg's

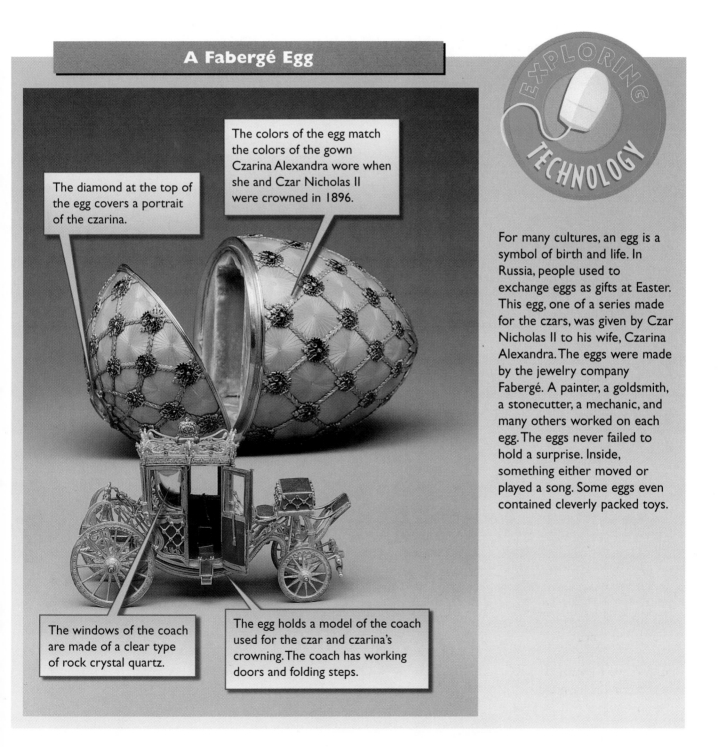

A Fabergé Egg

The diamond at the top of the egg covers a portrait of the czarina.

The colors of the egg match the colors of the gown Czarina Alexandra wore when she and Czar Nicholas II were crowned in 1896.

The windows of the coach are made of a clear type of rock crystal quartz.

The egg holds a model of the coach used for the czar and czarina's crowning. The coach has working doors and folding steps.

EXPLORING TECHNOLOGY

For many cultures, an egg is a symbol of birth and life. In Russia, people used to exchange eggs as gifts at Easter. This egg, one of a series made for the czars, was given by Czar Nicholas II to his wife, Czarina Alexandra. The eggs were made by the jewelry company Fabergé. A painter, a goldsmith, a stonecutter, a mechanic, and many others worked on each egg. The eggs never failed to hold a surprise. Inside, something either moved or played a song. Some eggs even contained cleverly packed toys.

grandest sight, the Winter Palace, is on the Neva. This 1,000-room palace, shown in the pictures below, was the winter home of Russia's czars. Part of the palace is the Hermitage (HUR mih tij) Museum. This museum houses one of the world's finest art collections.

Education in Russia   One of the few strengths of the old Soviet Union was its offer of free public education. Under this system, the number of Russians who could read and write rose from about 40 percent to nearly 100 percent.

Russian Treasures

Visitors to St. Petersburg's Hermitage Museum can view priceless art objects in the Emblem Hall (below) and climb the Grand Staircase where czars once walked (left). **Critical Thinking** Why do you think it is important to Russians to preserve the homes of czars even though Russia is no longer ruled by a czar?

The new Russia has continued free public schooling for children between ages 6 and 17. Schools are updating their old courses of study, which told only the communist point of view. New courses, such as business management, are preparing students for the new, non-communist Russia. Some private schools run by the Orthodox Church offer similar courses, as well as religious instruction.

These changes show that Russia is trying to recover the riches of its past even as it prepares for a new future. Religion and art, two important parts of Russia's cultural heritage, can now be freely expressed. And Russia's young people, unlike their parents, can grow up deciding their future for themselves.

▼ In his 1996 run for reelection, Russian President Boris Yeltsin campaigned in a Western way— he combined a political rally with a rock concert.

SECTION 3 REVIEW

1. **Define** (a) heritage, (b) repress, (c) propaganda.

2. **Identify** (a) Leo Tolstoy, (b) Peter Tchaikovsky, (c) St. Petersburg.

3. (a) What is Russia's major ethnic group? (b) How has the government treated Russia's smaller ethnic groups?

4. What are some examples of ways in which Russians are reconnecting with their past?

Critical Thinking

5. **Recognizing Cause and Effect** How have the political changes in Russia led to changes in education?

6. **Expressing Problems Clearly** How has Russia's ethnic mix created challenges for the new Russian government?

Activity

7. **Writing to Learn** What predictions might you make about Russia's culture in the next 10 years? Give reasons for your predictions.

Review and Activities

Reviewing Main Ideas

1. What features make many cities in Western Europe great centers for culture?

2. How do open borders and free trade affect the way Western Europeans live?

3. (a) Who are the Slavs? (b) Why are the Slavs an important part of the population of Eastern Europe?

4. How was the breakup of Czechoslovakia different than the breakup of Yugoslavia?

5. How have non-Russian ethnic groups reacted to recent events in Russia?

6. What traditions are Russians reviving following the collapse of the Soviet Union?

Reviewing Key Terms

Match the definitions in Column I with the key terms in Column II.

Column I

1. to put down

2. the movement of people from place to place

3. people who share a language, culture, and religion

4. a variation of a language

5. customs passed on from one generation to the next

6. influenced by many different cultures

7. spread of ideas designed to support a cause

8. a fee that the government charges for goods entering the country

Column II

a. multicultural

b. migration

c. heritage

d. ethnic group

e. dialect

f. propaganda

g. repress

h. tariff

Critical Thinking

1. **Drawing Conclusions** Why do Western Europeans generally have a higher standard of living than Eastern Europeans?

2. **Identifying Central Issues** How has life changed for the Russian people since the collapse of the Soviet Union?

Graphic Organizer

Copy the chart onto a separate sheet of paper. Then fill in the empty boxes to complete the chart.

	How the Lives of Its People Are Changing	What Is Special About Its Cultures	Relations Among Different Ethnic Groups or Countries
Western Europe			
Eastern Europe			
Russia			

Map Activity

Europe and Russia

For each place listed below, write the letter from the map that shows its location. Use the maps in the Activity Atlas to help you.

1. France
2. Ukraine
3. Russia
4. Germany
5. Slovakia
6. St. Petersburg

Place Location

Writing Activity

Writing a Travel Guide

If you had friends who were visiting Europe and Russia for the first time, what information would you want to share with them? Starting with the title "A Guide to Europe and Russia," write a brief travel guide your friends can use to plan an educational and enjoyable trip. Mention places and activities your friends will not want to miss. Also, provide background information that will help them understand the cultures and daily lives of the people they will meet.

Internet Activity

Use a search engine to find **Russian Cities on the Net.** Explore several Russian cities. What did you find most interesting about Russian culture? How does Russian culture differ in the various cities? Make a brochure with text and pictures highlighting the cultural events in a Russian city of your choice.

Skills Review

Turn to the Skills Activity.

Review the steps for summarizing information. Then, write a one-paragraph summary of your last weekend.

How Am I Doing?

Answer these questions to help you check your progress.

1. Do I understand how and why the people of Western Europe are coming together?
2. Can I identify different ethnic groups in Eastern Europe?
3. Can I describe the heritage of the Russian people?
4. What information from this chapter can I use in my book project?

Exploring Western Europe

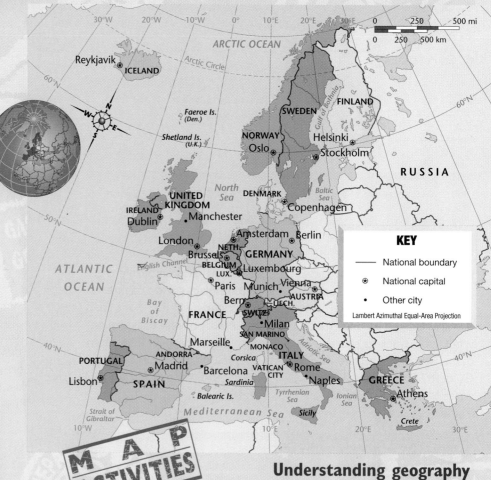

MAP ACTIVITIES

This map shows Western Europe, the region you will be reading about in this chapter. To help you get to know Western Europe, complete the following activities.

Understanding geography

Western Europe is sometimes called a "peninsula of peninsulas." Use information from the map to explain why.

Study the map

Follow the outlines of the countries. Look for familiar shapes. For example, Italy looks like a boot. Spain and Portugal look like a square attached to the rest of Europe. Describe the shapes of other countries.

Great Britain

A DEMOCRATIC TRADITION

BEFORE YOU READ

Reach Into Your Background

What does the word *tradition* mean to you? Identify two or three American traditions.

Compare them to the British traditions you read about in this section.

Questions to Explore

1. How did democracy develop in Britain?
2. How does Britain's status as an island nation affect the way of life of its people?

Key Terms

Parliament
representative
constitutional monarchy

Key People and Places

Queen Elizabeth II
King John
Buckingham Palace

The line of tourists seems to go on forever. Every few feet along the line, a different language is spoken. You can hear English, French, Arabic, and Japanese. Despite the difference in languages, all the tourists are talking about the same thing: the British crown jewels.

The jewels are kept under guard in a large building called the Tower of London. The beautiful collection includes crowns worn by Great Britain's kings and queens. After a long wait, the tourists reach a motorized walkway, which slowly carries them past the bulletproof case. Their eyes widen with wonder at the sight of huge diamonds, bright rubies, and cool sapphires (SAF eyerz).

British history comes alive in and around the Tower. On Tower Green, nobles went to their deaths on the executioner's block. In the Bloody Tower, the young King Edward V and his brother were said to have been murdered. The Wakefield Tower holds rings and royal symbols of

▼ St. Edward's crown, one of several crowns kept at the Tower of London, is a copy of a crown worn by Edward the Confessor. He ruled England from 1042 to 1066.

kings and queens. All these places are watched over by guards called Beefeaters. They wear colorful red costumes like those worn by the guards in the 1500s.

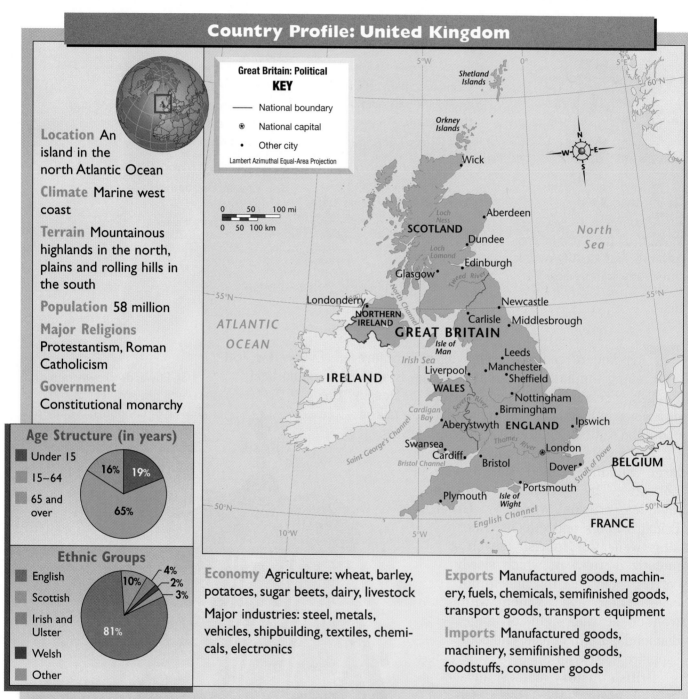

Country Profile: United Kingdom

Location An island in the north Atlantic Ocean

Climate Marine west coast

Terrain Mountainous highlands in the north, plains and rolling hills in the south

Population 58 million

Major Religions Protestantism, Roman Catholicism

Government Constitutional monarchy

Great Britain: Political
KEY
— National boundary
⊛ National capital
• Other city
Lambert Azimuthal Equal-Area Projection

0   50   100 mi
0   50 100 km

Age Structure (in years)
- Under 15
- 15–64
- 65 and over

16% 19% 65%

Ethnic Groups
- English
- Scottish
- Irish and Ulster
- Welsh
- Other

81% 10% 4% 2% 3%

Economy Agriculture: wheat, barley, potatoes, sugar beets, dairy, livestock

Major industries: steel, metals, vehicles, shipbuilding, textiles, chemicals, electronics

Exports Manufactured goods, machinery, fuels, chemicals, semifinished goods, transport goods, transport equipment

Imports Manufactured goods, machinery, semifinished goods, foodstuffs, consumer goods

Map and Chart Study This map shows the countries of England, Scotland, Northern Ireland, and Wales. These four countries make up the United Kingdom. They share one monarch and one Parliament, but they are separate countries within the United Kingdom. The United Kingdom is commonly called Great Britain. However, officially, the term Great Britain refers to Scotland, England, and Wales. **Regions** What three countries in the United Kingdom are connected by land? **Critical Thinking** Look at the graph of Great Britain's ethnic groups. Based on the chart, where do you think most people in Great Britain live?

A Democratic Heritage

Visitors standing inside the Tower of London may forget that Great Britain is a modern nation. In the Tower, Britain's long tradition of kings and queens seems as strong as ever. Great Britain is still a monarchy, headed by Queen Elizabeth II. She is a symbol of Britain's past and its customs. But Great Britain also has a strong democratic government. This country served as one of the first models of a modern democracy.

The roots of British democracy go back many hundreds of years. During the Middle Ages, British kings could not take major actions without the approval of a group of rich nobles. Over time, the power of this group grew. In 1215, the group forced one English monarch, King John, to sign a document called the Magna Carta, or "Great Charter." The Magna Carta strengthened the power of the nobles and limited the power of the king.

In time, the group of nobles became known as the **Parliament.** This word comes from the French word *parler* (PAHR lay), which means "to talk." The Parliament later gained more power. It helped to decide the kinds of taxes paid by citizens. It elected people from each area to serve as **representatives.** A representative represents, or stands for, a group of people. In time, the people themselves elected these representatives. Such changes helped to make Britain a true democracy.

READ ACTIVELY

Ask Questions What questions would you like answered about Great Britain's system of government?

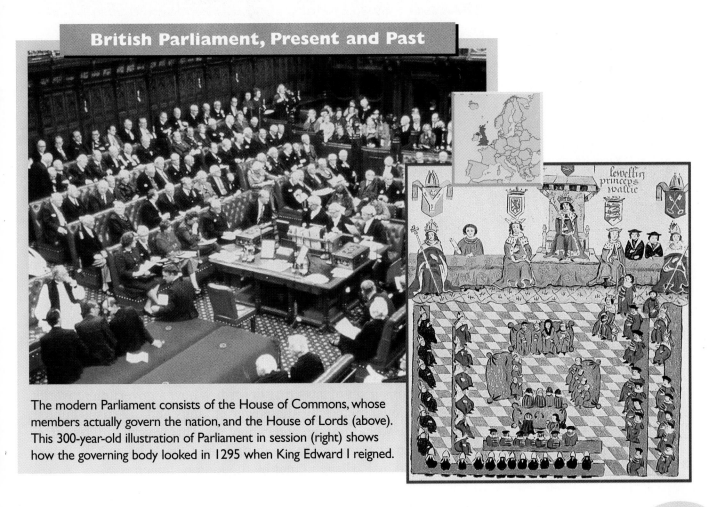

British Parliament, Present and Past

The modern Parliament consists of the House of Commons, whose members actually govern the nation, and the House of Lords (above). This 300-year-old illustration of Parliament in session (right) shows how the governing body looked in 1295 when King Edward I reigned.

A Ceremonial Monarchy

Britain's Queen Elizabeth II (above left) was crowned in 1953. The red-coated officers (above right) who guard her stand at stiff attention. The Queen may approve or reject laws passed by Parliament, but no British monarch has rejected a law since the 1700s. The Queen and members of her family also sponsor charity events, participate in important national ceremonies and parades, and represent Britain on trips to other countries.

Democracy and Monarchy

Today, the monarchy serves as an important symbol of Britain's past. It also helps to unify, or bring together, the British people. The British honor the monarchy in many ways. When the queen is in London, a royal flag is flown over her home at Buckingham (BUK ing um) Palace. Whether she is there or not, a short ceremony called the changing of the guard takes place every day. Trumpets blare and guardsmen march back and forth at the palace gate.

However, Britain's monarchs today do not have the power to make laws or collect taxes. Great Britain is now a **constitutional monarchy.** A constitution is a set of laws that describes how a government works. In a constitutional monarchy, the power of kings and queens is limited. The laws state what they can and cannot do. This is very different from the absolute monarchy in France during the time of Louis XIV. British laws are made by Parliament, not by the king or queen.

Britain Looks Outward

Parliament today governs all of the United Kingdom, which includes Great Britain (England, Scotland, and Wales) and Northern Ireland. The southern part of the island of Ireland became an independent country in the 1920s. Though *United Kingdom* is the country's official name, people often use *Britain* or *Great Britain* instead. This is because most of the people live on the island of Great Britain.

Building an Empire As an island nation, Great Britain is more difficult to invade than other European countries. During World War II, it was one of the few European countries that was not captured by the Germans. But as an island, Britain has limited natural resources. It must trade with other nations for resources. For this reason, trade has always been important to Britain.

In the 1500s, Britain began building a large empire. Its empire grew to include colonies on six continents. The colonies provided Britain's factories with raw materials. They also provided places to sell the goods made in Britain's factories. The colonies, then, helped Britain become a world economic power.

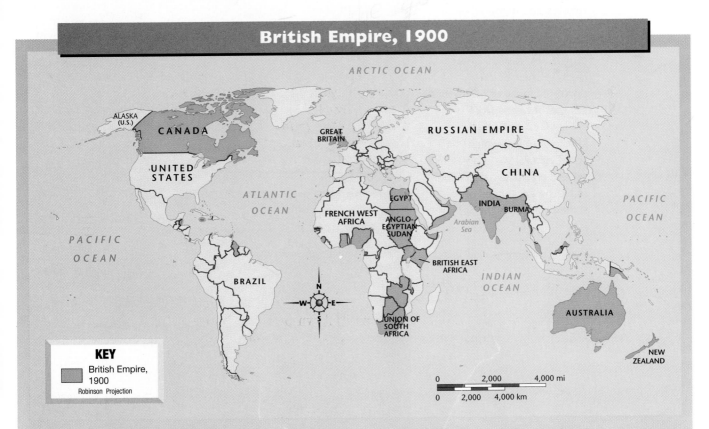

British Empire, 1900

ARCTIC OCEAN

ALASKA (U.S.)

CANADA

GREAT BRITAIN

RUSSIAN EMPIRE

UNITED STATES

ATLANTIC OCEAN

CHINA

EGYPT

FRENCH WEST AFRICA

ANGLO-EGYPTIAN SUDAN

Arabian Sea

INDIA

BURMA

PACIFIC OCEAN

PACIFIC OCEAN

BRITISH EAST AFRICA

INDIAN OCEAN

BRAZIL

UNION OF SOUTH AFRICA

AUSTRALIA

NEW ZEALAND

KEY

British Empire, 1900

Robinson Projection

0   2,000   4,000 mi

0   2,000   4,000 km

Map Study By 1900, the British Empire had reached its high point. At that time, it included approximately one fourth of the world's land and people. As the 1900s dawned, one writer noted that the area under British control had grown by "over two acres of new territory every time the clock has ticked since 1800." **Location** List, along with their continents, at least three British colonies.

At one point, Britain had so many colonies around the world that people said, "The sun never sets on the British Empire." Fighting the two World Wars weakened Britain, however. After the World Wars, Great Britain's empire fell apart. Most of its colonies gained their independence. Britain maintained close economic ties with its former colonies. However, it now had to compete with other countries to buy and sell in these markets.

A Community Member   Britain's industrial base remains strong. It has good supplies of fossil fuels—especially oil from deposits beneath the North Sea. It continues to export many manufactured goods, such as clothing and electronic products. However, Britain is not as strong a world power as it was before the World Wars.

A Natural Gas Refinery

Great Britain uses natural gas in factories that produce automobiles, ships, steel, textiles, and many other products. Several deposits of natural gas lie under the North Sea, east of Great Britain. Great Britain produces most of the natural gas that it needs from these fields. **Critical Thinking** Unlike gasoline, which is a liquid, natural gas is a gas, like air and steam. What do you think the challenges of shipping a gas might be?

In 1997, the European Union had 15 members. Their flags are shown here (left). European passports (below) allow EU citizens freedom of movement among member countries. **Critical Thinking** By the early 2000s, the EU expects to include all the countries of Europe. How might membership in such an organization benefit the British economy?

Great Britain is trying to improve its economy. In 1973, it became a member of what is now called the European Union (EU). Nations belonging to the EU are trying to promote trade among and unite the nations of Europe.

Britain hopes that trade with the rest of Europe will replace the trade it lost when the empire collapsed. With new links to the resources and markets of other European countries, the British economy may again prosper.

SECTION 1 REVIEW

1. **Define** (a) Parliament, (b) representative, (c) constitutional monarchy.

2. **Identify** (a) Queen Elizabeth II, (b) King John, (c) Buckingham Palace.

3. How did Britain become a constitutional monarchy?

4. How has the location of Great Britain affected how the country has developed?

Critical Thinking

5. **Drawing Conclusions** Why do you think Britain holds on to its monarchy even though the monarch now has very little power?

Activity

6. **Writing to Learn** Write one or two paragraphs describing the places you would go and the things you would do if you visited London.

France

PRESERVING A CULTURE

Reach Into Your Background

Do you have a special way of doing something? Is it dancing, playing a sport, dressing, or something else? As you read this section, you will see that the French, too, have special ways of doing things.

Questions to Explore

1. In what parts of their culture do the French people take special pride?
2. How is the culture of other nations affecting French culture?

Key Terms
emigrate

Key Places
Aix-en-Provence
Paris

▼ Carrying baguettes—long, crusty loaves of bread—two young girls stroll through France's countryside.

Catherine and Victoire are sisters. Both are in their 20s—just one year apart in age. The two look so much alike that some people think they are twins. They grew up in the south of France, in a city called Aix-en-Provence (eks ahn praw VAHNS). It is a quiet, pretty town, a trading center for olives, almonds, and wine.

Catherine and Victoire may look alike, but they are very different. Catherine still lives in Aix. She is married and has two children. Her husband works as a pastry chef, making cakes and other desserts. He learned how to make them from a master chef. He follows French recipes that were created 150 years ago.

Victoire is single and lives in Paris, the capital of France. She works for a publisher. Her job is to get American books translated into French. She has worked on science fiction books, westerns, and even vampire novels! Of course, she speaks English very well. In her apartment, she listens to American rock bands or watches American television programs. Her favorite restaurant serves only American food.

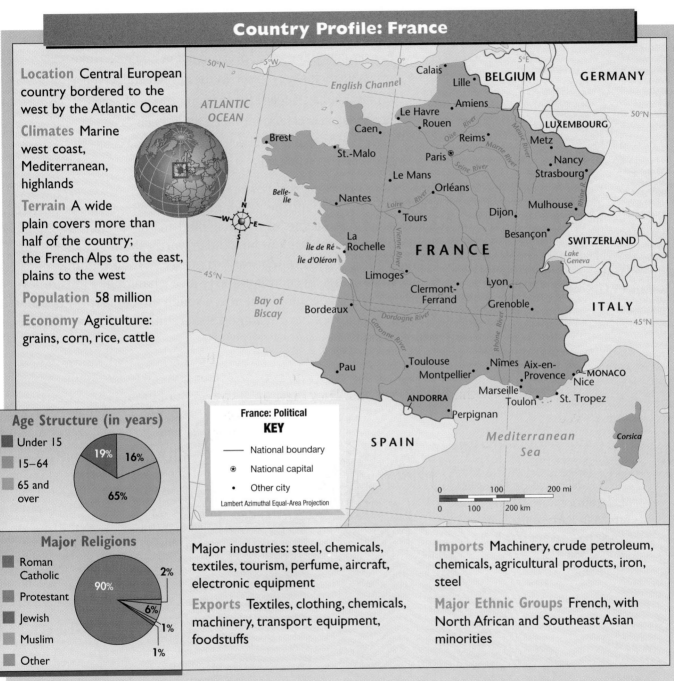

Country Profile: France

Location Central European country bordered to the west by the Atlantic Ocean

Climates Marine west coast, Mediterranean, highlands

Terrain A wide plain covers more than half of the country; the French Alps to the east, plains to the west

Population 58 million

Economy Agriculture: grains, corn, rice, cattle

Age Structure (in years)
- Under 15
- 15–64
- 65 and over

19% 16%
65%

Major Religions
- Roman Catholic
- Protestant
- Jewish
- Muslim
- Other

90% 2% 6% 1% 1%

France: Political
KEY
— National boundary
⊛ National capital
• Other city
Lambert Azimuthal Equal-Area Projection

0   100   200 mi
0   100   200 km

Major industries: steel, chemicals, textiles, tourism, perfume, aircraft, electronic equipment

Exports Textiles, clothing, chemicals, machinery, transport equipment, foodstuffs

Imports Machinery, crude petroleum, chemicals, agricultural products, iron, steel

Major Ethnic Groups French, with North African and Southeast Asian minorities

Map and Chart Study This map shows the borders and major cities of France. **Movement** Note that two large bodies of water, the Atlantic Ocean and the Mediterranean Sea, border France. How do you think these bodies of water affect France's economy?

Location What large island is part of France? Where is it located? **Critical Thinking** In recent years, immigration has become a major issue in France. What information in the Country Profile reflects this?

Pride in French Culture

Catherine and Victoire show us two sides of the French character. Each side values French culture differently. Catherine sums up her attitude this way:

> "We French are as modern as anyone else. But there is something very special about our culture. Take our language. It's very exact. In the seventeenth century [we] invented a standard for speaking correct French. Since then, an organization called the French Academy has tried to keep our language as correct as possible. We French love our traditions."

Catherine is right about the Academy. Since 1635, it has published dictionaries that give all the words accepted in the French language. The Academy makes rules about how these words should be used. This is an example of how the French work to preserve their culture.

On the other hand, French culture is also changing. Films, television, tourists, and trade have put the French in contact with other cultures. These cultures have changed the traditional French lifestyle. As Victoire explains:

READ ACTIVELY

Connect Think of two or three foreign words that are part of the American language.

▶This billboard on Galeries Lafayette, a huge department store in Paris, announces to English speakers that it is the "Capital of Fashion."

"There are plenty of articles in the French papers about the need to keep the French language pure. How are we going to do that, is what I want to know! At my publishing company most of us use a few foreign words to describe some of our activities. In the new France there are plenty of modern things that we didn't have any words for. We had to borrow them from the Americans!"

"The bigger the better" may have been the motto of architects and builders in the Middle Ages. Without the help of modern machinery or electric power, they built towering cathedrals like this one at Chartres, France. At the time, many people could not read or write, so cathedrals were built with scenes from the Bible carved in stone or shown in stained-glass windows. It took over 100 years to build most cathedrals, but the people of Chartres built this one in only 30 years. What part of the cathedral do you think was the hardest to build? Why?

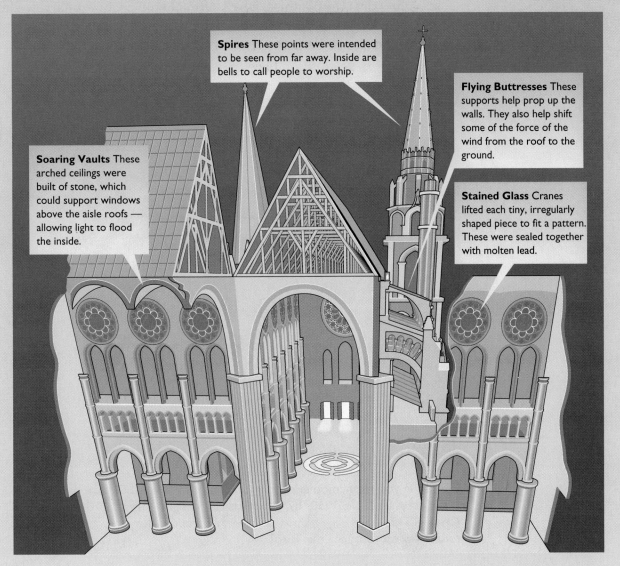

Spires These points were intended to be seen from far away. Inside are bells to call people to worship.

Flying Buttresses These supports help prop up the walls. They also help shift some of the force of the wind from the roof to the ground.

Soaring Vaults These arched ceilings were built of stone, which could support windows above the aisle roofs — allowing light to flood the inside.

Stained Glass Cranes lifted each tiny, irregularly shaped piece to fit a pattern. These were sealed together with molten lead.

LINKS TO ART

Going Home to Paint Paul Cézanne was one of the greatest painters of his time. He lived in both Paris and Aix-en-Provence—where he was born—for most of his life. In 1883, he went to the countryside near his home town. He painted mountains, seashores—even his gardener. When he was outdoors, Cézanne tried to learn from nature. He believed that nature showed him what he needed to paint.

Victoire is referring to words like *sandwich, weekend, toast,* and *parking.* These words are a sign of France's close ties with other nations. These close ties mean that other cultures affect life in France. They also mean that French culture affects life in other nations.

Highlights of French Culture In 1805, a French pastry chef named Marie-Antoine Carême (muh REE ahn TWAHN kuh REM) began making desserts for rich and powerful people in France. His cakes and puddings delighted all. Some cakes looked like buildings or monuments. Some puddings looked like birds or flowers.

In 1833, Carême wrote a book on the art of French cooking. His book was similar to the dictionary of the French Academy. It set strict standards of excellence. Ever since Carême's book was published, French cooking has been one of the most respected kinds of cooking in the world.

The French have also set standards in the fashion industry. In 1947, a French fashion designer named Christian Dior (dee OR) caught the attention of the industry. His clothing designs were fresh and new. During World War II, women had worn shoulder pads and short, straight skirts. In contrast, Dior's "New Look" featured narrow shoulders and long, full dresses. His fashions became popular all over the world. Dior made Paris the center of the fashion industry.

Fashion's "New Look"

Women in your grandmother's generation might have worn evening dresses such as these, designed in the 1950s by French fashion designer Christian Dior (center). **Critical Thinking** High-fashion clothing by European designers remains popular today. Why do you think this is so?

◀▼ Paris's beautiful Opera House glitters by day or night. One of the world's largest theaters, the Opera opened in 1875.

French cooking and fashions are only two examples of the influence of French culture on the rest of the world. France has also produced world-famous poets, philosophers, painters, and politicians. And some of the best wine in the world comes from France. The roots of this success go back centuries. They are based on the French system of education, methods of farming, and outlook on life.

Holding on to Tradition   In Aix, many French traditions continue. Catherine feels that the city of her birth is an important part of who she is. Her father, grandmother, and great-grandmother live in Aix. Her family has lived there since the 1400s! Catherine says that good French pastry chefs, like her husband, are born with the talent "in their blood." Once she even checked the city's records to see if her husband's ancestors were pastry chefs.

Changes in French Life

Like many French citizens, Catherine believes French culture is unique and valuable. Yet she, too, agrees that life in France is changing. And the French people and government are beginning to deal with the changes.

Predict When immigrants move to a new place, how do they change the culture?

The New Immigrants Immigrants have been moving to Western Europe since World War II. Many people in French colonies started **emigrating,** or moving away, from their homelands to France. They came from Algeria (al JIR ee uh), Senegal (sen ih GAWL), Vietnam (vee ut NAHM), and other former French colonies.

When France joined the European Union, immigrants from other countries in Europe moved to France in search of work. The native French people had questions about the immigrants. Would the newcomers take jobs away from people already in France? Would the newcomers understand French culture? Would the cultures of the newcomers change French traditions?

The debate about the new immigrants continues. But their influence can be seen, especially in the big cities. In Paris, Arab, African, and Asian cultures are very strong. In other large cities in France, it is common to hear people speaking languages other than French. Every year, there are more and more restaurants and grocery stores that sell foreign food.

Paris Street Scenes

In an immigrant neighborhood in Paris, people buy and sell foods that are both new and familiar (below). Immigrants from West and North Africa, some of France's newest residents, can browse at book shops that feature Arabic and French-language books about Islam and Africa (right).

Some French people, like Catherine, continue to follow traditional French ways. And some French politicians support her point of view. The French government passed a law that makes it illegal to use certain foreign words in advertisements, business, and education. This law aims to protect the French language from foreign influences. Another law was passed to deal with citizenship. This law states that children born in France of parents born in other countries are not all French citizens.

Like her sister, Victoire is proud of French culture. But Victoire disagrees with the new language law. She believes France should accept foreign influences. Victoire also disagrees with the citizenship law. A few years ago, she and some friends protested against it in public.

American Influence In 1992, a strong foreign influence showed up just outside of Paris: the EuroDisney (YOO roh diz nee) theme park. This was the first Disney park to be built in Europe. Many French people cannot believe how big it is. The park is one fifth of the size of Paris.

At EuroDisney, visitors from all over Europe get to sample American culture. EuroDisney has a section called Main Street, U.S.A., with an American-style city hall. It also has a hotel that looks like a Wild West town, a camp with log cabins, and a California-style restaurant.

When the theme park opened, French reactions were mixed. Some French people loved it and brought their families to enjoy the rides, exhibits, and food. Other people were not so happy. They disliked the bright colors, cartoon characters, and fake scenery in the park.

After a slow start, EuroDisney has become a success. However, most visitors come from Great Britain, Germany, and other European countries—not France. Many French people prefer to go to another, smaller theme park called Parc Astérix (uhs STA riks). It is based on a French comic strip character.

▲ The theme park based on France's favorite cartoon character, Astérix, has added a new attraction every year since it opened.

SECTION 2 REVIEW

1. **Define** emigrate.

2. **Identify** (a) Aix-en-Provence, (b) Paris.

3. How has Catherine shown pride in French culture?

4. How has Victoire shown that she is open to new ideas from outside of France?

Critical Thinking

5. **Recognizing Bias** Describe the views of those who agree and those who disagree with France's language law.

Activity

6. **Writing to Learn** Think about making a visit to Catherine or Victoire. What would you like to talk about? What would you like to see in Aix or Paris?

Using the Writing Process

James ran the entire three blocks home from the library. He threw open the front door and dropped his books and coat in the hall. Then he ran upstairs. His uncle Steven found him an hour later at his desk, scribbling madly.

"What are you doing, James?"

James barely looked up from his paper. "I'm writing about the Berlin Wall. I can't believe it stood in place for all those years and then the people just knocked it down!"

Uncle Steven picked up the paper. He read a few sentences and frowned.

"James, I can see in your writing that you're very excited about it, but it's kind of a jumble. What are you trying to say?"

James shrugged. "I just want to write down everything I know."

"It's tempting, I know, but you can't just throw everything into one pot like a soup. You have to plan your work. Remember, writing is a process."

Get Ready

Using the writing process means following a certain kind of method when writing. It means that people do not just sit down and write a paper all at once. Writing is not a single act. Instead, writing is a process, or a series of steps.

Most things you do in life are processes. For example, when you brush your teeth, you might follow these steps: 1) pick up your toothbrush and toothpaste, 2) put toothpaste on the brush, 3) brush your teeth, and 4) rinse. When you think about it, you can see how you go through processes every day of your life.

Writing is the same way. It involves a series of steps called the writing process. By simply following the steps, you can complete any writing assignment.

Try It Out

The writing process is shown in the diagram at right. Refer to the diagram as you read the description of each step. Use it to complete the activity that follows.

A. Prewriting This first step is what you do before you start to write. (*Pre-* means "before.") Prewriting involves two steps: deciding what you will write about, and finding the information you will need.

B. Drafting Drafting means organizing your information in a logical and interesting way. Make an outline and write a rough draft of your work. If you discover that you need more information, return to the prewriting step.

C. Revising Revising is, in many ways, the most important step. Professional writers often revise their work three, four, or even more times until they are happy with it. When you revise, you change your writing to make it clearer and more enjoyable to read. If necessary, you can reorganize your ideas by returning to the drafting stage.

D. Proofreading Reread your writing and correct any errors in grammar, usage, spelling, and punctuation. Fix even the smallest problems to make your writing as good as it can be. This step is especially important because a lot of little mistakes can hurt a piece of writing as much as a few big mistakes can.

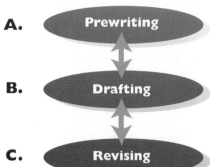

The Writing Process

A. Prewriting
B. Drafting
C. Revising
D. Proofreading
E. Publishing

E. Publishing Publishing is the final step. Publishing means sharing your writing with an audience. You might do this by turning it in to the teacher, posting it on the bulletin board, or reading it aloud to your classmates.

To help you apply the skill next time you have a writing assignment, do the following now. On a clean sheet of paper, copy the flowchart that shows the writing process. Write a brief description of each step underneath the step in the flowchart.

Apply the Skill

Use the writing process every time you have a writing assignment, from one-paragraph reports to long themes. You should even use it to answer essay questions on tests.

Now that you understand the writing process, put it to work. Your assignment is to use the writing process to write a paragraph that describes life in present-day rural France.

Sweden

A WELFARE STATE

BEFORE YOU READ

Reach Into Your Background

Do you know someone who has received some kind of help from the government? Do you think people need more government help, or should they do more for themselves? In Sweden, the government provides many services—such as hospital care and a college education—at little or no cost.

Questions to Explore

1. How does the Swedish government care for the needs of its people?

2. What economic challenges face the Swedish government, and how is it meeting these challenges?

Key Terms

benefit
welfare state
national debt

O lof Hylten-Cavallius (OHL uhf HIL tuhn kuh VAHL yuhs) is a Swedish banker. He thinks his third heart attack was the luckiest thing that ever happened to him. That is because it was not until the third heart attack that doctors agreed to give Olof an operation. Now his heart is close to normal.

The doctors who performed Olof's operation were experts in their field. The hospital had all the latest equipment, and the care afterwards was excellent. The operation would have cost Olof about $20,000 in the United States. But in Sweden, it cost him next to nothing. How did Olof manage to get such an expensive operation at such a low cost?

▼ Highly skilled surgeons use the most up-to-date equipment to perform heart surgery.

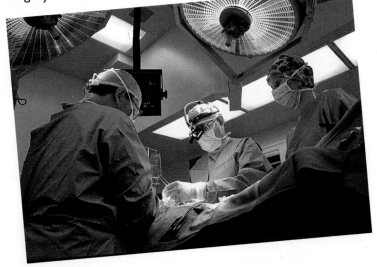

Life in a Welfare State

Olof's operation is just one example of the free—or nearly free—services in Sweden. Elisabet Ray, a school teacher, provides another example. She is happy that her daughter is going to college. This education costs nothing. Does this sound amazing to you? As you may know, college in the United States can cost more than $20,000 a year.

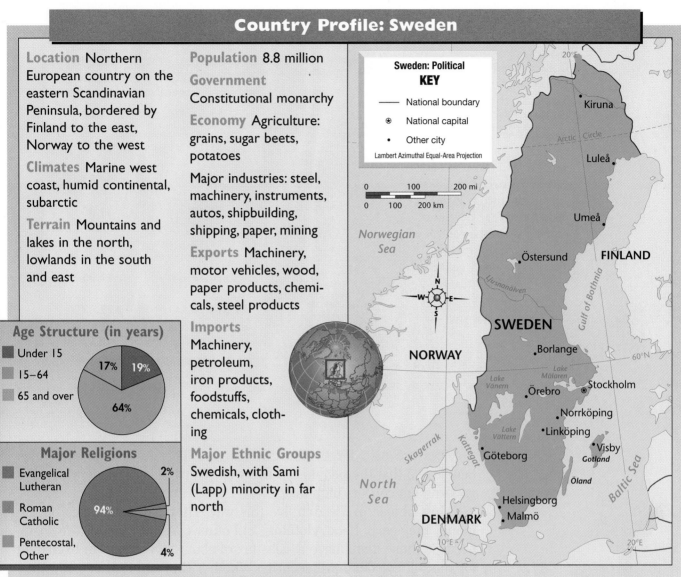

Location Northern European country on the eastern Scandinavian Peninsula, bordered by Finland to the east, Norway to the west

Climates Marine west coast, humid continental, subarctic

Terrain Mountains and lakes in the north, lowlands in the south and east

Population 8.8 million

Government Constitutional monarchy

Economy Agriculture: grains, sugar beets, potatoes

Major industries: steel, machinery, instruments, autos, shipbuilding, shipping, paper, mining

Exports Machinery, motor vehicles, wood, paper products, chemicals, steel products

Imports Machinery, petroleum, iron products, foodstuffs, chemicals, clothing

Major Ethnic Groups Swedish, with Sami (Lapp) minority in far north

Age Structure (in years)

- Under 15
- 15–64
- 65 and over

19%, 17%, 64%

Major Religions

- Evangelical Lutheran
- Roman Catholic
- Pentecostal, Other

94%, 2%, 4%

Sweden: Political
KEY

—— National boundary
⊛ National capital
• Other city

Lambert Azimuthal Equal-Area Projection

0 100 200 mi
0 100 200 km

Map and Chart Study This map shows the borders and major cities of Sweden. **Place** The northernmost farms in the world are in Sweden and Norway. Most countries this far north have climates that are too cold for farming. What physical feature shown on this map might warm Sweden's climate? **Critical Thinking** Look at the graph of Sweden's age structure. How might Sweden's age structure affect its economy?

Elisabet's family received other forms of help, too. When Elisabet's son Patrick was born, she took nine months off work so that she could take care of him. Her husband also took the time off from his job. During their time away from work, they received monthly checks for 90 percent of their salaries.

When Elisabet went back to work, she needed to take her son to a childcare center. Elisabet's family received help for this care, too. Until her son reaches the age of 16, Elisabet will receive more than $100 a week to pay for child care. Most countries do not have such benefits. A **benefit** is a free service or a payment.

Where do all of these benefits come from? In Sweden, they come from the government. Sweden is a **welfare state.** This means that many

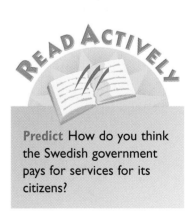

Predict How do you think the Swedish government pays for services for its citizens?

Consumer goods are expensive in Sweden. For the most part, this is because of the taxes the Swedish government collects. First, consumer goods are more expensive to make because companies pay heavy taxes on the raw materials they need. Second, a sales tax is charged when the goods are sold in stores. **Critical Thinking** Suppose you had to pay Swedish prices for the goods listed in the chart. How might your life be different?

Item	Price in United States	Price in Sweden
half gallon of milk	$1.51	$1.88
loaf of bread	$1.19	$1.92
pizza	$8.74	$4.83
fast food lunch	$3.49	$9.00
2 liters of cola	$1.39	$3.77
newspaper	$0.35	$1.06
compact disk	$12.99	$22.43
movie ticket	$8.00	$9.63

services are paid for by the government. The government provides benefits so that the people can live well. To pay for these services, the government collects high taxes.

Most people in Sweden live this way. They pay high taxes on the money they earn. Food, clothing, and other consumer goods are costly because these items have a sales tax of about 20 percent. In exchange for this, all Swedes have security. Whether they are rich or poor, they know their children will get a good education. Medical costs are low. Rents are affordable.

Sweden's Difficult Past

Life in Sweden was not always so secure. By the late 1800s, industry had grown in the United States and most of Europe. But Sweden was far behind. There were few factories or railroad lines or good roads. Farming methods had not changed much since the Middle Ages. Many people were very poor. By the end of the century, 1.5 million Swedes had left the country in search of a better life. Most of them settled in the United States.

Building a Welfare State

After World War II, a political party called the Social Democrats became powerful in Sweden. The Social Democrats promised a better life for Swedes. From 1946 to 1976, the party changed Sweden into a welfare state.

As part of the government benefits program, all workers receive five weeks of paid vacation. Most workers generally take their vacation at the same time during the summer. For five weeks in the summer, the nights in this far-northern country are very short. It is daylight for most of the day. Many factories and businesses shut down during this period.

Swedish people take more days off for being sick—and get paid for them—than the workers of any other Western country. Some of this money comes from the government. And when Swedish workers retire, they receive a monthly payment from the government that nearly equals the pay they received when they were working.

In Sweden, welfare benefits are for everyone. Many Swedes do not mind paying high taxes because they enjoy the benefits. Mona Sahlin (MOH nuh SAH lin), a Swedish politician, summed up the Swedish way of thinking:

> **"I**f you are a Social Democrat, you think it is terrific to pay taxes. For me, taxes are the finest expression of what politics are all about."

A welfare system means something very different in the United States than it does in Sweden. Our welfare system only helps people in great need—people who cannot afford medical care or food. And the rules about who can receive welfare benefits in the United States are becoming stricter. Sweden, too, is changing its rules about welfare benefits.

The Forecast: Sunny All Day and Night Near the Earth's polar regions, the sun can be seen 24 hours a day in six-month periods. At the North Pole, the sun is out from about March 20 to September 23. At the South Pole, the sun remains above the horizon from September 23 to March 20. In the northern part of Sweden, the sun stays out day and night for a few days around June 21. The Swedes celebrate this as Midsummer's Eve, with maypoles, dancing, and music.

▼ In midsummer, when the sun shines 24 hours a day, many people in Sweden stay up and celebrate with traditional dances.

Peter Wallenberg is a Swedish banker. His family owns more than 40 percent of Sweden's large corporations. Most businesses in Sweden, like most businesses in the United States, are owned by individuals. **Critical Thinking** How do businesses help people in the community?

Problems and Solutions

Everyone in Sweden receives benefits, but some people are wealthier than others. The Wallenberg family, for instance, owns 40 percent of the large corporations in Sweden. Families like the Wallenbergs live in great luxury. But in Sweden, some people are struggling with the costs of living. Lately, a number of Swedes have been just getting by.

Sweden's Troubles For the last 20 years, Sweden's economic growth has stalled. Because of the high taxes on groceries, clothing, and other goods, people buy fewer items than they would like to. Thus there is less spending to boost the economy. Also, Sweden's long vacations mean that workers spend less time on the job. This makes Swedish companies less productive.

There are also problems with the health care system. Medical care is not always available when it is needed. People often wait a long time to receive help.

The government is facing budgetary problems. To supply more benefits, the government has had to borrow money. Some Swedes think the amount their government owes, or the **national debt,** has gotten out of control. Higher taxes would lower the national debt, but most Swedes would not be able to afford them.

READ ACTIVELY

Connect What would you do if you had to wait a long time for medical help when you really needed it?

Finding Solutions Government and private businesses must both try to solve these problems. The government needs to reduce benefits and spend less money. And businesses need to earn more. The more money businesses earn, the more money, in the form of taxes, will go to the government.

One way for businesses to grow is to take advantage of Sweden's natural resources. Sweden has high-grade iron ore and makes enough steel for itself and for export. Each year, half of Sweden's electricity is made by hydroelectric turbines that use Sweden's fast rivers and many waterfalls. Sweden's vast forests support the timber industry, which supplies Sweden's needs and those of other countries.

Swedish companies have had trouble competing with firms in other countries. Most Swedish products are of high quality. But the Swedes have not been able to make them as quickly and cheaply as other countries. Some companies have found a solution to this problem. A Swedish automaker, for example, has made a partnership with an American company. Using the methods of American auto factories, the Swedes can now make a car in less than 40 hours. It used to take them four days.

The Graying of Sweden
Sweden has 2 million retired people out of a population of 8.8 million. This means that about one out of four people is retired. This is the highest proportion in the world. The Swedish government is having trouble taking care of so many retired people. Some studies say that unless the government reforms its welfare benefits, there will not be any money left by 2015. Raising taxes to cover benefits for everyone has been proposed—but it is not a popular idea.

◀▼ Natural resources, such as large forests (left), helped Sweden to build thriving industrial cities such as Stockholm (below). Wood products make up about 20 percent of Sweden's exports.

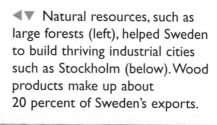

Sweden's Dala Horses

In this picture, a craftworker puts the finishing touches to a dala horse. These small figures are carved out of wood, painted red or blue, and decorated with floral designs. For Swedes, the dala horse is a symbol of hope and good luck. And for Swedes who no longer live in Sweden, it represents their homeland. In fact, the dala horse has become an important export item. Some 20 percent of dala horses made in Sweden are exported to the United States alone.

Improving the economy means changing the ways things are done in Sweden. Mats Thourslund (mahts THORZ luhnd), a professor at a Swedish university, said:

> "Sweden will not be that different from other countries in the future. We have been used to having our kids in day-care centers and old people cared for by the system, leaving the rest of us free to do whatever we want. But the party is over."

When Thorslund says, "the party is over," he means the country will be providing fewer services in order to spend less money. Making this happen is Sweden's biggest challenge today.

SECTION 3 REVIEW

1. **Define** (a) benefit, (b) welfare state, (c) national debt.

2. Describe some of the benefits that Swedish citizens receive.

3. What natural resources can help the Swedish economy?

Critical Thinking

4. **Recognizing Cause and Effect** What has caused Sweden to want to change its welfare system?

Activity

5. **Writing to Learn** Think about the welfare systems in the United States and Sweden. Write a paragraph about what you think the United States and Sweden might learn from each other.

Italy
TWO WAYS OF LIFE

BEFORE YOU READ

Reach Into Your Background

Do you think the region in which you live should help other regions develop new industries? Why or why not?

Questions to Explore

1. How have the differences in the environments of northern and southern Italy affected the lives of Italians?
2. How are Italians attempting to speed the development of southern Italy?

Key Term
manufacturing

Key Places
the Vatican
Rome
Milan
Locorotondo

Can you solve this riddle? A magazine photographer spent about a year exploring a certain country, yet the country is so tiny that he was able to walk around it in 40 minutes. Its population is only about 800. But one billion people look to its leader for guidance. What is the country?

The tiny nation is called the Vatican (VAT ih kun). It is the world headquarters of the Roman Catholic Church. Its leader is the pope. Every day, Roman Catholics all over the world look to him for leadership.

Country Within a Country

The Vatican is a country within a country. Located within Rome, the capital of Italy, the Vatican is an independent city-state. A city-state is both a city and an independent nation. The Vatican has its own money and stamps. It is a member of the United Nations. It also has its own radio station, newspaper, fire department, and supermarket.

▼ This aerial view of Vatican City shows the grand dome of St. Peter's Church, which dominates the skyline.

Country Profile: Italy

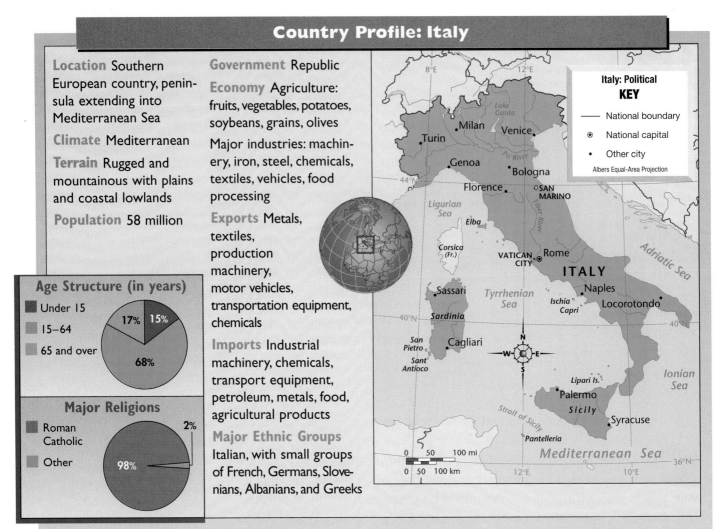

Location Southern European country, peninsula extending into Mediterranean Sea

Climate Mediterranean

Terrain Rugged and mountainous with plains and coastal lowlands

Population 58 million

Government Republic

Economy Agriculture: fruits, vegetables, potatoes, soybeans, grains, olives

Major industries: machinery, iron, steel, chemicals, textiles, vehicles, food processing

Exports Metals, textiles, production machinery, motor vehicles, transportation equipment, chemicals

Imports Industrial machinery, chemicals, transport equipment, petroleum, metals, food, agricultural products

Major Ethnic Groups Italian, with small groups of French, Germans, Slovenians, Albanians, and Greeks

Age Structure (in years)
- Under 15
- 15–64
- 65 and over

17% | 15%
68%

Major Religions
- Roman Catholic
- Other

2%
98%

Italy: Political
KEY
— National boundary
⊛ National capital
• Other city
Albers Equal-Area Projection

Map and Chart Study This map shows the borders and major cities of Italy. **Location** What two large islands are part of Italy? Which small country, other than Vatican City, is completely surrounded by Italy? **Place** Cities such as Genoa and Venice have a long history as important trading centers. Why do you think this is so? **Critical Thinking** Look at the graph of Italy's major religions. Then look again at the map and find Vatican City. How are this location and Italy's major religion related?

READ ACTIVELY

Visualize What would it be like to visit the Sistine Chapel? What would it feel like to be surrounded by art?

Every day, Catholics and non-Catholics stream into this little country. They come here to see St. Peter's Church. The Vatican's palace and art museum, which covers 13 acres (5 hectares), is also a popular attraction.

The Sistine (SIS teen) Chapel, located inside the Vatican, contains many world-famous paintings, sculptures, and other works of art. Tourists crowd into this chapel, but there is nearly perfect silence inside. No one is allowed to speak above a whisper. Everyone leans back to see the scenes painted on the ceiling. Some scenes were painted by the famous artist Michelangelo. Others are by another painter of the Renaissance period, Sandro Botticelli (SAHN dro baht uh CHEL ee). Visitors stare in wonder at the colors, figures, and designs until their necks get stiff and their eyes get blurry. It is the most famous and perhaps the most beautiful ceiling in the world.

Church and Family

Roman Catholicism unites about one billion people around the world. And it especially unites Italians. Not every Italian is Catholic, but Italy's history is closely tied to the history of Catholicism. Until recently, Catholicism was the official religion of the country.

The Roman Catholic Church provides a common focus for Italians throughout the country. For most Italians, the pope is symbolic of a father. The Church is a giant family to which they belong. Many Italians expect the Church to help them with their daily decisions—just as good parents help their children.

This way of living has existed for hundreds of years. Today, in the small towns of the countryside, life is organized around the larger family of the Church and the smaller family in the home. In the cities, these ties may not be as strong.

Divisions Between North and South

A common belief in Catholicism has helped Italians unify their nation. Until the 1800s, Italy was made up of many separate city-states, territories, and small kingdoms. In 1870, the Italian people unified these areas into one nation. Still, the Italy of today seems divided into two different countries—the north and the south. The ways of life in the two areas set them apart.

The Risorgimento: "Rising Again" The Risorgimento was a movement in the 1800s to inspire the Italian people to unite as one nation. Poets and philosophers tried to create a sense of nationalism. Today, Italian schoolchildren learn about and celebrate the movement. Cities have streets and squares that bear the names of many of the Risorgimento's heroes.

The Pope

Pope John Paul II, the leader of the Roman Catholic Church, greets visitors to Vatican City. John Paul, who is Polish, was the first non-Italian to become pope in 450 years. John Paul travels much more than previous popes did. In addition to Polish, he speaks English, Spanish, French, German, Italian, Latin, and several Slavic languages. **Critical Thinking** Why might the ability to speak many languages help a pope who often travels to other countries?

A Cross Between Art and Fashion Futurism was an artistic movement that centered in Italy in the early 1900s. Futurists celebrated the future and criticized traditions. They glorified technology by painting images of a speeding car or the motion of a powerful train. An artist named Fortunato Depero, a Futurist painter, also designed men's vests. These vests had "Futurist" designs on them—such as mechanical figures.

Life in the North   Milan (mih LAN) is typical of northern Italy. Abundant minerals, fast rivers, and a developed economy have brought wealth to the area. Many international businesses are located here.

Milan is one part of a triangle of cities—with the cities of Turin and Genoa—that are home to most of Italy's **manufacturing** industries. Manufacturing is the process of turning raw materials into finished products.

Milan has a flashier side, too. Every season, people interested in fashions crowd into Milan to see collections from clothing designers. Italian fashion has become so important that Milan is second only to Paris as a fashion capital. Milan's factories also produce cars, planes, leather goods, and plastics.

Like many European cities, Milan is a mix of the old and the new. In a 300-year-old palace, you can see what may be the oldest public library in Europe. Millions of dollars have been spent to keep it in good condition. Less than a mile away, you can drive past modern steel-and-glass office buildings. These buildings cost millions of dollars to construct.

▼▶ Italy has both new and old attractions, such as this high-tech shoe factory in Milan (below) and a centuries-old burial place in Rome (right).

▲ This band is playing music for the tarantella, one of southern Italy's most popular folk dances. Tarantella music is lively, so the dancers must skip, run, and hop as they dance. Italian legend states that dancing the tarantella can cure someone who has been bitten by a tarantula spider.

A Town in Southern Italy Southern Italy is very different from Milan. Southern Italy is mostly agricultural. Fertile areas near the coast get enough rainfall to grow abundant crops. Olives, tomatoes, fruits, and other crops are grown here. Inland, people barely make a living because of the thin soil and dry climate. These people follow a traditional way of life.

Locorotondo (loh koh roh TAWN doh) is a small town located in the southernmost part of Italy. It is on the "heel" of the Italian "boot." Farming is the way most people here make a living. Wheat, olives, and fruits are grown here. Fishing is also an important industry.

The people here talk about northern Italy as if it were another country. They know little of the high fashions of Milan or the noisy city of Rome. Southern Italian traditions and the family still rule everyday life.

Many religious events are celebrated in the streets of town. The procession of the Feast of Corpus Christi takes place every year, several weeks after Easter. It celebrates the presence of Jesus Christ. In this festival event, women hang their wedding clothes over their balconies and place flowers on them. Additional such displays are set up on the streets around town. People walk together around the town, from church to church and display to display.

The traditional way of life may change as the economy of southern Italy changes. After World War II, Puglia (POOL yah)—the region that Locorotondo lies within—became one of the main areas for land reform. Large farms were divided into smaller farms and sold. Today the Italian government is using tax money to modernize parts of the southern region. New schools and hospitals are being built. The government is also rebuilding factories in the south's large cities, such as Naples (NAY pulz) and Syracuse (SIHR uh kyoos).

Politics and the Two Italys

Northern and southern Italy are so different that some Italians think the two regions should be separate countries. In 1996, a political party known as the Northern League won 10 percent of the vote in a national election. The Northern League wants to turn northern Italy into a separate country. If this happens, people in northern Italy will no longer have to support the poorer southern part of Italy with their taxes.

It is not likely that the Northern League will get its way. No matter how much Italians disagree, they will never lose their strong Italian identity. Religion and family will probably keep the people of Italy unified for many years to come.

A Call for Independence

During a speech in Venice in 1996, Umberto Bossi, the leader of the Northern League, demanded independence for Padania, the League's name for northern Italy.

SECTION 4 REVIEW

1. **Define** manufacturing.
2. **Identify** (a) the Vatican, (b) Rome, (c) Milan, (d) Locorotondo.
3. List three differences between life in Milan and life in a southern Italian village.
4. How has the government tried to help the development of southern Italy?

Critical Thinking
5. **Drawing Conclusions** Do you think northern Italy should try to help develop southern Italy? Why or why not?

Activity
6. **Writing to Learn** Work with a partner. One of you will write a letter to a relative about life in northern Italy. The other will write a response from the point of view of a southern Italian.

Germany

A NATION REUNITED

BEFORE YOU READ

Reach Into Your Background

What is it like to see a friend whom you have not seen in a long time? Do you sometimes find that you do not know the person as well as you once did? As you read this section, you will see how two parts of Germany separated and then came together again.

Questions to Explore

1. Why was Germany divided and how did it become reunited?

2. How are Germans dealing with the issues of a reunited nation?

Key Terms

Holocaust
reunification

Key People and Places

Adolf Hitler
Berlin

One day in 1961, Conrad Schumann, a 19-year-old policeman, stood guard at a barbed-wire fence. His job was to shoot anyone who tried to get across the fence. East Berlin (bur LIN), where Schumann was standing, was part of East Germany. East Germany had a communist government. The fence was built to prevent East Berliners from escaping to West Berlin. From West Berlin, people could reach democratic West Germany.

To Schumann, the fence was a terrible thing. He could see the buildings of West Berlin on the other side. They seemed very beautiful. On television, he had seen a program from West Berlin. It showed people dancing to American music, shopping for colorful clothing, and speaking their views freely. In East Germany, the government did not approve of American music and free speech. The stores had few interesting things to buy.

Schumann thought about all these things. Then he made a decision and jumped over the barbed wire. A moment later, he was on the other side—in the freedom of the West.

Just a few days after Schumann jumped to freedom, the barbed-wire fence was replaced by a concrete wall. The Berlin Wall separated families and friends. On one side of it, communism ruled. On the other side, the people did.

▼ At first, the Berlin Wall was only barbed wire. As you can see, Conrad Schumann jumped over it easily. Later, he said, "I had no desire to shoot my fellow citizens, and I knew that they were about to put up a much stronger wall."

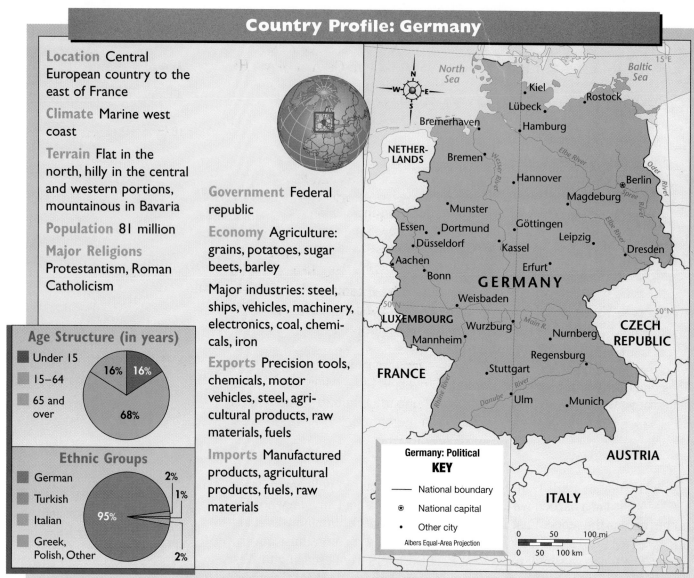

Location Central European country to the east of France

Climate Marine west coast

Terrain Flat in the north, hilly in the central and western portions, mountainous in Bavaria

Population 81 million

Major Religions Protestantism, Roman Catholicism

Government Federal republic

Economy Agriculture: grains, potatoes, sugar beets, barley

Major industries: steel, ships, vehicles, machinery, electronics, coal, chemicals, iron

Exports Precision tools, chemicals, motor vehicles, steel, agricultural products, raw materials, fuels

Imports Manufactured products, agricultural products, fuels, raw materials

Age Structure (in years)

- Under 15
- 15–64
- 65 and over

16% 16%
68%

Ethnic Groups

- German
- Turkish
- Italian
- Greek, Polish, Other

95% 2% 1% 2%

Germany: Political
KEY

— National boundary
⊗ National capital
• Other city
Albers Equal-Area Projection

0   50   100 mi
0   50 100 km

Map and Chart Study This map shows Germany's borders and major cities. **Location** How are the locations of Bonn, Bremen, Hamburg, and Dresden similar? **Critical Thinking** Most non-Germans who live in Germany are guest workers, people who have moved there temporarily to find work. What countries do you think most of Germany's guest workers come from?

Germany's Tragic Past

To understand the importance of the Berlin Wall, you need to understand part of Germany's past. After losing World War I in 1918, the German government had to pay billions of dollars as punishment for attacking other countries. To make things even worse, the German economy collapsed. Prices soared. Germans everywhere felt desperate.

Hitler and World War II Adolf Hitler (AY dahlf HIT lur), a young German soldier, had wept bitterly in 1918 when he learned that Germany had lost the war. He promised himself that his country would never suffer such a defeat again. Hitler became deeply involved in politics. In speech after speech, he promised to make Germany great again. By 1933, this once unknown soldier was dictator of Germany.

Hitler blamed Germany's economic problems on German Jews. He spread hateful theories about Jews, Gypsies, and other ethnic groups in Germany. He claimed they were inferior to, or not as good as, other Germans. He claimed that Germans were a superior ethnic group—and should lead Europe.

Many people did not believe Hitler's threats. But Hitler was deadly serious. He ordered attacks on neighboring countries and forced them under German rule. His actions led to the start of World War II in 1939. Great Britain, the Soviet Union, and the United States joined other nations to stop Hitler and the Germans. By the end of the war, Europe was in ruins. People around the world learned that the Germans had forced countless Jews, Gypsies, Slavs, and others into brutal prison camps. Millions of people were murdered in these camps. Most of them were Jews. This horrible mass murder of six million Jews is called the **Holocaust** (HAHL uh kawst).

The Cold War   At the end of the war, the Americans, the British, the French, and the Soviets divided Germany. The American, British, and French sections were joined into a democratic country called West Germany. The Soviet Union created a communist system in East Germany.

LINKS TO SCIENCE

Albert Einstein Born in 1879 to Jewish-German parents, Albert Einstein was a quiet child who grew into one of the greatest scientists of all time. His famous equation, $E=mc^2$, describes the relationship between mass and energy and led the world into the atomic age. Einstein settled in the United States in 1933 and gave up his German citizenship. He became a citizen of the United States in 1940.

Divided Berlin

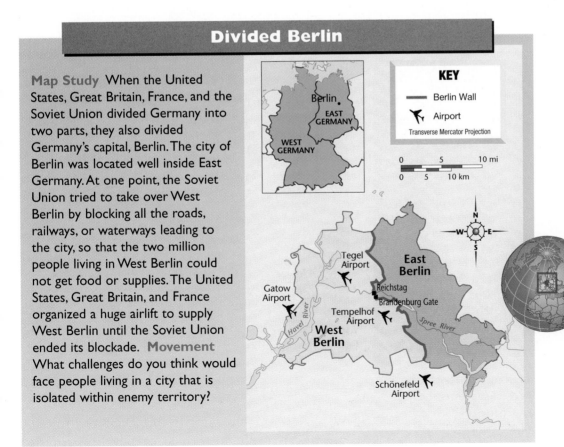

Map Study When the United States, Great Britain, France, and the Soviet Union divided Germany into two parts, they also divided Germany's capital, Berlin. The city of Berlin was located well inside East Germany. At one point, the Soviet Union tried to take over West Berlin by blocking all the roads, railways, or waterways leading to the city, so that the two million people living in West Berlin could not get food or supplies. The United States, Great Britain, and France organized a huge airlift to supply West Berlin until the Soviet Union ended its blockade. **Movement** What challenges do you think would face people living in a city that is isolated within enemy territory?

Berlin was in the Soviet part of Germany. But the western half of it, called West Berlin, became part of democratic West Germany. This turned the Western half into an island of democracy in the middle of communism. The Berlin Wall separated the two halves of the city. But it divided more than Berlin. It was a symbol of a divided world. Little wonder that some people called it the "Wall of Shame."

During the Cold War, the United States and Western Europe became partners. These countries had democratic governments and were against communism. Eastern European countries had communist governments and were partners with the Soviet Union. Soviet troops stayed in Eastern Europe to make sure that these countries remained communist.

Think about the effects of the Cold War on European countries. Recall that these countries are small and close together. Family, friends, and relatives were separated by Cold War borders. Even some who had managed to escape to the West suffered. For example, Conrad Schumann, who jumped over to the western side, could no longer see his sister, brother, and mother. They remained in East Berlin. The idea that he could not even visit his mother filled him with sadness.

East Germans led far different lives than West Germans. The communist government required people to obey without asking questions. It even encouraged people to spy on family members and

Easing International Tensions

Soviet and Western leaders often met to try to ease tensions. Soviet leader Nikita Khrushchev is shown meeting with French President Charles de Gaulle (above right) and U.S. President John F. Kennedy (above).

During the summer of 1989, many East Germans took vacations in other Eastern European countries. They had no intention of returning, however. Rather, they planned to flee to West Germany. Here, a group of East Germans celebrate as they prepare to go through the Czech-West German border. **Critical Thinking** In the summer of 1989, the Soviet Union and Eastern European countries such as Czechoslovakia were still under communist rule. Why do you think that no efforts were made to prevent East Germans from fleeing to the West?

neighbors. Children were taught to respect only those things that helped communism. Things from the West—including movies, music, books, and magazines—were seen as harmful to communism.

The Communists Weaken In time, communist rule started to change. One reason was that the East German economy was falling further behind the West German economy. The average West German had a much better life than the average East German. To keep East Germans happy, the government softened its rules. Some East Germans could then visit West Germany. Conrad Schumann's mother, who was then in her late seventies, was allowed to see him. But he still was not allowed to go to East Berlin to see her. If he crossed the border, he would be arrested and put in prison.

In the late 1980s, changes in the Soviet Union helped to cause the collapse of East Germany. Soviet leader Mikhail Gorbachev made it clear that he would not use force to protect communism in Eastern Europe. Fear of the Soviets had helped keep the East German government in power. Now this fear was gone. Gorbachev told the East German leaders to make more reforms, but they refused. Without any support from the people, East Germany's government collapsed.

The Berlin Wall collapsed as well. On November 9, 1989, crowds of Germans began scrambling over the wall. Some people raced to see friends and relatives. Others just wanted to enjoy a different life. People

READ ACTIVELY

Visualize Visualize the collapse of the Berlin Wall. Describe some of the sights and sounds of this momentous event.

Crowds began to destroy the Berlin Wall on November 9, 1989. They held a huge party on and around the wall, while people from both sides helped each other up and over. Three million people from East Germany visited West Germany the first weekend after the wall came down, and 2,500 decided to stay there permanently. **Critical Thinking** Judging from the behavior of the crowds, how do you think Germans felt about the Berlin Wall?

Ask Questions What questions might you ask East Germans about their views on reunification?

helped each other over the top of the wall to the other side. Crowds tore at the wall and took it apart block by block. Less than a year later, the governments of East and West Germany united. Germany had become a single country again.

Germany Reunited

Most Germans were thrilled about the fall of the Berlin Wall. The cultures of East and West Germany had remained similar in many ways. People in both Germanys spoke the same language and ate the same foods. They knew the same German composers, writers, and painters. Still, the process of becoming unified again, called **reunification** (ree yoo nuh fih KAY shun), would not be easy.

Germans spent millions of dollars to rebuild the economy of what was East Germany. For the first time since World War II, East Germans are enjoying modern televisions, cars, and washing machines. They have new shopping malls and better roads.

Easterners may have more televisions and cars, but they have fewer jobs. In communist East Germany, people were guaranteed a job and

▲ Since the fall of communism, many new stores and coffee shops have opened in Alexanderplatz, East Berlin's main shopping area.

food to eat. There are no such guarantees under the Western democratic system. Former East Germans also do not like losing free child care and paying higher prices for apartments and homes.

Many Westerners think the Easterners should be more grateful. After all, the Westerners helped pay to rebuild the Eastern economy. Westerners also feel that the East will get used to these changes in time. On the other hand, Westerners, too, must get used to their new and larger country. Creating a new Germany will require the effort of all Germans.

SECTION 5 REVIEW

1. **Define** (a) Holocaust, (b) reunification.
2. **Identify** (a) Adolf Hitler, (b) Berlin.
3. Describe (a) the events that led to the division of Germany and (b) the events that led to its reunification.
4. How has the reunification of Germany affected life in the former East Germany?

Critical Thinking
5. **Making Comparisons** Compare personal freedom in East and West Germany during the Cold War.

Activity
6. **Writing to Learn** Write a journal entry from the point of view of an East Berliner. Describe the night the Berlin Wall was torn down. How did you feel? Whom and what did you want to see?

Review and Activities

Reviewing Main Ideas

1. How does the monarchy unify Great Britain?

2. If Great Britain were on the European continent, would life for the British be different? Explain your answer.

3. Why have the French made laws forbidding the use of foreign words?

4. What aspects of foreign culture are becoming a part of France?

5. How do Sweden's mineral reserves benefit its economy?

6. Why have most Swedes not worried about medical care or money for retirement in the past?

7. Why might a person from Milan have a hard time adapting to life in southern Italy?

8. How has northern Italy tried to develop southern Italy?

9. (a) How was Germany divided? (b) Why was it reunified?

10. What kept Germans unified in their thinking even when their country was divided?

Reviewing Key Terms

Decide whether each statement is true or false. If it is true, write *true*. If it is false, change the underlined term to make the statement true.

1. <u>Parliament</u> is the group of people that governs Britain.

2. A <u>representative</u> is someone who represents, or stands for, a group of people.

3. In a <u>welfare state,</u> the power of kings and queens is controlled by laws about what they can and cannot do.

4. To <u>immigrate</u> is to move away from a country.

5. Swedes enjoy the <u>national debt</u> they receive from the government.

6. Milan is a <u>manufacturing</u> center.

7. Many European Jews were killed during the <u>Holocaust</u>.

8. Germans celebrated the <u>reunification</u> of their nation.

Critical Thinking

1. **Making Comparisons** (a) How is Sweden like the former East Germany? (b) How is it different?

2. **Drawing Conclusions** How do you think Germany will change in the future? How might Germans react to these changes?

Graphic Organizer

Copy the chart onto a separate sheet of paper. Then fill in facts you have learned about each country.

Country	Government	Economy	Culture
United Kingdom			
France			
Sweden			
Italy			
Germany			

Map Activity

Western Europe
For each place listed below, write the letter from the map that shows its location.

1. Aix-en-Provence

2. London

3. Sweden

4. Italy

5. Berlin

Writing Activity

Writing a Travel Journal
Imagine that you have traveled to each country in this chapter. Write a journal entry describing some of the traditions you encountered.

Internet Activity
Use a search engine to find **Paris Pages.** Choose **Culture** and use the interactive map to take a day trip around virtual Paris. Explore other links. Use the interactive map as a guide to make your own city map including sights and events you would recommend to a friend.

Skills Review

Turn to the Skills Activity.
Review the steps for using the writing process. Then, follow the steps to write a one-page paper about one aspect of life in Western Europe.

How Am I Doing?

Answer these questions to help you check your progress.

1. Do I understand why tradition is important in Great Britain?

2. Do I understand why France has tried to preserve its traditional culture?

3. Do I understand what kind of welfare state Sweden is?

4. Do I understand how and why people are working to unify two separate regions in both Italy and Germany?

5. What information from this chapter can I use in my book project?

Tracking the Midnight Sun

In Hammerfest, Norway, people who look up in the middle of a December afternoon see a dark sky full of stars. In the summer, though, people who go to bed at midnight can see the sun shining through their windows.

All around the world, the length of daylight changes throughout the year. The amount of change in daylight is greatest in areas near the North or South Pole. Because Hammerfest is in the Arctic, near the North Pole, there is a huge difference in the number of light hours during summer days and winter days.

Purpose

The length of daylight changes as the Earth makes its yearly orbit around the sun. Because of the tilt of the Earth's axis, the Northern Hemisphere faces the sun during summer. It faces away from the sun during winter. In this activity, you will make a model that shows why arctic Scandinavia and Russia have midnight suns in summer and dark days in winter.

Materials

- unshaded lamp
- tangerine or orange
- masking tape
- marker
- pencil
- metric tape measure

Procedure

STEP ONE

Make a model of the Earth. Holding your tangerine or orange around its middle, push your pencil through the fruit's core. The fruit represents the Earth. The pencil represents the Earth's axis, or the imaginary line around which the Earth turns. The point where the pencil emerges represents the North Pole. With your marker, draw a line all the way around the fruit, halfway between the two ends of the pencil. This circle represents the Equator. Next, measure the distance in centimeters between the "Equator" and the "North Pole." Then use your marker to draw a circle around the fruit approximately seven ninths of the distance from the "Equator" to the "North Pole." This circle represents the 70° latitude. Areas north of the 70° latitude are considered arctic areas. Make a dot just above this line to represent Hammerfest, Norway.

STEP TWO

Make a model of the Earth's path around the sun. Place the unshaded lamp on the floor. With the masking tape, mark a circle on the floor with the lamp at its center. This line shows the Earth's orbit. Next, mark the tape at four points equally spaced around the orbit. Label the points "arctic spring," "arctic summer," "arctic autumn," and "arctic winter." Turn on the lamp.

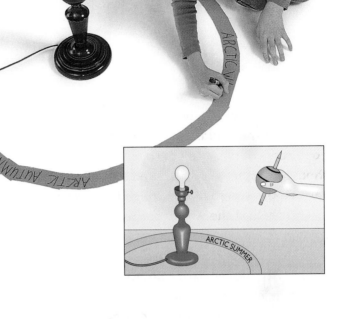

STEP THREE

Show what happens when it is summer in the Arctic. Hold the fruit at the level of the lamp's lightbulb and place it above the spot on the floor labeled "arctic summer." Refer to the diagram to tilt the "Earth's" axis correctly. The Earth turns on its axis about once every 24 hours, or once each day. Where the Earth faces the sun, it is daytime. Where the Earth faces away from the sun, it is night. Slowly turn the "Earth" on its axis. Notice where the lamp's light hits the fruit. Notice what parts of the fruit are in shadow. Study the amount of light and shadow in the Arctic.

STEP FOUR

Show what happens when it is winter in the Arctic. Hold the fruit at the level of the lightbulb and place it above the spot on the floor marked "arctic winter." Line up the axis as before. Slowly turn the fruit on its axis. Study the amount of light and shadow that hits the Arctic.

Observations

1. In the Arctic, is the length of daylight more affected by the Earth's rotation or the tilt of the Earth's axis? Explain your answer.

2. During summer, how much of the day is light in Hammerfest? How much is light during winter? Why?

ANALYSIS AND CONCLUSION

1. If the Earth were not tilted on its axis, how do you think life in the Arctic would be different? Explain your answer.

2. Suppose that the Earth orbited around the sun but never rotated on its axis. How much daylight would Hammerfest receive during the summer? Autumn? Winter? Spring? Explain your answer.

CHAPTER 5

Exploring Eastern Europe and Russia

PICTURE ACTIVITIES

This picture shows Red Square in Russia's capital, Moscow. The large building on the right is the Kremlin. This was the headquarters of the Communist government during Soviet times. Decisions made here often affected people throughout Eastern Europe. To begin your study of Russia and Eastern Europe, complete the following activities.

Study the picture

Notice that there are many tourists milling around Red Square. One of the major tourist attractions in the square is St. Basil's Cathedral, the building on the left. As you read this chapter, consider why a cathedral might be of interest to people living in a former communist country.

Write a postcard

Put yourself in the place of one of the tourists in the picture. What are your reactions to what you see in Red Square? Write a postcard to a friend telling of your visit to Red Square.

Poland

TRADITION AND CHANGE

Reach Into Your Background

Think of your own hometown 20 years from now. Do you think it will be very different?

What things about it would you like to see changed? What would you like to stay the same?

Questions to Explore

1. What traditions remain strong in the Polish countryside?
2. How is life changing in Polish towns and cities?

Key Terms

free enterprise
shrine

Key People

Pope John Paul II

In 1989, Poland's communist government came to an end, and many things changed. Meet two brothers-in-law who are like the two faces of Poland. One man has changed with the times. The other sticks to old ways.

The first is Janusz Rajtar (YAHN uhsh RY tuhr). He owns a grocery store in a small city. The new non-communist government lets him keep most of his profits. He has saved money and gotten a loan. Now he is thinking of expanding his business. You can tell how well he is doing when you see his family. He and his wife dress in the latest fashions. His three young sons have new clothes, too.

Janusz Rajtar's brother-in-law, whose name is Janusz Podolak, has not been quite so lucky. He still wears the loose-fitting overalls that people wore during communist days. When the communist government fell, he grew poorer. He is a peasant farmer in a region where most farmers still use horses to plow the land. During the time of communist rule, the government kept his farm going by paying some of his costs. Now all of that is over.

▼ Now that Poland is no longer communist, its businesses are thriving.

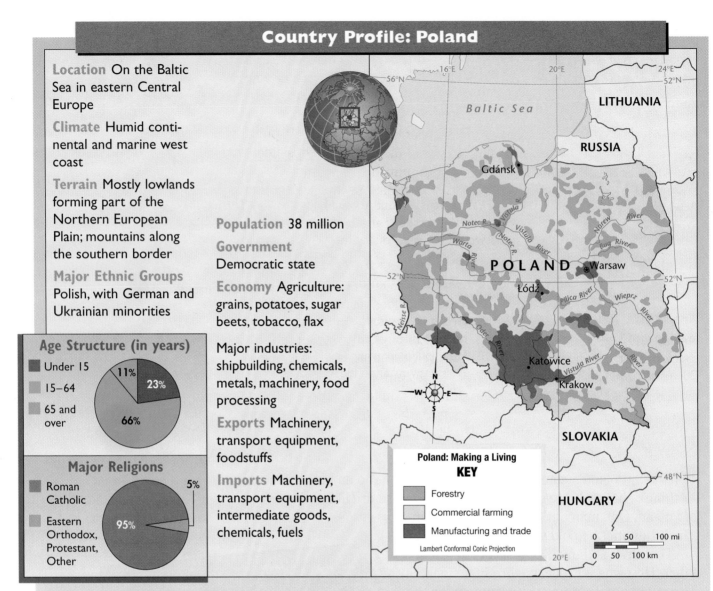

Country Profile: Poland

Location On the Baltic Sea in eastern Central Europe

Climate Humid continental and marine west coast

Terrain Mostly lowlands forming part of the Northern European Plain; mountains along the southern border

Major Ethnic Groups Polish, with German and Ukrainian minorities

Population 38 million

Government Democratic state

Economy Agriculture: grains, potatoes, sugar beets, tobacco, flax

Major industries: shipbuilding, chemicals, metals, machinery, food processing

Exports Machinery, transport equipment, foodstuffs

Imports Machinery, transport equipment, intermediate goods, chemicals, fuels

Age Structure (in years)
- Under 15
- 15–64
- 65 and over

11%
23%
66%

Major Religions
- Roman Catholic
- Eastern Orthodox, Protestant, Other

5%
95%

Poland: Making a Living
KEY
- Forestry
- Commercial farming
- Manufacturing and trade

Lambert Conformal Conic Projection

0   50   100 mi
0   50   100 km

Map and Chart Study This map shows the ways people make a living in different parts of Poland. **Location** How do you think most people make a living in the cities that are shown on this map? **Place** Look at the key. What clues does this map give you about the vegetation and terrain of Poland? What can you learn from these clues? **Critical Thinking** Look at the graph of Poland's major religions. What is the most common religion in Poland?

Tradition in Poland

Since Poland's communist government fell, the country has moved away from a communist economy in which the government owned and ran all the businesses. Instead, Poland has adopted the **free enterprise** system, or capitalism. In it, people can run their own businesses. But not all of life in Poland has changed. As you travel in the countryside, you see signs of a way of life that existed long before communist rule.

The Polish Countryside For a look at tradition in Poland, you might visit the northeast corner of the country. Here, the Polish border has shifted many times. Again and again, other countries have seized this area. Sometimes, it belonged to Russia. At other times, it was controlled by Lithuania (lith oo AY nee uh) or Germany. There were even times when other countries took over all of Poland. But no matter what happened, the traditions of Polish life stayed the same. This is true even today.

After World War II, Poland became a communist nation. At public festivals, Poles had to pledge loyalty to communism. When crops did not grow, Poles relied on money from the communist government. When Poles were sick, they went to doctors who were paid by the government. When they were too old to farm, they knew they would receive a government pension.

Now all that has changed. It is up to the farmer to save money for old age. If the crops fail, the farmer must try to borrow money to start again. Learning this new way of life has been hard for some Poles.

Polish Catholicism   The years of communist rule did not change the love most Poles have for the Roman Catholic Church. For hundreds of years, Catholicism has been at the center of Polish tradition. The communist government tried to discourage Catholicism, but it did not succeed. Today, most Poles still are Catholic.

Polish Catholicism is unique. Poles have their own way of observing Catholic holidays and their own way of prayer. An example of Polish religious life can be seen in northeastern Poland, in the forest of

Ask Questions What questions might you ask about life in Poland under communism?

Poland's Solidarity Movement

Polish workers put pressure on the Communist government throughout the 1980s by rallying under the banner of Solidarity, an independent labor union (left). Their rallies often were broken up by the police (below). Today, Solidarity is a leading political party with many representatives in the Polish parliament.

Brightly Colored Eggs

Christians across the world give decorated eggs as gifts at Easter. The brightly colored eggs pictured here are similar to those Polish people might exchange. Don't try to peel off the shells, however. These eggs are made of wood. **Critical Thinking** What other celebrations or religious holidays involve the exchange of special gifts?

The Wisent For centuries the European bison, or wisent, roamed forests from Western Europe to Siberia. These animals are related to the North American buffalo. The wisent eat grasses, ferns, leaves, and tree bark. By 1600, loss of habitat wiped out almost all of the wisent. Now, thanks to special programs, about 1,500 wisent live in Poland. They make their home in the forest of Biaolowiza.

Biaolowiza (bee AHL uhv yezh uh). Not far from the forest is the holy mountain of Grabarka. A church sits at the top of the mountain. In mid-August, visitors climb this mountain to visit the church. Each visitor plants a cross in the earth. Among the trees on the mountainside are hundreds of crosses. Some are as tall as trees, others as tiny as flowers. You can see such **shrines,** or holy places, all over Poland.

Polish Catholics felt tremendous pride in 1978, when a Pole was selected as pope of the Catholic Church. Pope John Paul II quickly became the most widely traveled Catholic leader in history. He also made the world more aware of Poland, which was struggling under communism. On his visit to Poland in 1979, about one million Poles went wild with joy in greeting him. Mothers held babies over their heads for the pope's blessing. The crowd sang hymns and threw flowers toward the stage on which he sat. For most of these people, the pope stood for traditional Poland. He was a symbol of a part of Poland that they hoped would never die.

The Polish Language Like Roman Catholicism, the language of the Poles has also stood the test of time. Some foreign rulers banned the use of Polish in schools and in the government. The communists did not ban Polish but did force Polish schoolchildren to learn Russian, the main language of the Soviet Union.

Today, the Polish language is alive and well. It ties the people of the nation together. And it gives them the strong feeling that being Polish is something different and special. As a Slavic language, it also links the nation to other Slavic nations in Eastern Europe.

Changes in the Towns and Cities

If you are looking for the newer Poland, you will find it in the larger towns and cities. Ever since the fall of communism, Poland has undergone rapid change. The biggest of these changes have come in Poland's economy.

Making Business Grow With the end of communist rule, Poles were free to find new ways to make money. Small businesses soon blossomed all over Poland's capital, Warsaw. At first, traders set up booths on the streets. They sold everything they could find, from American blue jeans to old Soviet army uniforms.

Slowly but surely, some traders earned enough money to take over stores that the government had once owned. Poland's economy began growing faster than any other in Eastern Europe. Today, the standard of living of its people is growing stronger every day.

Predict What do you think new businesspeople in Poland must do to succeed?

Standard of Living in Eastern European Countries		
Country	Percent of Population with Televisions	Percent of Population with Telephones
Albania	10%	2%
Czech Republic	33%	33%
Hungary	50%	20%
Lithuania	33%	25%
Poland	25%	14%
Romania	17%	13%
Serbia	17%	20%
United States	83%	77%

Chart Study One way to study a country's economic health is to take a look at its basic services, such as communications. Televisions and telephones are two important tools of communication in today's world. This chart lists several Eastern European countries and shows what percentage of people have TVs and telephones in each. It also shows the same for the United States. **Critical Thinking** Study the information in the chart. Which country probably has the weakest economy?

People like store owner Janusz Rajtar are doing well in the new Poland. To find the best products for his store, Rajtar rises at 4:00 A.M. to buy fruits and vegetables at the local farmers' market. By 7:00 A.M., he is behind his desk at a second job, working in an office. Then, at 3:00 P.M., he is back at the grocery store.

Looking Toward the Future Janusz Rajtar is benefiting from his hard work. But people like Janusz's brother-in-law are working harder and are not benefiting. Farmers, with no government support, find it hard to compete in the European market. Many young people in rural areas feel that they have little chance to make a decent living. Some have moved to the city in the hope of finding jobs.

Migration to the cities, however, can cause overcrowding. Today, 60 percent of all Poles live in towns or cities, a huge increase from just 50 years ago. In response, the government is building apartment buildings and expanding suburban areas.

The new life is good in some ways and hard in others. Many Poles have things they never had before. In 1989, only half of the homes in Poland had color televisions. Now, almost every home has one. On the streets of Warsaw, some people make telephone calls on cellular phones and wear the new clothing fashions. For these people, the new way of life is good.

▼ Forests once covered Poland's flat landscape, but for centuries most of the country has been cleared for farming. This picture shows Poland's fertile farmland and the traditional wooden houses near the city of Krakow, in the foothills of the Carpathian Mountains. Many of Poland's farmers still sow their fields by hand.

Old Market Square, Warsaw, Poland

Years ago, merchants sold their wares in Warsaw's Old Market Square. People did their shopping on special market days. Today, Old Market Square is not only a shopping area, but also a place to meet friends and watch free entertainment. Street performers regularly attract large and enthusiastic audiences.

But in Warsaw, you can also see people with nothing to do. This, too, is a change. There are more people without jobs than there were under communism. The Poles will have to find ways to deal with such challenges. The Polish people are ready to do whatever is needed because for the first time in many years, their future is in their own hands.

SECTION 1 REVIEW

1. **Define** (a) free enterprise; (b) shrine.

2. **Identify** Pope John Paul II.

3. What features of country life show the traditional side of Poland?

4. What are some of the changes taking place in Poland?

Critical Thinking

5. **Making Predictions** What do you predict will happen to the Polish economy in the future? Give reasons for your predictions.

Activity

6. **Writing to Learn** Use library resources to find a book or encyclopedia article about Polish history. Read about the fall of communism in Poland. Then, write a brief summary of what you have read.

Bosnia-Herzegovina

A TRAGIC CONFLICT

BEFORE YOU READ

Reach Into Your Background

Have you ever been separated from a family member or close friend? Try to imagine the many troubles an entire nation must have when people are separated and the country is divided.

Questions to Explore

1. What impact has ethnic conflict in the former Yugoslavia had on the people of the region?

2. What divides Bosnians, Croatians, and Serbians, and what unites them?

Key Terms
icon
United Nations

Key People and Places
Marshal Tito
Sarajevo
Belgrade

▼ This bridge in Mostar, Bosnia-Herzegovina, stood for more than 400 years. It was destroyed in 1993 during a war between ethnic groups.

Bosko and Admira were a beautiful couple. Born in the late 1960s, they fell in love during high school. A graduation picture shows them in each other's arms, smiling at the camera. At the time, both lived in the city of Sarajevo (sah ray YAY voh), in a country called Yugoslavia. Bosko came from one ethnic group, and Admira from another.

On their graduation day, neither could have guessed what the future held in store. Just a few years later, their country would be ripped apart. The nation's ethnic groups would be at war with each other.

Life in a Divided Country

Yugoslavia is in a region of southeastern Europe called the Balkans. Most people there are Slavs. However, the Slavs are made up of many ethnic groups. Before the breakup of Yugoslavia, the largest groups there were the

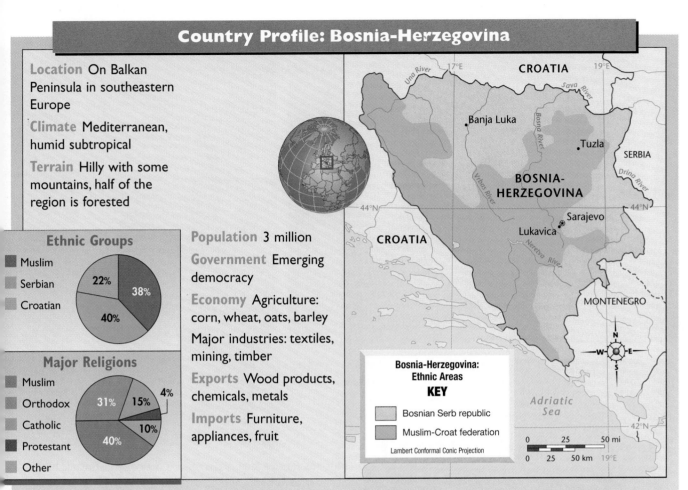

Country Profile: Bosnia-Herzegovina

Location On Balkan Peninsula in southeastern Europe

Climate Mediterranean, humid subtropical

Terrain Hilly with some mountains, half of the region is forested

Ethnic Groups
- Muslim
- Serbian
- Croatian

38% 22% 40%

Major Religions
- Muslim
- Orthodox
- Catholic
- Protestant
- Other

31% 15% 4% 10% 40%

Population 3 million

Government Emerging democracy

Economy Agriculture: corn, wheat, oats, barley Major industries: textiles, mining, timber

Exports Wood products, chemicals, metals

Imports Furniture, appliances, fruit

Bosnia-Herzegovina: Ethnic Areas
KEY
- Bosnian Serb republic
- Muslim-Croat federation

Lambert Conformal Conic Projection

0 25 50 mi
0 25 50 km

Map and Chart Study This map shows the areas occupied by various ethnic groups in Bosnia-Herzegovina. **Location** The ethnic groups of Bosnia-Herzegovina were at war with each other for several years. The capital, Sarajevo, was caught in the middle. Explain why Sarajevo's location would make it likely to be attacked. **Critical Thinking** Look at the graphs of Bosnia-Herzegovina's major religions and ethnic groups. Does any one ethnic group or religion form a majority?

Serbians, Croatians (kroh AY shunz), and Muslims. Smaller groups include the Slovenes, Macedonians (mas uh DOH nee unz), and Montenegrins (mahn tuh NEH grinz).

Serbians, Croatians, Slovenes, Macedonians, and Montenegrins have some things in common but also have differences. First, let's look at language. Bosko is a Serbian, and Admira is not, but they both speak Serbo-Croatian. Croatians speak this language, too. But the Serbians use a different alphabet for this language than the Croatians do. Having two alphabets for the same language causes confusion.

Another thing that separates the groups is religion. Most Serbians, like Bosko, belong to the Christian Orthodox Church. It is closely related to the Russian Orthodox Church but has its own practices. For example, its ceremonies use **icons** (EYE kahnz), or paintings of saints and holy people. The icons were designed to give believers a sense of personal contact with Jesus and the saints. Most Croatians, on the other hand, are Roman Catholic Christians. They follow the Christian traditions of Western Europe.

Muslims (above left) make up the majority in Bosnia, but Serbs (above right) and Croats (left) also live and worship here. In a diary about the war in Bosnia, 11-year-old Zlata Filipović wrote, "Among my girlfriends, among our friends, in our family, there are Serbs and Croats and Muslims. It's a mixed group and I never knew who was a Serb, a Croat or a Muslim." The war, however, painfully revealed these ethnic and religious differences.

But not all the people of Yugoslavia are Christians. Many are Muslims. This is because much of Eastern Europe was controlled by Muslims for several hundred years. During that time, many people living in Bosnia adopted the religion of Islam. Admira was from a Muslim family.

After World War II, Yugoslavia fell under communist control, as did other Eastern European countries. During the communist years, life in Yugoslavia was stable. One leader, Marshal Tito (TEE toh), headed the country and united the ethnic groups. Tito stressed the many things that people in Yugoslavia had in common. For example, many Yugoslavians spoke the same language and dressed in similar ways. Even so, below the surface, there were serious differences. These began to rise after Tito's death in 1980 and the collapse of communism in 1989.

READ ACTIVELY

Connect What kinds of ideas can cause barriers between people?

The Breakup of Yugoslavia In 1991, tensions among the Serbians, the Croatians, and other groups in Yugoslavia came to a breaking point. The Serbians controlled the government of Yugoslavia, and some provinces did not want to live under Serbian rule. First, the northern provinces declared their independence. One province formed the republic of Croatia. Another formed the new country of Slovenia (sloh VEE nee uh). Soon after, the central region, Bosnia-Herzegovina, declared its independence, too.

The Serbians did not want any of the provinces to break away. Instead, they wanted to keep control of the entire country. Also, Serbians who lived in Croatia and Bosnia-Herzegovina became nervous when those regions set up their own governments. Croatians living in Serbia and Bosnia-Herzegovina feared what would happen to them. No group trusted any other group. No group wanted to live in a country that was ruled by people from another group. Political leaders of these groups did not work to reduce tensions. Instead they frightened people even more, in order to build up their own power.

A Time of War

In Bosnia-Herzegovina, tensions among different ethnic groups led to a long and bitter war. Sometimes Serbians and Croatians fought on the same side to win land controlled by Bosnian Muslims. At other times, Serbians and Croatians fought against each other for land. There was much bloodshed on all sides, and people on all sides were mistreated by their enemies. But the worst killing was done by Serbians who wanted Bosnia to stay part of Yugoslavia. Most of the victims were Bosnian Muslims.

TO LANGUAGE ARTS

Writer in War During World War II, Germany invaded Yugoslavia. To protest against this, people in Sarajevo started a newspaper called *Oslobodjenje* in 1943. It is still published today, despite the civil war. *Oslobodjenje's* office has been bombed. The newspaper has suffered from shortages of electricity, paper, and ink. It has few reporters left. And still it continues, keeping hope alive.

▼ During the war, bursting bombshells were an almost daily occurrence in Sarajevo, Bosnia-Herzegovina's capital.

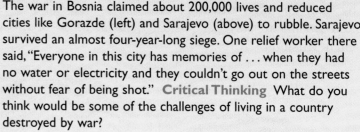

The war in Bosnia claimed about 200,000 lives and reduced cities like Gorazde (left) and Sarajevo (above) to rubble. Sarajevo survived an almost four-year-long siege. One relief worker there said, "Everyone in this city has memories of . . . when they had no water or electricity and they couldn't go out on the streets without fear of being shot." **Critical Thinking** What do you think would be some of the challenges of living in a country destroyed by war?

READ ACTIVELY

Connect How would you feel if you and some of your friends or members of your family were on opposite sides in a war?

During the war, Sarajevo, the capital of Bosnia-Herzegovina, was almost completely destroyed. Homes and schools were bombed. People were shot as they went about their daily business. Life in Sarajevo became so dangerous that Bosko's mother decided to leave. She moved to Belgrade, capital of Serbia. She felt she would be safer with her fellow Serbians around her.

Although his mother left, Bosko decided to stay. He could not leave Admira, whose Muslim family still lived in Bosnia-Herzegovina. Admira told her mother that the war would never separate her from Bosko. To Bosko and Admira, the war made no sense. Yes, he was a Serbian Christian and she was a Muslim, yet they loved one another. If they could live in peace, other people could, too.

However, things kept getting worse. Serbian armies had cut Sarajevo off from the rest of the world. People began to run out of food and other supplies. In 1992, the United Nations sent troops to the city to bring in supplies. The **United Nations** is a group of countries that work together to bring about peace and cooperation.

Bosko and Admira stayed on in Sarajevo. They knew that their lives were in danger, but they did not know what else to do. They prayed for a quick end to the war.

Other nations offered suggestions on how to end the war. Some thought that Bosnia-Herzegovina should be divided into three parts, one each for Serbians, Croatians, and Bosnian Muslims. Few people liked this idea or any other ideas that were suggested. Finally, in the mid-1990s, the Serbians, Croatians, and Bosnian Muslims signed a peace treaty. After years of war, the people of what had once been Yugoslavia hoped that the peace would last.

Lessons for Other Nations

Most countries contain different ethnic and religious groups. However, the groups do not often use violence against each other. They find ways to work together. They focus on things that they share, such as language or hopes for the future.

What happened in Bosnia-Herzegovina made the world watch other areas closely. Would the violence spread? People began to wonder if the growth of nationalism in other parts of the world might cause new wars.

With such questions in mind, most people are hoping that Bosnia-Herzegovina will serve as a lesson. They hope new nations will be born without bloodshed and that old nations will keep people united without war.

UN Aid

The United Nations tried, but failed, to keep the peace in Bosnia-Herzegovina during the war. However, UN soldiers were able to airlift food and medicine to areas under siege.

SECTION 2 REVIEW

1. **Define** (a) icon, (b) United Nations.

2. **Identify** (a) Marshal Tito, (b) Sarajevo, (c) Belgrade.

3. How has the war in the former Yugoslavia affected people there?

4. What do Bosnians, Croatians, and Serbians have in common? How do they differ?

Critical Thinking

5. **Recognizing Bias** Differences in religion seem to be one of the causes of the war in Bosnia-Herzegovina. Why do you think this is so?

Activity

6. **Writing to Learn** In your journal, write a letter from Bosko to his mother in Belgrade explaining why he is not going to follow her to that city.

SKILLS ACTIVITY

Recognizing Cause and Effect

Have you ever played with dominoes? It's fun to stand them up in a line and then topple them over. **By pushing just the first domino, you set up a chain reaction that eventually knocks all of the dominoes down. In 1988, students in the Netherlands set up 1.5 million dominoes! By pushing just one, they were able to topple nearly all the rest.**

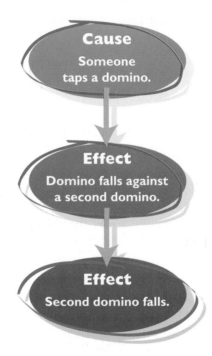

Cause
Someone taps a domino.

Effect
Domino falls against a second domino.

Effect
Second domino falls.

Get Ready

Toppling dominoes is fun, but it also teaches a lesson in cause and effect. A *cause* is something that makes something else happen. The *effect* is what happens. Someone taps the first domino. It falls over. The falling domino hits a second domino and it falls, too. The tapping of the first domino is the cause, and the effect is the fall of the second domino.

Cause and effect can explain the relationship between events. History is full of causes and effects. For example, a big cause of the French Revolution was the fact that a small number of people owned most of the country's wealth. An effect of the revolution was that France's king, who was very wealthy, was thrown out of power.

A single event can have more than one cause or more than one effect. In France, for example, the revolution had many effects besides the fall of the monarchy.

Also keep in mind that not all events are linked by cause and effect. For example, if a girl claps her hands, and it then begins to rain, her claps did not cause it to rain. Learning to correctly recognize causes and effects will help you understand history.

Try It Out

Causes and effects can be shown in cause-effect diagrams, like the one pictured to the left. You can see how events can have more than one cause or more than one effect.

To understand how cause-effect relationships work, make a cause-effect diagram about the most recent presidential election. You can learn about this event by looking it up in an almanac or other source. To make your cause-effect diagram, complete the following steps:

A. Identify the event. Your diagram will explain the most recent presidential election. Write the event in the middle of a clean sheet of paper and circle it.

B. Identify the causes. What caused the election to take place? You should be able to identify at least two causes. Write them to the left of the event, and draw a circle around each one. Then, draw an arrow from each cause to the event to show that they made the event happen.

C. Identify the effects. Identify at least two effects of a presidential election. For example, was the President reelected? Write the effects to the right of the event, and circle each one. Then, draw an arrow from the event to each effect to show that they resulted from the event.

Now look your diagram over to see how it works. Notice that it reads from left to right, just as books do. By following the arrows, you can trace the causes and effects of events.

▼ A line of falling dominoes is an example of the relationship between cause and effect.

Apply the Skill

Read the paragraph below. Look for cause-and-effect relationships between the events. Words and phrases such as "because," "so," and "as a result" will give you clues that a cause-and-effect relationship exists.

Poland After Communism

In 1989, communism in Poland ended, and Poland adopted the free enterprise system. In this kind of system, people can open and run their own businesses free from government control. The fall of communism meant that <u>the government no longer controlled the creation of jobs.</u> As a result, <u>many government jobs disappeared.</u> The loss of jobs forced people to look for jobs elsewhere. Because of free enterprise, <u>small companies now have the freedom to grow naturally.</u> Growing companies have created new and better jobs for some people, but other people remain jobless.

When you have finished reading the paragraph, go back and read the underlined events. Find at least one cause and one effect of each underlined event, and write them down. As you are looking, remember that the effect of one event can also be the cause of another.

153

Ukraine

PEOPLE WORKING TOGETHER

How many people, linked hand-to-hand, would it take to cover 300 miles (483 km)? The people of Ukraine can tell you, because they did it in 1990. It took about 500,000 Ukrainians to make a human chain this long. It stretched from Kiev, Ukraine's capital, to the city of Lvov (lvawf). The chain was a symbol of their protest against Soviet control of Ukraine. It also proved that Ukrainians know how to work together to solve their problems. Today, people in Ukraine are still eager to be independent and to work together.

▼ In 1990, the people of Ukraine rallied to protest Soviet control of their country.

Ukraine's Path to Freedom

For hundreds of years, Ukraine has struggled to be independent. You can see why if you look at Ukraine's location. This huge land lies between the nations of Europe and Russia. In fact, the name *Ukraine* means "borderland." Look at the political map of Europe in the Atlas at the back of the book. Notice that to the west of Ukraine are Poland, Slovakia, and Hungary. To the east of Ukraine is Russia. The map makes it easy to see that Ukraine is open to invasion by its neighbors.

Country Profile: Ukraine

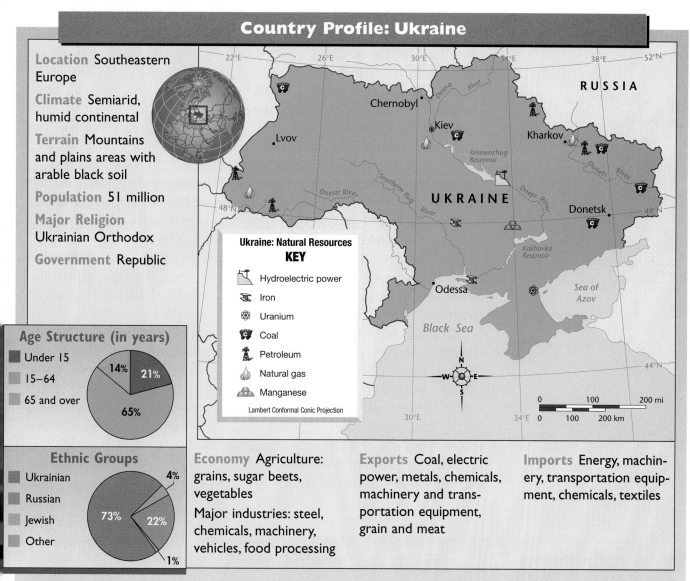

Location Southeastern Europe

Climate Semiarid, humid continental

Terrain Mountains and plains areas with arable black soil

Population 51 million

Major Religion Ukrainian Orthodox

Government Republic

Age Structure (in years)

- Under 15
- 15–64
- 65 and over

14%
21%
65%

Ethnic Groups

- Ukrainian
- Russian
- Jewish
- Other

4%
73%
22%
1%

Ukraine: Natural Resources
KEY

- Hydroelectric power
- Iron
- Uranium
- Coal
- Petroleum
- Natural gas
- Manganese

Lambert Conformal Conic Projection

RUSSIA

Chernobyl
Kiev
Lvov
Kharkov
Kremenchug Reservoir
UKRAINE
Donetsk
Kakhovka Reservoir
Odessa
Sea of Azov
Black Sea

Desna River
Dniestr River
Southern Bug River
Dnepr River
Donets River

0   100   200 mi
0   100   200 km

Economy Agriculture: grains, sugar beets, vegetables

Major industries: steel, chemicals, machinery, vehicles, food processing

Exports Coal, electric power, metals, chemicals, machinery and transportation equipment, grain and meat

Imports Energy, machinery, transportation equipment, chemicals, textiles

Map and Chart Study This map shows the natural resources of Ukraine. Although Ukraine is famous for its agricultural production, it is also one of the world's leading manganese producers. Manganese and iron are used to make steel. **Location** In what part of Ukraine can manganese and iron be found? **Critical Thinking** While Ukraine was part of the Soviet Union, its official language was Russian. Look at the graph of Ukraine's ethnic groups. What percentage of people in Ukraine are Russian?

Location has been only part of the problem. The other has been Ukraine's vast natural resources, which attract invaders. As a result, at one time or another, Poland, Czechoslovakia, and Romania have taken slices of Ukraine. During World War II, the German army invaded Ukraine to gain its natural resources. But the most difficult neighbor of all has been Russia. It ruled Ukraine for much of the time between the late 1700s and the fall of the Soviet Union in 1991.

Supplying the Soviets A hundred years ago, Ukraine, which then was part of the Russian empire, was one of Europe's leading grain producing regions. Ukraine produced so much grain that people

READ ACTIVELY

Predict What kinds of natural resources would encourage one country to try to take over another?

called it the "breadbasket of Europe." Why is Ukraine so productive? Over half of the country is covered by a rich, black soil called **chernozem** (CHER nuh zem).

In 1922, Ukraine was forced to become part of the Soviet Union. Ukrainian farmers began supplying the rest of the Soviet Union with food. By the end of the 1980s, they were producing 25 percent of the country's grain and 30 percent of its meat.

Under Soviet rule, Ukrainian industries grew. In time, factories in Ukraine were making about 25 percent of the country's goods. Further, many of the weapons, ships, and machines for the Soviet Union's armed forces came from Ukraine. And Ukrainian mines supplied much of the iron ore, coal, and other minerals for Soviet industries.

The Soviets used other Ukrainian resources as well. Ships used Ukraine's ports on the Black Sea to bring goods into and out of the Soviet Union. Several of Ukraine's rivers reach like highways into other countries. The Soviets made use of these rivers to ship goods.

All the economic changes under Soviet rule changed the lives of Ukraine's people. The Soviet rulers took farms away from farmers and created huge government-owned farms called **collectives.** Most farmers were forced to become workers on these collective farms. (Some farmers were sent instead to cities to work in the new factories.) All the crops from the collectives went to the government. The people who worked the land got very little of the food they grew. As a result, in the 1930s millions of Ukrainians died of hunger. Over the years, however, life improved on the farms.

Golden Fields of Wheat

Visit southern Ukraine and this view will greet you—vast fields of wheat stretching almost to the horizon. Under Soviet rule, Ukrainian farmers grew wheat to meet production figures set by communist officials. Today, they grow whatever they can sell. **Critical Thinking** Why is Ukrainian farmland so productive?

The city of Odessa is one of Ukraine's greatest assets. Located on the Black Sea, it is a center of shipping and manufacturing.

Building an Independent Economy   Ukrainians won their independence from the Soviets in 1991. Since then, they have worked together to build up their economy and change to a new way of life. Like people in other former Soviet republics, Ukrainians are having to learn how to start new businesses, make goods, and keep prices under control. However, they have had some important successes. For example, very few Ukrainians are without work. Recently, less than 3 percent of the people who could work were unemployed. In contrast, 5 to 15 percent of workers are unemployed in the rest of Europe.

Issues After Independence

Now that Ukrainians are independent, they must decide many important issues for themselves. For example, should their national language be Russian or Ukrainian?

Choosing a Language   Under Soviet rule, the official language was Russian. Books and newspapers were published only in Russian. Lessons in school were taught only in Russian, using Russian textbooks. As a result, many Ukrainians speak only Russian, especially in the cities and in the eastern part of the nation. Russian is also the language of ethnic Russians, who make up about one fifth of the people. Ukrainian is widely spoken only in rural areas and in the western part of the nation.

In the days after the Chernobyl nuclear power accident, there was always at least one helicopter in the air near the reactor. From the helicopters, people used hand-held radiation counters (right) to check the levels of radiation in the air. Despite the unsafe conditions, the Soviet Union began operating the Chernobyl reactor again six months later. People returned to Chernobyl to work, but not to live. Years after the accident, the Chernobyl area (below) remained deserted. **Critical Thinking** What challenges do you think might face people who returned to work at Chernobyl after the accident?

READ ACTIVELY

Ask Questions What do you want to know about the explosion at the nuclear power plant in Chernobyl?

Still, many people want the country to return to its own language. Speaking Ukrainian could tie the country together. It could also free Ukraine from its Soviet past. Elementary schools have begun using Ukrainian in the early grades. In later grades and high school, Russian is still used. In the coming years, however, that will change. Most Ukrainians are pleased about the change. One teacher said, "Language is the anchor of our independence."

Accident at Chernobyl One of the biggest issues facing independent Ukraine grew out of a terrible event during the Soviet period. When it was under Soviet rule, Ukraine sent resources to the Soviet Union. In return, it received Soviet natural gas and oil. But Ukraine's industries needed even more energy. So the Ukrainians built five nuclear power plants. These supply about one third of the country's electricity.

Nuclear power is created with a special radioactive metal called uranium. When atoms, or very tiny pieces, of uranium are split, heat is released. The heat turns water into steam. The steam turns large machines called generators, which produce electricity.

This process must be kept under tight control. If too much heat is produced too quickly, it could destroy the entire building. Then poisonous gas would escape into the air.

In 1986, there was an explosion at the Chernobyl (CHER noh bul) nuclear plant, 65 miles (105 km) from the city of Kiev. Poisonous gases filled the air. Some people died at once. Others had serious health problems that killed them slowly or left them suffering. More than 100,000 people had to be moved out of the area because it was no longer safe to live there.

Even after 10 years, much of Ukraine's soil and water was still poisoned. Some towns and farmland remain abandoned to this day. With the help of other nations, the Ukrainians are cleaning up the poison around Chernobyl. It may take up to a hundred years to repair the damage. But the Ukrainians are determined to bring back the land they love.

Ukraine has a strong antinuclear movement. Some Ukrainians who are opposed to nuclear power wear masks and hoist banners in protest.

Life in Ukraine

Independence has already changed life in Ukraine. For example, the Kreshchatik (kree SHAH tik), the main street in Kiev, often is jammed with people. Along this street are many parks, stores, and restaurants. People sell ice cream and hot dogs covered with a thin red sauce that Ukrainians love. Newsstands are filled with magazines and newspapers, many of which have been published only since independence. At a local market, farmers sell cheese or produce from their own farms. This, too, only became possible after independence.

LINKS ACROSS THE WORLD

The Spread of Poison Winds blew Chernobyl's poisonous gases across Europe. In England, Germany, and Spain the gases poisoned milk, meat, and leafy vegetables. In Belarus, one fifth of the farmland was poisoned. And in Norway, Sweden, and Finland, the reindeer herds of the Laplanders, ate poisoned grasses. Almost the whole herd— about 180,000 animals— had to be killed.

◀ To symbolize the deadly nature of the Chernobyl accident, a protester plants crosses near a nuclear power station.

Folk Museum in Ukraine

Near Kiev, Ukraine, the Museum of Folk Architecture features a traditional farmhouse. A loom, used to weave cloth, sits in the middle of the room shown here. It reminds visitors of a time when people made cloth, furniture, and tools for themselves. People on farms also grew the vegetables and grains that they ate, collected eggs from the chickens they raised, and raised cows and goats for milk and meat. **Critical Thinking** Life in Ukraine and elsewhere has changed in many ways since the days when this traditional farmhouse was used. Name some aspects of life that have not changed.

Other Ukrainian cities are also alive with the new spirit of freedom. Not far from Kiev is the city of Kharkov. Located near huge reserves of iron ore and coal, it is the busiest industrial center in the nation. But Kharkov is not all work. While you are there, you can listen to fine music or watch a play.

As you travel through Ukraine, you can see that it is in the early stages of a new time in its history. The people have always wanted freedom, and now they have it in their grasp. They know that independence is not easy. But with the land's great resources and the people's ability to work together, the Ukrainians have a good chance to make independence work.

SECTION 3 REVIEW

1. **Define** (a) chernozem, (b) collective.

2. **Identify** (a) Kiev, (b) Chernobyl, (c) Kharkov.

3. How has Ukraine's location affected its history?

4. Why do many Ukrainians want to make Ukrainian the official national language?

Critical Thinking

5. **Distinguishing Cause and Effect** In recent years, some Russian leaders have declared that they want Ukraine to become a part of Russia. Why would they want this to happen?

Activity

6. **Writing to Learn** Write a letter to one of the people who was forced to leave his or her home because of the Chernobyl explosion. You can offer comfort or advice and/or ask questions about the accident.

Russia

A LARGE AND DIVERSE COUNTRY

BEFORE YOU READ

Reach Into Your Background

What other states in the United States have you visited? What other towns or cities have you seen? Were they very different from where you live? In Russia, as you will see, there are great differences from one region of the nation to another.

Questions to Explore

1. How do ways of life differ in a land as large as Russia?

2. What problems do Russians have today in unifying their country?

Key Terms
investor

Key Places
Kemerovo
Moscow

Inessa Krichevskaya (in ES uh kree CHEV sky uh) has surprising feelings about change in Russia. "You know," she says, "it's a very difficult period in our country right now, but we will just have to live through it, because this is the right direction. . . . We can never go back to what was before."

Why are Inessa's feelings so surprising? For more than 30 years, she was a loyal Communist. She lived and worked in the city of Moscow as an engineer. Like all other Russians, she always expected that the government would send her monthly checks when she grew too old to work. That was part of the communist system. But then Russia switched to the free enterprise system. Now Inessa is in her 60s and is retired. The amount she receives from the government is much less than she expected. Inessa gets about 1,300 rubles a month—only about $8.

The fall of communism caused other hardships for Inessa. During a march for democracy, her son was killed by soldiers. Still, Inessa believes that the changes are moving her country in the right direction, toward freedom. "My son, and the others who turned out that night, just wanted some sort of free life," she explains.

What kind of life have the people of Russia found as their country has turned toward a new system? To answer that question, let's look at two parts of Russia: Siberia and Moscow.

▼ After the collapse of communism, Russia's people joyfully used their right to speak freely about politics.

161

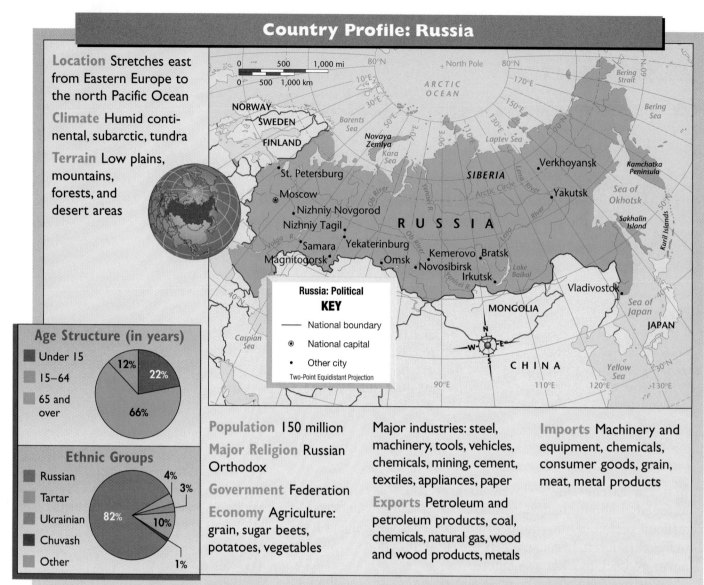

Country Profile: Russia

Location Stretches east from Eastern Europe to the north Pacific Ocean

Climate Humid continental, subarctic, tundra

Terrain Low plains, mountains, forests, and desert areas

Russia: Political
KEY
— National boundary
⊛ National capital
• Other city
Two-Point Equidistant Projection

Age Structure (in years)
- Under 15
- 15–64
- 65 and over

12% · 22% · 66%

Ethnic Groups
- Russian
- Tartar
- Ukrainian
- Chuvash
- Other

82% · 10% · 4% · 3% · 1%

Population 150 million

Major Religion Russian Orthodox

Government Federation

Economy Agriculture: grain, sugar beets, potatoes, vegetables

Major industries: steel, machinery, tools, vehicles, chemicals, mining, cement, textiles, appliances, paper

Exports Petroleum and petroleum products, coal, chemicals, natural gas, wood and wood products, metals

Imports Machinery and equipment, chemicals, consumer goods, grain, meat, metal products

Map and Chart Study This map shows the borders and major cities of Russia. Notice that Russia's territory is not all connected. One very small region of Russia is separated from the rest of the country by the countries of Eastern Europe. At one time, the Russian empire extended that far west. **Regions** As you know, Russia extends over part of two continents: Europe and Asia.

Name two Asian countries that share borders with Russia. **Critical Thinking** People whose ethnic background is Russian have ancestors from the European part of Russia. Look at the graph of Russia's ethnic groups. What percentage of Russia's people are ethnically Russian? In what part of Russia do you think most of the people of Russia live?

Life in Siberia

During the Soviet years, the government tried to change Siberia, the huge region of eastern Russia. It built factories to take advantage of the region's rich reserves of coal, gold, iron, oil, and natural gas. The government built the Trans-Siberian Railroad to transport materials to and from Siberia. But today, many of the factories are outdated. In the Siberian city of Kemerovo (KEM uh roh voh), factories still release black smoke into the air. Other buildings in the town are crumbling. Rusty cars move slowly down the muddy streets.

Black smoke belches into the cool air in the Siberian town of Ulan Ude (oo LAHN oo DAY) along the Trans-Siberian Railroad. The railroad, completed in 1904, helped to link Siberia's rich natural resources to more densely populated areas of Europe. When towns along the tracks of this railroad became industrial centers, the number of available jobs increased. But so did pollution.

In the Villages As Kemerovo shows, the changes of free enterprise have come slowly to cities in this region. Change is even slower in rural areas. Life in many villages is almost like life on the American frontier more than 100 years ago. Many homes have no running water, so water has to be hauled from wells once a week. Sometimes the wells freeze in the winter. Then people have to drink and cook with melted snow.

Despite problems like these, Siberians know how to survive and enjoy life in their frigid climate. They follow a strict timetable so they can take advantage of changes in the seasons. Before winter comes they start collecting nuts and honey. Tractors work overtime to harvest crops before the frost. In winter, some families hang huge pieces of meat from their porches. Temperatures in winter are so cold that the meat freezes solid and does not spoil.

During winter, women wearing many layers of clothing leave their log cabins to fetch firewood. Inside the log cabins, it is warm and cozy. That is because many cabins have large stoves used both for cooking and for heating. When the nights become really cold, the family may spread a straw mat on top of the stove and sleep there to stay warm.

During the winter, the meals are hearty. To catch fresh fish, men cut holes through the ice that covers the rivers. At home, the women may also cook homemade goose soup or dumplings stuffed with meat. Or perhaps the family will make a meal of some of the meat they have frozen.

READ ACTIVELY

Visualize Visualize life in a Siberian village.

Believe it or not, some Siberians start their day by bathing in a pitcher of ice-cold water! They believe that it strengthens their body against the cold. Sometimes, they pour water to make a huge puddle in front of their houses. The water freezes quickly, and the children then play ice hockey.

While the children are playing, the adults might decide to have a Siberian-style sauna (SAW nuh), or steam bath. They crowd into a shack filled with hot steam scented with pine. There they sit until they can stand the heat no longer. Then they rush out of the sauna dripping with sweat and roll in the snow to cool down.

Changing Ways Traditional ways still continue in Siberia. But the fall of communism and the arrival of free enterprise are starting to affect life in the region. Under the communist system, everyone was guaranteed a job. Now Siberians who work in factories and coal mines must worry about losing their jobs. On the other hand, for the first time in more than 70 years, Siberians are able to buy their own homes. Before, they had to live in houses that belonged to the state. People can also now buy stock in the companies in which they work.

Life in Moscow

In Moscow, where Inessa lives, buying shares in businesses is a big business in itself. Investors from everywhere, including the United States, have come to Moscow to make money. An **investor** is someone who spends money on improving a business in the hope of getting more money when the business succeeds. Some investors have become very

READ ACTIVELY

Ask Questions What do you want to know about how the fall of the Soviet Union affected life in Siberia?

▼ During the long Siberian winter, a horse-drawn sleigh hauls supplies (right) and a red-cheeked Siberian child plays on his toboggan (below).

Building Anew in Moscow

Since the fall of communism, people in Moscow, Russia's capital, have started over. They have constructed new buildings and started many new businesses. As a result, more jobs and consumer goods are available to people than ever before. **Critical Thinking** How does starting a new business create jobs?

wealthy. When the first American fast-food chain in Russia opened in Moscow, people lined up in the streets to try it out. The restaurant served 30,000 people on the first day.

New Wealth   Moscow is the capital of Russia. It is also the third-largest city in the world, with more than 8 million people. In big cities like Moscow, investors have brought big changes. Just outside the city, a new skyscraper reaches the sky. At its top is a fine restaurant, enclosed in stone and glass. The building is the world headquarters of Gazprom (GAHS prahm), Russia's only natural gas company. Started by a former Communist official, it makes a huge amount of money.

Like the head of Gazprom, some of Russia's richest people used to work for the Soviet government. Other Russians say this is unfair. They say these people used their influence to get a head start in the move to a free-market economy. Another group of newly rich Russians is also causing concern. These are leaders of criminal gangs. The rise in crime has worried ordinary Russians.

Still, most Russians are using hard work to get ahead. They dream of starting new businesses or opening small factories. To get ideas on how to succeed, they study Western ways of doing business.

READ ACTIVELY

Connect What things make a business in your neighborhood a success?

Some Russians take bold actions to succeed. Vlad Olkhovski (vlad ohl HAWV skee) is starting a new travel agency. There used to be only one travel agency for all of Russia. But Vlad hopes that he can attract customers to his new agency. Vlad explains his approach this way:

> "We have learned that the only way you can prosper is to be the best in your market, be professional and be reliable. In America, of course, these are old lessons. But it's an entirely new [way of thinking] for people here."

Tradition and Change   Free enterprise is changing Moscow. But old Russian ways survive alongside the new. After all, Russia is a huge country with many different ways of life. On Moscow's streets you will see Muslim women whose faces are covered by veils. You will see people from Mongolia wearing the traditional padded silk jackets of their region. And you will see young Russians wearing blue jeans, with haircuts in the latest American style.

On very cold winter days, some people in Moscow go to the parks to celebrate an old tradition: picnicking in the snow. At these picnics they make shish ke-bab by piercing pieces of meat with a sharp stick. Then they roast the meat over an open fire.

Moscow's art, theater, and dance also show great variety. On one evening, people might attend the Bolshoi (BOHL shoy) Ballet. Dancers from this famous Russian school of ballet have performed around the world. On another evening, people might go to see a group of folk dancers

▶GUM, Moscow's biggest department store, stands at the city's center. In the new free enterprise economy, business is picking up. On weekends, 25,000 people a day shop here.

Russian Art

The collapse of communism has freed artists to experiment with bold modern styles in painting (left) and sculpture (above).

from northern Russia. Wearing jeweled caps and robes with laced sleeves, the dancers twirl and stamp their feet to traditional folk songs.

The differences between Siberia and Moscow show us the challenges that Russia must meet in the future. Can a country with many different ethnic groups and an area of more than 6 million square miles (9 million sq km) hold itself together? Will the old ways and new ways become one common way for everyone? The answers to these questions are not yet clear. But Russians are united in the hope for a better future for all.

SECTION 4 REVIEW

1. **Define** investor.

2. **Identify** (a) Kemerovo, (b) Moscow.

3. What do Siberians do to survive in their very cold climate?

4. How does Moscow show the variety of Russian life?

Critical Thinking

5. **Recognizing Cause and Effect** What problems might a country have if it includes many ethnic groups that speak many different languages?

Activity

6. **Writing to Learn** Choose and conduct research on one of Russia's 100 ethnic groups. Find answers to these questions: Where do the people live? What language do they speak? What is their religion? What is their relationship to the rest of the country? Then write a brief report on the group.

Review and Activities

Reviewing Main Ideas

1. What parts of Polish life have not changed?

2. What forces are changing some basic parts of Polish town life and country life?

3. What conflicts led to the breakup of Yugoslavia?

4. (a) Name some things that Bosnians, Croatians, and Serbians in Bosnia-Herzegovina have in common. (b) Name some differences.

5. (a) What are the natural resources of Ukraine? (b) How have they affected its history?

6. How did the explosion at Chernobyl damage Ukraine's rich soil?

7. What are some differences between the lifestyle in Siberia and that in Moscow?

8. How have recent events affected the people of Russia in different ways?

Reviewing Key Terms

Use each key term below in a sentence that shows the meaning of the term.

1. free enterprise

2. shrine

3. icon

4. United Nations

5. chernozem

6. collective

7. investor

Critical Thinking

1. **Making Comparisons** Compare life in a Polish village to life in Siberia. How are they alike? How are they different?

2. **Expressing Problems Clearly** What do you think would help bring lasting peace to Bosnia-Herzegovina?

Graphic Organizer

Copy the chart onto a separate sheet of paper. Then fill in the empty boxes to complete the chart.

	Country	Recent Challenges	Possible Solutions
Warsaw			
Sarajevo			
Chernobyl			
Moscow			

Map Activity

Eastern Europe
For each place listed below, write the letter from the map that shows its location.

1. Ukraine
2. Kiev
3. Sarajevo
4. Bosnia-Herzegovina
5. Serbia

Writing Activity

Writing an Advertisement
Write an advertisement for Janusz Rajtar's shop in Warsaw. In the advertisement, explain why people should buy from Rajtar instead of from older stores that used to be run by the government.

Internet Activity
Use a search engine to find the **Polish Home Page.** Explore the various links to learn about Polish history and culture. Think about how Poland has managed to preserve its traditions while moving into the 21st century. Use the links to research this idea and then write a newspaper article on the subject.

Skills Review

Turn to the Skills Activity. Review the steps for recognizing cause and effect. Then, list three unrelated events of your own life history. For each event, name at least one cause and one effect.

How Am I Doing?

Answer these questions to help you check your progress.

1. Do I understand the clash between tradition and change in both Poland and Russia?

2. Do I understand some of the causes of the war in Bosnia-Herzegovina?

3. Do I understand how Ukraine's natural resources have helped and hurt that country?

4. Do I know some of the changes talking place in Russia?

5. What information from this chapter can I use in my book project?

Plan a New Railroad Line

Siberia, the vast Asian region of Russia, has many natural resources, but it has few transportation routes. The region's major rail line, the Trans-Siberian Railroad, was completed in 1905. The route is thousands of miles long, but it covers only a part of Siberia. An addition to the rail line would make it easier for people to move throughout the region.

Purpose

In this activity, you will plan a new branch of the Trans-Siberian Railroad. As you work on the activity, you will learn about Siberia's resources.

Draw a Resource Map

A new rail line in Siberia would transport some of the region's many natural resources to other parts of Russia. Look in an encyclopedia for Siberia and for Russia. Make a list of Siberian mineral resources. Next to each item on the list, note its uses. Draw a small symbol, or picture, to represent each resource. Then draw a map of Siberia. Put the symbols on the map to show where these resources can be found.

Make a Circle Graph

Money to build a new rail line will come from cities and towns located along the line, from the Siberian regional government, and from the Russian national government. Using the figures below, draw a circle graph to show the percentages of the total money each source would contribute.

- Cities and towns   15%
- Regional government   32%
- National government   53%

Decide on a Route

Look at some maps of Siberia, including your mineral resources map. Then decide where you think a new rail line should run.

▶ A Trans-Siberian Railroad station

Trans-Siberian Railroad

KEY

— Trans-Siberian Railroad
— National boundary
⊛ National capital
• Other city

Two-Point Equidistant Projection

Write down a list of cities and towns the route might pass through. On your list, write the distances between the cities and towns. Figure out the total distance of the route. Finally, circle the places where the line will start and end.

Write a Proposal

Write a proposal to persuade the national government to build a new rail line in Siberia. Start with a brief history of the Trans-Siberian Railroad. Then tell where the new rail line will run, what purpose it will serve, and how the project will be paid for.

Write a Railroad Song

Once a new rail line is built, people need to hear about it. Write a song that will advertise the new railroad. In your song lyrics, describe the features of the new train. Tell about the resources and wildlife of Siberia. Try to use the rhythm and sounds of a train in your own rhythm and melody.

Links to Other Subjects

Making a mineral resource chart	**Earth Science**
Making a circle graph	**Math**
Determining routes and distances	**Math**
Writing a proposal	**Language Arts**
Writing a song	**Language Arts & Music**

ANALYSIS AND CONCLUSION

Write a summary explaining what you've learned from planning and proposing the railroad extension. Be sure to answer the following questions in your summary:

1. What have you learned about the geography of Siberia and its mineral resources?

2. What did you learn about writing an effective proposal and song?

FROM

Zlata's Diary
A Child's Life in Sarajevo

BY ZLATA FILIPOVIĆ

BEFORE YOU READ

Reach Into Your Background

To whom do you tell your secret thoughts? Many people write in a diary or journal what they would tell no other person. Diaries can give people hope and courage, especially during hard times.

Zlata Filipović (ZLAH tah FIL uh POH vich) kept a diary from 1991 through 1993, during the civil war in the country of Bosnia. She was eleven years old when she began her diary, which she called Mimmy. At that time, life in the city of Sarajevo (sar uh YEH voh) was normal for Zlata and her parents. In the spring of 1992, however, their lives changed when war broke out around them. Schools closed. Zlata's family, like many others, spent their days in the basement to avoid gunfire. Food and water became scarce. In December of 1993, Zlata and her parents were able to leave Bosnia safely.

Questions to Explore

1. What do these diary entries tell you about war?
2. How do you think the experience of living through a war affected Zlata?

shrapnel *n.:* fragments of a bomb, mine, or shell

Thursday, May 7, 1992

Dear Mimmy,

I was almost positive the war would stop, but today . . . Today a shell fell on the park in front of my house, the park where I used to play and sit with my girlfriends. A lot of people were hurt. From what I hear Jaca, Jaca's mother, Selma, Nina, our neighbor Dado and who knows how many other people who happened to be there were wounded. Dado, Jaca and her mother have come home from the hospital, Selma lost a kidney but I don't know how she is, because she's still in the hospital. AND NINA IS DEAD. A piece of shrapnel lodged in her brain and she died. She was such a sweet, nice little girl. We went to kindergarten together, and we used to play together in the park. Is it possible I'll never see Nina again? Nina, an innocent eleven-year-old little girl—the victim of a stupid war. I feel sad. I cry and wonder why? She didn't do anything. A disgusting war has destroyed a young child's life. Nina, I'll always remember you as a wonderful little girl.

Love, Mimmy,
Zlata

Thursday, December 3, 1992

Dear Mimmy,

Today is my birthday. My first wartime birthday. Twelve years old. Congratulations. Happy birthday to me!

The day started off with kisses and congratulations. First Mommy and Daddy, then everyone else. Mommy and Daddy gave me three Chinese vanity cases—with flowers on them!

As usual there was no electricity. Auntie Melica came with her family (Kenan, Naida, Nihad) and gave me a book. And Braco Lajtner came, of course. The whole neighborhood got together in the evening. I got chocolate, vitamins, a heart shaped soap (small, orange), a key chain with a picture of Maja and Bojana, a pendant made of a stone from Cyprus, a ring (silver) and earrings (bingo!).

The table was nicely laid, with little rolls, fish and rice salad, cream cheese (with Feta), canned corned beef, a pie, and, of course—a birthday cake. Not how it used to be, but there's a war on. Luckily there was no shooting, so we could celebrate.

It was nice, but something was missing. It's called peace!

Your Zlata

READ ACTIVELY

Connect How can people celebrate one thing while being sad about another? Explain why you think people do this.

Melica (MEE lit zuh)
Kenan (KEN ahn)
Naida (NY duh)
Nihad (NEE hahd)
Braco Lajtner (BRAHT zoh LYT nur)
Maja (MY uh)
Bojana (BOY ah nuh)

EXPLORING YOUR READING

Think It Over

2. How would you describe Zlata's outlook on her world?

3. Why do you think Zlata treats her diary as a friend?

Go Beyond

4. How do you think the war has changed Zlata?

Ideas for Writing: Diary

5. Keep a diary for a week, writing one entry each day. Write about what makes you happy as well as things that bother or upset you. At the end of the week, write an entry telling what you think about keeping a diary.

Look Back

1. What bad experiences does Zlata record in her entries? What good experiences does she write about?

EUROPE AND RUSSIA
PROJECT POSSIBILITIES

The following questions will help you direct your reading about Europe and Russia:

- ☛ **How has physical geography affected the environment and cultures of Europe and Russia?**

- ☛ **How have the people of Europe and Russia been shaped by historical experiences?**

- ☛ **What values and traditions do the people of Europe and Russia have in common?**

- ☛ **How have modern times changed the ways of life in the region?**

- ☛ **How do different people in Europe and Russia get along?**

These projects will give you the chance to show what you know about Europe and Russia!

GEO LEO

Project Menu

The chapters in this book have some answers to these questions. Now it's time for you to find your own answers by doing projects on your own or with a group. You can make your own discoveries about Europe and Russia.

Changing Climates It's not always easy to get used to life in a new climate. Someone who moved from Norway to Greece, for example, might be surprised about the way the climate affects how the Greek people live. Choose a European country near the Arctic or one near the Mediterranean. Find out about ways of life that have to do with the climate. Look for details about housing, clothing, food, and recreation.

Based on what you find, write a guide for someone moving to that region from the other end of the continent. Include special tips for things like very hot or cold days, comfortable sleeping, or special snacks.

From Questions to Careers

INTERNATIONAL TRADE

The United States trades many goods and services with Europe and Russia. This trade is important to people in both places. Many international businesspeople work to make this trade happen. Some Americans work in Europe, and some stay here.

There are many careers in international trade. People with careers in international marketing and sales sell products and services to customers in other countries. Shipping companies transport products by boat or by plane. Sailors, pilots, shippers, and handlers make shipping possible.

When people work in other countries, they often need translators. English is the most common language for international business, so some Americans can work in Europe without knowing other languages. However, all who work with other countries must know something about those countries. International managers train workers in the cultures of their trade partners.

▼ Many people have careers in international shipping, as this man does.

Olympic Cities Plan an Olympic season in a European city. As you read this book, keep track of cities that you find interesting. Research them at the library or on the Internet.

After you have gathered your information, choose a city that you think would do a good job of hosting either the summer or winter Olympics. Write a proposal to Olympic officials, explaining what the city has to offer to the Olympics. Include maps or pictures of your city with your proposal.

Tourism in Eastern Europe Many former communist countries would like to have more tourists, who bring money to their economies. Choose a country in Eastern Europe. Read about parts of the culture and landscape that might interest visitors—for example, ski slopes in Slovakia.

Create a travel advertisement for that country. Write your own text and use pictures that you draw or cut out from magazines.

Folklore Corner Create a library of folk and fairy tales from countries throughout Europe. As you read about a country in this book, find a traditional tale from that country. Think about how the stories reflect the country's culture.

With your classmates, build a Folklore Corner in your classroom. Create a display of books of folk tales. Include objects, drawings, and photographs that represent the culture in these tales. Label each tale with its country of origin.

Reference

TABLE OF CONTENTS

Handbook

MAP AND GLOBE

This Map and Globe Handbook is designed to help you develop some of the skills you need to be a world explorer. These can help you whether you explore from the top of an elephant in India or from a computer at school.

You can use the information in this handbook to improve your map and globe skills. But the best way to sharpen your skills is to practice. The more you practice the better you'll get.

GEO CLEO and GEO LEO

Table of Contents

Five Themes of Geography

Studying the geography of the entire world can be a huge task. You can make that task easier by using the five themes of geography: location, place, human-environment interaction, movement, and regions. The themes are tools you can use to organize information and to answer the where, why, and how of geography.

1 Location answers the question, "Where is it?" You can think of the location of a continent or a country as its address. You might give an absolute location such as "22 South Lake Street" or "40°N and 80°W." You might also use a relative address, telling where one place is by referring to another place. "Between school and the mall" and "eight miles east of Pleasant City" are examples of relative locations.

2 Place identifies the natural and human features that make one place different from every other place. You can identify a specific place by its landforms, climate, plants, animals, people, or cultures. You might even think of place as a geographic signature. Use the signature to help you understand the natural and human features that make one place different from every other place.

1. Location
Chicago, Illinois, occupies one location on the Earth. No other place has exactly the same absolute location.

2. Place
Ancient cultures in Egypt built distinctive pyramids. Use the theme of place to help you remember features that exist only in Egypt.

3 Human-Environment Interaction focuses on the relationship between people and the environment. As people live in an area, they often begin to make changes to it, usually to make their lives easier. For example, they might build a dam to control flooding during rainy seasons. Also, the environment can affect how people live, work, dress, travel, and communicate.

4 Movement answers the question "How do people, goods, and ideas move from place to place?" Remember that, often, what happens in one place can affect what happens in another. Use the theme of movement to help you trace the spread of goods, people, and ideas from one location to the next.

5 Regions is the last geographic theme. A region is a group of places that share common features. Geographers divide the world into many types of regions. For example, countries, states, and cities are political regions. The people in these places live under the same type of government. Other features can be used to define regions. Places that have the same climate belong to a particular climate region. Places that share the same culture belong to a cultural region. The same place can be found in more than one region. The state of Hawaii is in the political region of the United States. Because it has a tropical climate, Hawaii is also part of a tropical climate region.

PRACTICE YOUR WORLD EXPLORER SKILLS

1. What is the absolute location of your school? What is one way to describe its relative location?

2. What might be a "geographic signature" of the town or city you live in?

3. Give an example of human-environment interaction where you live.

4. Name at least one thing that comes into your town or city and one that goes out. How is each moved? Where does it come from? Where does it go?

5. What are several regions you think your town or city belongs in?

3. Human-Environment Interaction
Peruvians have changed steep mountain slopes into terraces suitable for farming. Think how this environment looked before people made changes.

4. Movement
Arab traders brought not only goods to Kuala Lumpur, Malaysia, but also Arab building styles and the Islamic religion.

5. Regions
Wheat farming is an important activity in Kansas. This means that Kansas is part of a farming region.

Understanding Movements of the Earth

Planet Earth is part of our solar system. The Earth revolves around the sun in a nearly circular path called an orbit. A revolution, or one complete orbit around the sun, takes 365 1/4 days, or a year. As the Earth revolves around the sun, it is also spinning around in space. This movement is called a rotation. The Earth rotates on its axis—an invisible line through the center of the Earth from the North Pole to the South Pole. The Earth makes one full rotation about every 24 hours. As the Earth rotates, it is daytime on the side facing the sun. It is night on the side away from the sun.

The Earth's axis is tilted at an angle. Because of this tilt, sunlight strikes different parts of the Earth at certain points in the year, creating different seasons.

Earth's Revolution and the Seasons

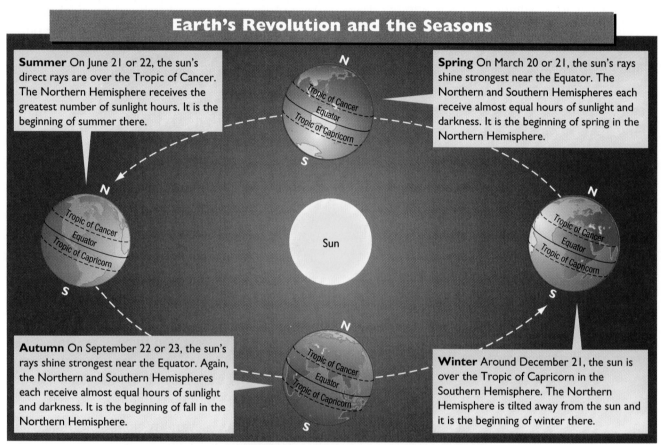

Summer On June 21 or 22, the sun's direct rays are over the Tropic of Cancer. The Northern Hemisphere receives the greatest number of sunlight hours. It is the beginning of summer there.

Spring On March 20 or 21, the sun's rays shine strongest near the Equator. The Northern and Southern Hemispheres each receive almost equal hours of sunlight and darkness. It is the beginning of spring in the Northern Hemisphere.

Autumn On September 22 or 23, the sun's rays shine strongest near the Equator. Again, the Northern and Southern Hemispheres each receive almost equal hours of sunlight and darkness. It is the beginning of fall in the Northern Hemisphere.

Winter Around December 21, the sun is over the Tropic of Capricorn in the Southern Hemisphere. The Northern Hemisphere is tilted away from the sun and it is the beginning of winter there.

▲ **Location** This diagram shows how the Earth's tilt and orbit around the sun combine to create the seasons. Remember, in the Southern Hemisphere the seasons are reversed.

PRACTICE YOUR WORLD EXPLORER SKILLS

1. What causes the seasons in the Northern Hemisphere to be the opposite of those in the Southern Hemisphere?

2. During which two months of the year do the Northern and Southern Hemispheres have about equal hours of daylight and darkness?

Maps and Globes Represent the Earth

Globes

A globe is a scale model of the Earth. It shows the actual shapes, sizes, and locations of all the Earth's landmasses and bodies of water. Features on the surface of the Earth are drawn to scale on a globe. This means a smaller unit of measure on the globe stands for a larger unit of measure on the Earth.

Because a globe is made in the true shape of the Earth, it offers these advantages for studying the Earth.

- The shape of all land and water bodies are accurate.
- Compass directions from one point to any other point are correct.
- The distance from one location to another is always accurately represented.

However, a globe presents some disadvantages for studying the Earth. Because a globe shows the entire Earth, it cannot show small areas in great detail. Also, a globe is not easily folded and carried from one place to another. For these reasons, geographers often use maps to learn about the Earth.

Maps

A map is a drawing or representation, on a flat surface, of a region. A map can show details too small to be seen on a globe. Floor plans, mall directories, and road maps are among the maps we use most often.

While maps solve some of the problems posed by globes, they have some disadvantages of their own. Maps flatten the real round world. Mapmakers cut, stretch, push, and pull some parts of the Earth to get it all flat on paper. As a result, some locations may be distorted. That is, their size, shape, and relative location may not be accurate. For example, on most maps of the entire world, the size and shape of the Antarctic and Arctic regions are not accurate.

PRACTICE YOUR WORLD EXPLORER SKILLS

1 What is the main difference between a globe and a map?

2 What is one advantage of using a globe instead of a map?

Global Gores

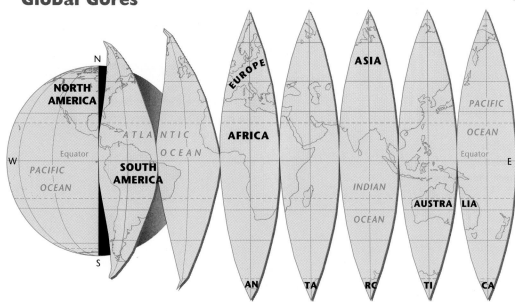

◄ **Location**
When mapmakers flatten the surface of the Earth, curves become straight lines. As a result, size, shape, and distance are distorted.

The Hemispheres

Another name for a round ball like a globe is a sphere. The Equator, an imaginary line halfway between the North and South Poles, divides the globe into two hemispheres. (The prefix *hemi* means "half.") Land and water south of the Equator are in the Southern Hemisphere. Land and water north of the Equator are in the Northern Hemisphere.

Mapmakers sometimes divide the globe along an imaginary line that runs from North Pole to South Pole. This line, called the Prime Meridian, divides the globe into the Eastern and Western Hemispheres.

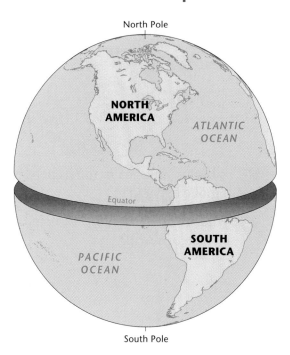

Southern Hemisphere

▲ The Equator divides the Northern Hemisphere from the Southern Hemisphere.

Western Hemisphere   **Eastern Hemisphere**

▲ The Prime Meridian divides the Eastern Hemisphere from the Western Hemisphere.

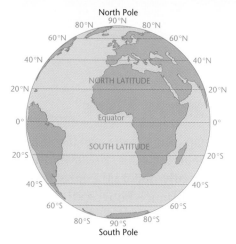

Parallels of Latitude

The Equator, at 0° latitude, is the starting place for measuring latitude or distances north and south. Most globes do not show every parallel of latitude. They may show every 10, 20, or even 30 degrees.

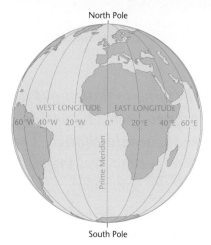

Meridians of Longitude

The Prime Meridian, at 0° longitude, runs from pole to pole through Greenwich, England. It is the starting place for measuring longitude or distances east and west. Each meridian of longitude meets its opposite longitude at the North and South Poles.

The Global Grid

Two sets of lines cover most globes. One set of lines runs parallel to the Equator. These lines, including the Equator, are called *parallels of latitude.* They are measured in degrees (°). One degree of latitude represents a distance of about 70 miles (112 km). The Equator has a location of 0°. The other parallels of latitude tell the direction and distance from the Equator to another location.

The second set of lines runs north and south. These lines are called *meridians of longitude.* Meridians show the degrees of longitude east or west of the Prime Meridian, which is located at 0°. A meridian of longitude tells the direction and distance from the Prime Meridian to another location. Unlike parallels, meridians are not the same distance apart everywhere on the globe.

Together the pattern of parallels of latitude and meridians of longitude is called the global grid. Using the lines of latitude and longitude, you can locate any place on Earth. For example, the location of 30° north latitude and 90° west longitude is usually written as 30°N, 90°W. Only one place on Earth has these coordinates—the city of New Orleans, in the state of Louisiana.

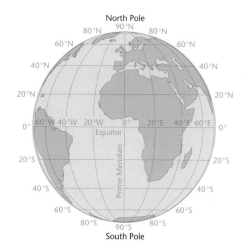

The Global Grid

By using lines of latitude and longitude, you can give the absolute location of any place on the Earth.

1. Which continents lie completely in the Northern Hemisphere? The Western Hemisphere?

2. Is there land or water at 20°S latitude and the Prime Meridian? At the Equator and 60°W longitude?

Map Projections

Imagine trying to flatten out a complete orange peel. The peel would split. The shape would change. You would have to cut the peel to get it to lie flat. In much the same way, maps cannot show the correct size and shape of every landmass or body of water on the Earth's curved surface. Maps shrink some places and stretch others. This shrinking and stretching is called distortion—*a change made to a shape.*

To make up for this disadvantage, mapmakers use different map projections. Each map projection is a way of showing the round Earth on flat paper. Each type of projection has some distortion. No one projection can accurately show the correct area, shape, distance, and direction for the Earth's surface. Mapmakers use the projection that has the least distortion for the information they are studying.

Same-Shape Maps

Some map projections can accurately show the shapes of landmasses. However, these projections often greatly distort the size of landmasses as well as the distance between them.

One of the most common same-shape maps is a Mercator projection, named for the mapmaker who invented it. The Mercator projection accurately shows shape and direction, but it distorts distance and size. In this projection, the northern and southern areas of the globe appear stretched more than areas near the Equator. Because the projection shows true directions, ships' navigators use it to chart a straight line course between two ports.

Mercator Projection

Equal-Area Maps

Some map projections can show the correct size of landmasses. Maps that use these projections are called equal-area maps. In order to show the correct size of landmasses, these maps usually distort shapes. The distortion is usually greater at the edges of the map and less at the center.

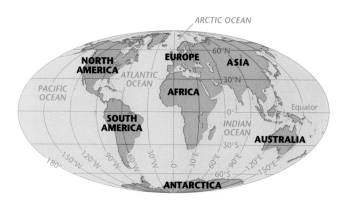

Equal-Area Projection

Robinson Maps

Many of the maps in this book use the Robinson projection. This is a compromise between the Mercator and equal-area projections. It gives a useful overall picture of the world. The Robinson projection keeps the size and shape relationships of most continents and oceans but does distort size of the polar regions.

Azimuthal Maps

Another kind of projection shows true compass direction. Maps that use this projection are called azimuthal maps. Such maps are easy to recognize—they are usually circular. Azimuthal maps are often used to show the areas of the North and South Poles. However, azimuthal maps distort scale, area, and shape.

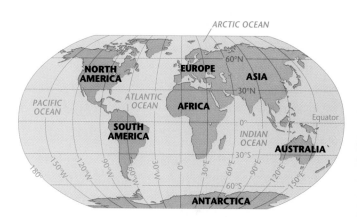

Robinson Projection

1 What feature is distorted on an equal-area map?

2 Would you use a Mercator projection to find the exact distance between two locations? Tell why or why not.

3 Which would be a better choice for studying the Antarctic—an azimuthal projection or a Robinson projection? Explain.

Azimuthal Projection

Parts of a Map

Mapmakers provide several clues to help you understand the information on a map. As an explorer, it is your job to read and interpret these clues.

Many maps show north at the top of the map. One way to show direction on a map is to use an arrow that points north. There may be an N shown with the arrow. Many maps give more information about direction by displaying a compass showing the directions, north, east, south, and west. The letters N, E, S, and W are placed to indicate these directions.

Title
The title of a map is the most basic clue. It signals what kinds of information you are likely to find on the map. A map titled *West Africa: Population Density* will be most useful for locating information about where people live in West Africa.

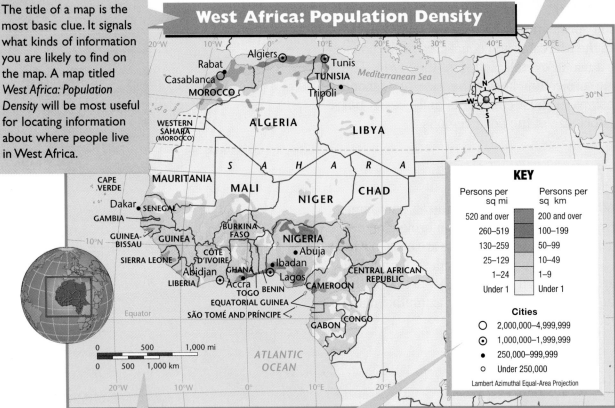

West Africa: Population Density

KEY

Persons per sq mi	Persons per sq km
520 and over	200 and over
260–519	100–199
130–259	50–99
25–129	10–49
1–24	1–9
Under 1	Under 1

Cities

○ 2,000,000–4,999,999
◉ 1,000,000–1,999,999
• 250,000–999,999
○ Under 250,000

Lambert Azimuthal Equal-Area Projection

Scale
A map scale helps you find the actual distances between points shown on the map. You can measure the distance between any two points on the map, compare them to the scale, and find out the actual distance between the points. Most map scales show distances in both miles and kilometers.

Key
Often a map has a key, or legend, that shows the symbols used on the map and what each one means. On some maps, color is used as a symbol. On those maps, the key also tells the meaning of each color.

PRACTICE YOUR **WORLD EXPLORER** SKILLS

❶ What part of a map tells you what the map is about?

❷ Where on the map should you look to find out the meaning of this symbol? •

❸ What part of the map can you use to find the distance between two cities?

Comparing Maps of Different Scale

Here are three maps drawn to three different scales. The first map shows Moscow's location in the northeastern portion of Russia. This map shows the greatest area—a large section of northern Europe. It has the smallest scale (1 inch = about 900 miles) and shows the fewest details. This map can tell you what direction to travel to reach Moscow from Finland.

Find the red box on Map 1. It shows the whole area covered by Map 2. Study Map 2. It gives a closer look at the city of Moscow. It shows the features around the city, the city's boundary, and the general shape of the city. This map can help you find your way from the airport to the center of town.

Now find the red box on Map 2. This box shows the area shown on Map 3. This map moves you closer into the city. Like the zoom on a computer or camera, Map 3 shows the smallest area but has the greatest detail. This map has the largest scale (1 inch = about 0.8 miles). This is the map to use to explore downtown Moscow.

Map 1

KEY

— National boundary

0   500   1,000 mi

0   500   1,000 km

One inch = about 900 miles

Map 2

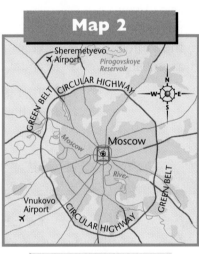

KEY

▨ Built-up area

— Road or street

0   5   10 mi

0   5   10 km

One inch = about 12.5 miles

Map 3

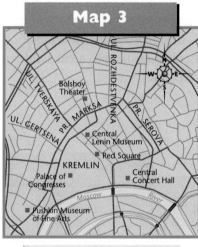

KEY

— Road or street

■ Point of interest

0   .5   1 mi

0   .5   1 km

One inch = about 0.8 miles

PRACTICE YOUR WORLD EXPLORER SKILLS

1 Which map would be best for finding the location of Red Square? Why?

2 Which map best shows Moscow's location relative to Poland? Explain.

3 Which map best shows the area immediately surrounding the city?

Political Maps

Mapmakers create maps to show all kinds of information. The kind of information presented affects the way a map looks. One type of map is called a political map. Its main purpose is to show continents, countries, and divisions within countries such as states or provinces. Usually different colors are used to show different countries or divisions within a country. The colors do not have any special meaning. They are used only to make the map easier to read.

Political maps also show where people have built towns and cities. Symbols can help you tell capital cities from other cities and towns. Even though political maps do not give information that shows what the land looks like, they often include some physical features such as oceans, lakes, and rivers.

Political maps usually have many labels. They give country names, and the names of capital and major cities. Bodies of water such as lakes, rivers, oceans, seas, gulfs, and bays are also labeled.

PRACTICE YOUR
WORLD EXPLORER
SKILLS

1 What symbol shows the continental boundary?

2 What symbol is used to indicate a capital city? A major city?

3 What kinds of landforms are shown on this map?

Russia: Political

KEY
— Continental boundary
— National boundary
⊛ National capital
• Other city
Azimuthal Equidistant Projection

▲ The keys of political maps may include symbols. Study the key to learn what the symbols on this map mean.

Physical Maps

Like political maps, physical maps show country labels and labels for capital cities. However, physical maps also show what the land of a region looks like by showing the major physical features such as plains, hills, plateaus, or mountains. Labels give the names of features such as mountain peaks, mountains, plateaus, and river basins.

In order to tell one landform from another, physical maps often show elevation and relief.

Elevation is the height of the land above sea level. Physical maps in this book use color to show elevation. Browns and oranges show higher lands while blues and greens show lands that are at or below sea level.

Relief shows how quickly the land rises or falls. Hills, mountains, and plateaus are shown on relief maps using shades of gray. Level or nearly level land is shown without shading. Darkly shaded areas indicate steeper lands.

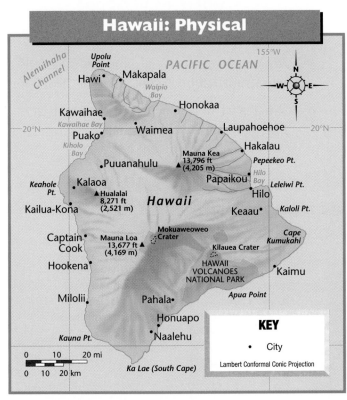

Hawaii: Physical

Alenuihaha Channel
Upolu Point
PACIFIC OCEAN
155°W
N · W E · S
Hawi
Makapala
Waipio Bay
Honokaa
Kawaihae
Kawaihae Bay
20°N
Waimea
Laupahoehoe
20°N
Puako
Kiholo Bay
Hakalau
Mauna Kea 13,796 ft ▲ (4,205 m)
Pepeekeo Pt.
Puuanahulu
Papaikou
Hilo Bay
Keahole Pt.
Kalaoa
▲ Hualalai 8,271 ft (2,521 m)
Hawaii
Hilo
Leleiwi Pt.
Kailua-Kona
Keaau
Kaloli Pt.
Captain Cook
Mauna Loa 13,677 ft ▲ (4,169 m)
Mokuaweoweo Crater
Cape Kumukahi
Kilauea Crater
Hookena
HAWAII VOLCANOES NATIONAL PARK
Kaimu
Milolii
Pahala
Apua Point
Honuapo
Naalehu
Kauna Pt.
Ka Lae (South Cape)

0 10 20 mi
0 10 20 km

KEY
• City

Lambert Conformal Conic Projection

▲ On a physical map, shading is sometimes used to show relief. Use the shading to locate the moutains in Hawaii.

PRACTICE YOUR WORLD EXPLORER SKILLS

1. How is relief shown on the map to the left?

2. How can you use relief to decide which areas will be the most difficult to climb?

3. What information is given with the name of a mountain peak?

▼ Mauna Kea, an extinct volcano, is the highest peak in the state of Hawaii. Find Mauna Kea on the map.

Special Purpose Maps

As you explore the world, you will encounter many different kinds of special purpose maps. For example, a road map is a special purpose map. The title of each special purpose map tells the purpose and content of the map. Usually a special purpose map highlights only one kind of information. Examples of special purpose maps include land use, population distribution, recreation, transportation, natural resources, or weather.

The key on a special purpose map is very important. Even though a special purpose map shows only one kind of information, it may present many different pieces of data. This data can be shown in symbols, colors, or arrows. In this way, the key acts like a dictionary for the map.

Reading a special purpose map is a skill in itself. Look at the map below. First, try to get an overall sense of what it shows. Then, study the map to identify its main ideas. For example, one main idea of this map is that much of the petroleum production in the region takes place around the Persian Gulf.

PRACTICE YOUR WORLD EXPLORER SKILLS

1. What part of a special purpose map tells what information is contained on the map?

2. What part of a special purpose map acts like a dictionary for the map?

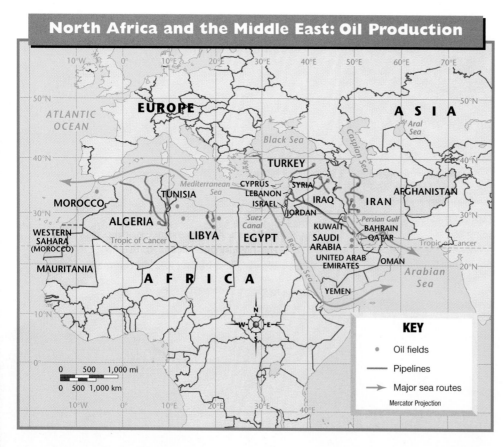

North Africa and the Middle East: Oil Production

ATLANTIC OCEAN
EUROPE
ASIA
Aral Sea
Black Sea
Caspian Sea
TURKEY
Mediterranean Sea
CYPRUS
LEBANON
SYRIA
AFGHANISTAN
ISRAEL
IRAQ
IRAN
TUNISIA
JORDAN
MOROCCO
Suez Canal
Persian Gulf
ALGERIA
KUWAIT
BAHRAIN
WESTERN SAHARA (MOROCCO)
Tropic of Cancer
LIBYA
EGYPT
SAUDI ARABIA
QATAR
Tropic of Cancer
MAURITANIA
UNITED ARAB EMIRATES
OMAN
AFRICA
Arabian Sea
Red Sea
YEMEN

0   500   1,000 mi
0   500 1,000 km

KEY
• Oil fields
— Pipelines
→ Major sea routes
Mercator Projection

◄ The title on a special purpose map indicates what information can be found on the map. The symbols used on the map are explained in the map's key.

Landforms, Climate Regions, and Natural Vegetation Regions

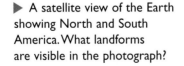

Maps that show landforms, climate, and vegetation regions are special purpose maps. Unlike the boundary lines on a political map, the boundary lines on these maps do not separate the land into exact divisions. A tropical wet climate gradually changes to a tropical wet and dry climate. A tundra gradually changes to an ice cap. Even though the boundaries between regions may not be exact, the information on these maps can help you understand the region and the lives of people in it.

Landforms

Understanding how people use the land requires an understanding of the shape of the land itself. The four most important landforms are mountains, hills, plateaus, and plains. Human activity in every region in the world is influenced by these landforms.

- **Mountains** are high and steep. Most are wide at the bottom and rise to a narrow peak or ridge. Most geographers classify a mountain as land that rises at least 2,000 feet (610 m) above sea level. A series of mountains is called a mountain range.

- **Hills** rise above surrounding land and have rounded tops. Hills are lower and usually less steep than mountains. The elevation of surrounding land determines whether a landform is called a mountain or a hill.

- A **plateau** is a large, mostly flat area of land that rises above the surrounding land. At least one side of a plateau has a steep slope.

- **Plains** are large areas of flat or gently rolling land. Plains have few changes in elevation. Many plains areas are located along coasts. Others are located in the interior regions of some continents.

▶ A satellite view of the Earth showing North and South America. What landforms are visible in the photograph?

Climate Regions

Another important influence in the ways people live their lives is the climate of their region. Climate is the weather of a given location over a long period of time. Use the descriptions in the table below to help you visualize the climate regions shown on maps.

Climate	Temperatures	Precipitation
Tropical		
Tropical wet	Hot all year round	Heavy all year round
Tropical wet and dry	Hot all year round	Heavy when sun is overhead, dry other times
Dry		
Semiarid	Hot summers, mild to cold winters	Light
Arid	Hot days, cold nights	Very light
Mild		
Mediterranean	Hot summers, cool winters	Dry summers, wet winters
Humid subtropical	Hot summers, cool winters	Year round, heavier in summer than in winter
Marine west coast	Warm summers, cool winters	Year round, heavier in winter than in summer
Continental		
Humid continental	Hot summers, cold winters	Year round, heavier in summer than in winter
Subarctic	Cool summers, cold winters	Light
Polar		
Tundra	Cool summers, very cold winters	Light
Ice Cap	Cold all year round	Light
Highlands	Varies, depending on altitude and direction of prevailing winds	Varies, depending on altitude and direction of prevailing winds

Natural Vegetation Regions

Natural vegetation is the plant life that grows wild without the help of humans. A world vegetation map tells what the vegetation in a place would be if people had not cut down forests or cleared grasslands. The table below provides descriptions of natural vegetation regions shown on maps. Comparing climate and vegetation regions can help you see the close relationship between climate and vegetation.

Vegetation	Description
Tropical rain forest	Tall, close-growing trees forming a canopy over smaller trees, dense growth in general
Deciduous forest	Trees and plants that regularly lose their leaves after each growing season
Mixed forest	Both leaf-losing and cone-bearing trees, no type of tree dominant
Coniferous forest	Cone-bearing trees, evergreen trees and plants
Mediterranean vegetation	Evergreen shrubs and small plants
Tropical savanna	Tall grasses with occasional trees and shrubs
Temperate grassland	Tall grasses with occasional stands of trees
Desert scrub	Low shrubs and bushes, hardy plants
Desert	Little or no vegetation
Tundra	Low shrubs, mosses, lichens; no trees
Ice Cap	No vegetation
Highlands	Varies, depending on altitude and direction of prevailing winds

PRACTICE YOUR WORLD EXPLORER SKILLS

1. How are mountains and hills similar? How are they different?

2. What is the difference between a plateau and a plain?

Atlas

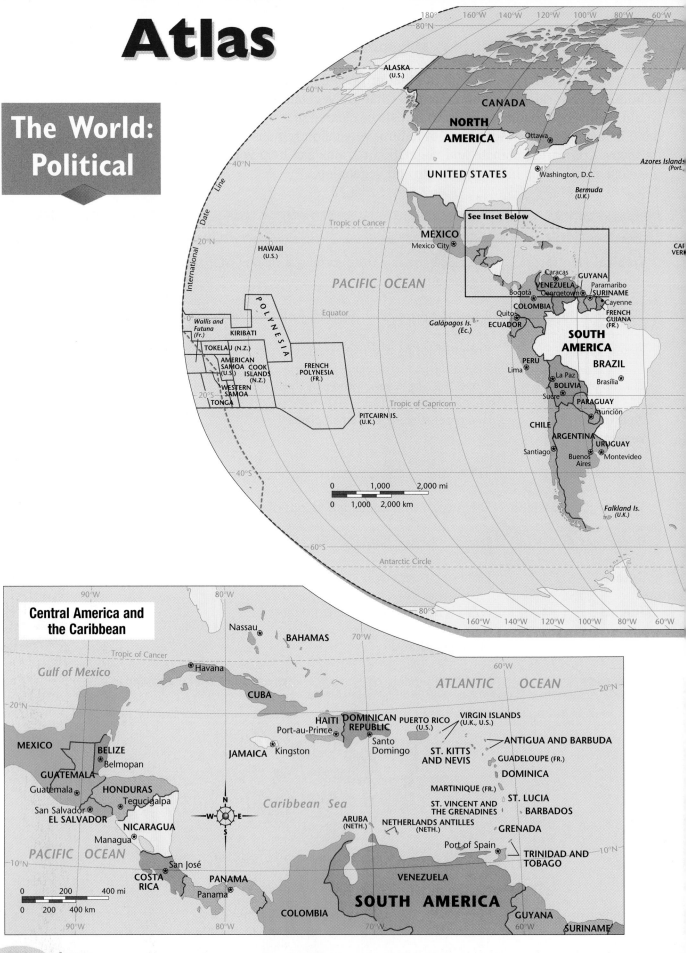

Central America and the Caribbean

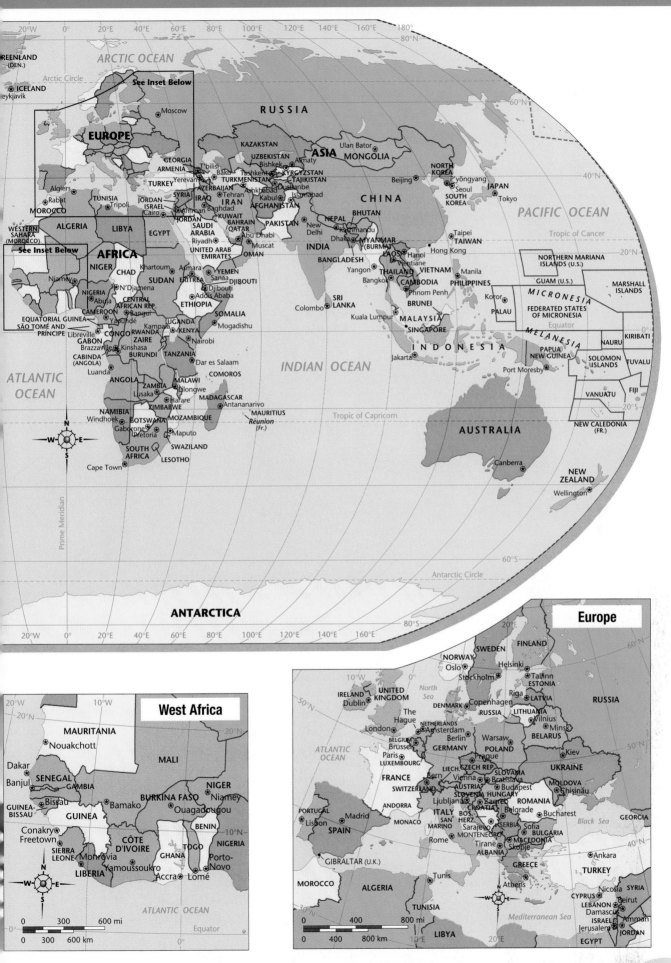

ARCTIC OCEAN
GREENLAND
(DEN.)
Arctic Circle
ICELAND
Reykjavik
See Inset Below
Moscow
RUSSIA
EUROPE
60°N
KAZAKSTAN
ASIA
Ulan Bator
GEORGIA
ARMENIA
T'bilisi
Baku
Bishkek
Almaty
MONGOLIA
40°N
Algiers
TURKEY
Yerevan
TURKMENISTAN
KYRGYZSTAN
TAJIKISTAN
Beijing
NORTH
KOREA
P'yŏngyang
Seoul
JAPAN
SYRIA
AZERBAIJAN
Ashkhabad
Dushanbe
Tokyo
Rabat
TUNISIA
Tripoli
IRAQ
IRAN
Kabul
Islamabad
CHINA
SOUTH
KOREA
PACIFIC OCEAN
MOROCCO
ISRAEL
JORDAN
Cairo
Amman
Baghdad
AFGHANISTAN
KUWAIT
PAKISTAN
New
Delhi
NEPAL
Kathmandu
BHUTAN
Taipei
TAIWAN
Tropic of Cancer
WESTERN
SAHARA
(MOROCCO)
ALGERIA
LIBYA
EGYPT
SAUDI
ARABIA
BAHRAIN
QATAR
Riyadh
Abu Dhabi
Muscat
INDIA
Dhaka
MYANMAR
(BURMA)
Hong Kong
20°N
See Inset Below
NIGER
CHAD
SUDAN
Khartoum
Asmara
UNITED ARAB
EMIRATES
OMAN
BANGLADESH
Yangon
LAOS
Hanoi
Vientiane
NORTHERN MARIANA
ISLANDS (U.S.)
AFRICA
ERITREA
YEMEN
Sanaa
THAILAND
VIETNAM
Manila
GUAM (U.S.)
MARSHALL
ISLANDS
Niamey
NIGERIA
Abuja
N'Djamena
CENTRAL
AFRICAN REP.
Djibouti
Addis Ababa
DJIBOUTI
Bangkok
CAMBODIA
Phnom Penh
PHILIPPINES
MICRONESIA
FEDERATED STATES
OF MICRONESIA
CAMEROON
ETHIOPIA
SOMALIA
BRUNEI
Koror
PALAU
EQUATORIAL GUINEA
SÃO TOMÉ AND
PRÍNCIPE
Yaoundé
UGANDA
Kampala
KENYA
Kuala Lumpur
MALAYSIA
SINGAPORE
Equator
KIRIBATI
Libreville
GABON
CONGO
Brazzaville
RWANDA
ZAIRE
BURUNDI
Nairobi
NAURU
CABINDA
(ANGOLA)
Kinshasa
TANZANIA
Dar es Salaam
INDONESIA
Jakarta
MELANESIA
PAPUA
NEW GUINEA
SOLOMON
ISLANDS
TUVALU
ATLANTIC
OCEAN
Luanda
ANGOLA
ZAMBIA
Lusaka
MALAWI
Lilongwe
COMOROS
INDIAN OCEAN
Port Moresby
VANUATU
FIJI
NAMIBIA
Windhoek
ZIMBABWE
Harare
MOZAMBIQUE
MADAGASCAR
Antananarivo
MAURITIUS
Réunion
(Fr.)
Tropic of Capricorn
20°S
NEW CALEDONIA
(FR.)
Gaborone
BOTSWANA
Pretoria
SWAZILAND
AUSTRALIA
SOUTH
AFRICA
Maputo
LESOTHO
Cape Town
Canberra
NEW
ZEALAND
Wellington
60°S
Antarctic Circle
ANTARCTICA
80°S

West Africa

MAURITANIA
Nouakchott
MALI
Dakar
SENEGAL
GAMBIA
Banjul
NIGER
Niamey
BURKINA FASO
Ouagadougou
GUINEA-
BISSAU
Bissau
Bamako
GUINEA
Conakry
Freetown
SIERRA
LEONE
Monrovia
LIBERIA
CÔTE
D'IVOIRE
Yamoussoukro
BENIN
TOGO
GHANA
Accra
NIGERIA
Porto-
Novo
Lomé
ATLANTIC OCEAN
Equator
0   300   600 mi
0   300   600 km

Europe

FINLAND
NORWAY
SWEDEN
Oslo
Helsinki
Stockholm
Tallinn
ESTONIA
IRELAND
UNITED
KINGDOM
North
Sea
Riga
LATVIA
RUSSIA
Dublin
DENMARK
Copenhagen
RUSSIA
LITHUANIA
Vilnius
Minsk
The
Hague
London
NETHERLANDS
Amsterdam
Berlin
Warsaw
BELARUS
ATLANTIC
OCEAN
BELGIUM
Brussels
Paris
GERMANY
POLAND
Kiev
LUXEMBOURG
Prague
UKRAINE
LIECH.
CZECH REP.
SLOVAKIA
FRANCE
Bern
Vienna
Bratislava
MOLDOVA
Chişinău
SWITZERLAND
AUSTRIA
Budapest
HUNGARY
ROMANIA
PORTUGAL
SLOVENIA
Ljubljana
Zagreb
Belgrade
Bucharest
GEORGIA
ANDORRA
ITALY
CROATIA
BOS.
HERZ.
SERBIA
Black Sea
Lisbon
Madrid
MONACO
SAN
MARINO
Sarajevo
Sofia
BULGARIA
SPAIN
Rome
MONTENEGRO
MACEDONIA
Tiranë
Skopje
ALBANIA
Ankara
GIBRALTAR (U.K.)
GREECE
TURKEY
MOROCCO
ALGERIA
Tunis
Athens
CYPRUS
Nicosia
SYRIA
Beirut
LEBANON
Damascus
TUNISIA
Mediterranean Sea
ISRAEL
Jerusalem
Amman
JORDAN
LIBYA
EGYPT
0   400   800 mi
0   400   800 km

The World: Physical

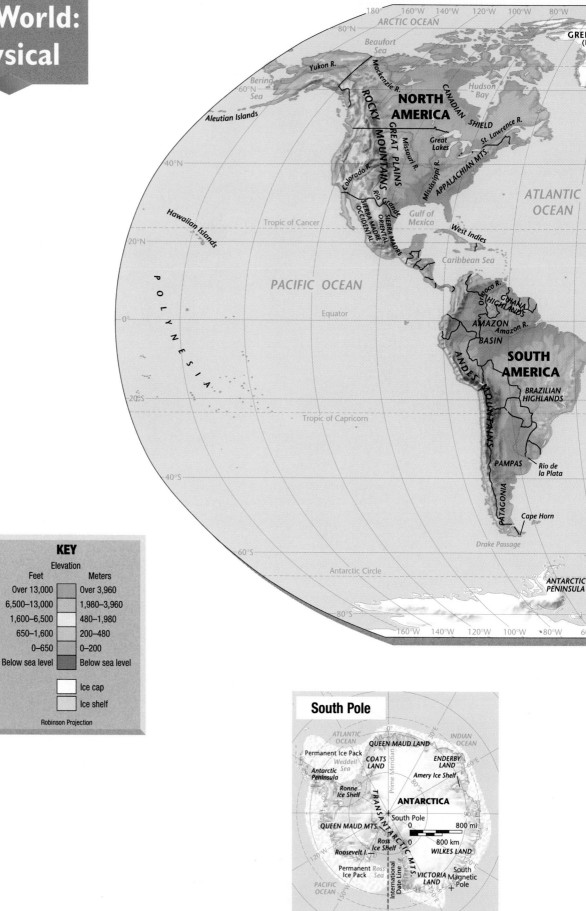

ARCTIC OCEAN

GREENL.
(DEN.

Beaufort
Sea

Yukon R.

Bering
Sea

Mackenzie R.

NORTH
AMERICA

Hudson
Bay

CANADIAN SHIELD

ROCKY MOUNTAINS

GREAT PLAINS

Missouri R.

Great
Lakes

St. Lawrence R.

Aleutian Islands

Colorado R.

Mississippi R.

APPALACHIAN MTS.

ATLANTIC
OCEAN

Rio Grande

SIERRA MADRE OCCIDENTAL

SIERRA MADRE ORIENTAL

Gulf of
Mexico

Tropic of Cancer

Hawaiian Islands

West Indies

Caribbean Sea

PACIFIC OCEAN

Equator

Orinoco R.

GUIANA HIGHLANDS

AMAZON
BASIN

Amazon R.

SOUTH
AMERICA

BRAZILIAN
HIGHLANDS

P O L Y N E S I A

ANDES MOUNTAINS

Tropic of Capricorn

PAMPAS

Rio de
la Plata

PATAGONIA

Cape Horn

Drake Passage

Antarctic Circle

ANTARCTIC
PENINSULA

KEY

Elevation

Feet		Meters
Over 13,000		Over 3,960
6,500–13,000		1,980–3,960
1,600–6,500		480–1,980
650–1,600		200–480
0–650		0–200
Below sea level		Below sea level

Ice cap

Ice shelf

Robinson Projection

South Pole

ATLANTIC
OCEAN

QUEEN MAUD LAND

INDIAN
OCEAN

Permanent Ice Pack

COATS
LAND

ENDERBY
LAND

Weddell
Sea

Amery Ice Shelf

Antarctic
Peninsula

Ronne
Ice Shelf

TRANSANTARCTIC MTS.

ANTARCTICA

South Pole

QUEEN MAUD MTS.

Ross
Ice Shelf

WILKES LAND

Roosevelt I.

Permanent
Ice Pack

Ross
Sea

VICTORIA
LAND

South
Magnetic
Pole

PACIFIC
OCEAN

International Date Line

Prime Meridian

0   800 mi

0   800 km

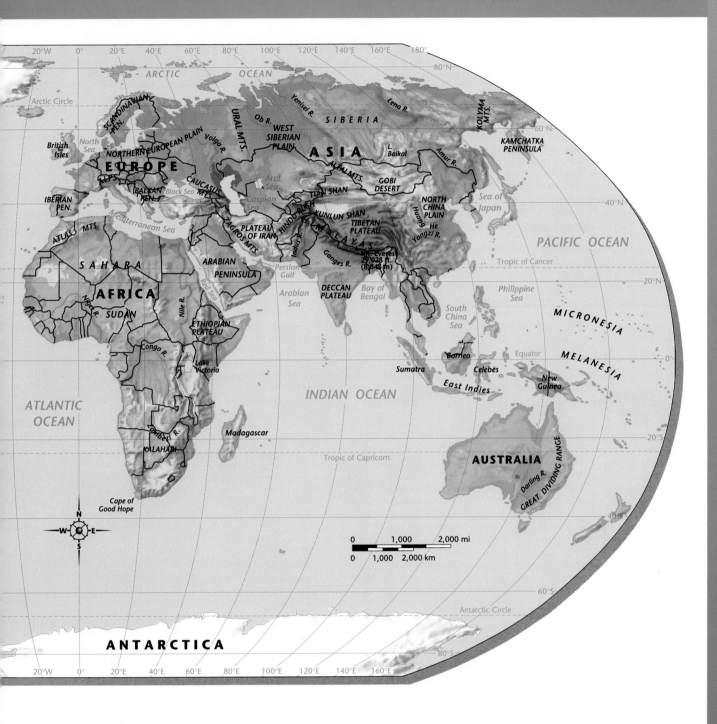

20°W 0° 20°E 40°E 60°E 80°E 100°E 120°E 140°E 160°E 180°

ARCTIC OCEAN

80°N

Arctic Circle

SCANDINAVIAN PEN.

British Isles

North Sea

NORTHERN EUROPEAN PLAIN

URAL MTS.

Ob R.

Yenisei R.

SIBERIA

Lena R.

60°N

KOLYMA MTS.

EUROPE

ALPS

Volga R.

WEST SIBERIAN PLAIN

ASIA

KAMCHATKA PENINSULA

IBERIAN PEN.

BALKAN PEN.

CAUCASUS MTS.

Black Sea

Caspian Sea

Aral Sea

ALTAI MTS.

L. Baikal

GOBI DESERT

Amur R.

NORTH CHINA PLAIN

Sea of Japan

PACIFIC OCEAN

40°N

ATLAS MTS.

Mediterranean Sea

ZAGROS MTS.

PLATEAU OF IRAN

HINDU KUSH

TIAN SHAN

KUNLUN SHAN

HIMALAYAS

TIBETAN PLATEAU

Huang He

Yangzi R.

SAHARA

Red Sea

ARABIAN PENINSULA

Persian Gulf

Indus R.

Mt. Everest 29,028 ft. (8,848 m)

Ganges R.

Tropic of Cancer

AFRICA

Nile R.

Arabian Sea

DECCAN PLATEAU

Bay of Bengal

20°N

Niger R.

SUDAN

ETHIOPIAN PLATEAU

South China Sea

Philippine Sea

MICRONESIA

Congo R.

Lake Victoria

Sumatra

Borneo

Celebes

East Indies

New Guinea

MELANESIA

Equator

0°

ATLANTIC OCEAN

INDIAN OCEAN

Zambezi R.

Madagascar

20°S

KALAHARI

Tropic of Capricorn

AUSTRALIA

Darling R.

GREAT DIVIDING RANGE

Cape of Good Hope

N
W E
S

0 1,000 2,000 mi
0 1,000 2,000 km

40°S

60°S

Antarctic Circle

ANTARCTICA

80°S

20°W 0° 20°E 40°E 60°E 80°E 100°E 120°E 140°E 160°E

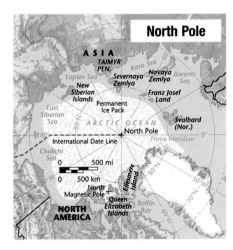

North Pole

ASIA

TAIMYR PEN.

Kara Sea

Laptev Sea

New Siberian Islands

Severnaya Zemlya

Novaya Zemlya

Barents Sea

Franz Josef Land

East Siberian Sea

Permanent Ice Pack

ARCTIC OCEAN

Svalbard (Nor.)

Chukchi Sea

North Pole

International Date Line

Prime Meridian

0 500 mi
0 500 km

North Magnetic Pole

Ellesmere Island

Baffin Bay

Queen Elizabeth Islands

NORTH AMERICA

United States: Political

ARCTIC OCEAN

RUSSIA

Arctic Circle

70°N

70°N

ALASKA

CANADA

Yukon River

60°N

Anchorage

Bering Sea

Gulf of Alaska

Juneau

160°W

0 250 500 mi

0 250 500 km

140°W

50°N

120°W

110°W

M

Bism

Seattle

Olympia

WASHINGTON

Spokane

Columbia

Missouri River

Helena

MONTANA

Portland

Salem

OREGON

Billings

IDAHO

Sheridan

Boise

Klamath Falls

Snake River

Jackson

Rapid

Eureka

Twin Falls

WYOMING

40°N

Winnemucca

Great Salt Lake

NEBR

Salt Lake City

Cheyenne

Carson City

Sacramento

NEVADA

UTAH

Denver

Grand Junction

COLORADO

San Francisco

Colorado River

Pueblo

CALIFORNIA

Cedar City

Las Vegas

Los Angeles

Santa Fe

Albuquerque

PACIFIC

ARIZONA

NEW MEXICO

OCEAN

Phoenix

San Diego

Roswell

Tucson

Rio Grande

El Paso

160°W

155°W

Honolulu

PACIFIC OCEAN

HAWAII

20°N

20°N

Hilo

0 50 100 mi

0 50 100 km

155°W

M E X I C O

Tropic of Cancer

120°W

110°W

198 **ATLAS**

CANADA

90°W   80°W   70°W

0   150   300 mi
0   150   300 km

Lake Superior

NORTH DAKOTA

Duluth •

Sault Ste. Marie •

MINNESOTA

MICHIGAN

Lake Huron

Presque Isle •

MAINE

Augusta ⊛

Portland •

Montpelier ⊛

VERMONT

NEW HAMPSHIRE

Concord ⊛

Boston •

Minneapolis • • St. Paul ⊛

WISCONSIN

SOUTH DAKOTA

Lake Michigan

Milwaukee •

Madison ⊛

Lansing ⊛

Detroit •

Missouri River

Mississippi River

Lake Ontario

NEW YORK

Albany ⊛

Buffalo •

MASSACHUSETTS

Providence ⊛

Hartford ⊛

RHODE ISLAND   40°N

New Haven •

CONNECTICUT

Lake Erie

Cleveland •

PENNSYLVANIA

Harrisburg ⊛

Pittsburgh •

New York City •

Trenton ⊛

NEW JERSEY

Philadelphia •

Chicago •

IOWA

Cedar Rapids •

Des Moines ⊛

INDIANA

OHIO

Columbus ⊛

Baltimore •

Dover ⊛

DELAWARE

Omaha •

ILLINOIS

Indianapolis ⊛

Cincinnati •

WEST VIRGINIA

Washington, D.C. ⊛

Annapolis ⊛

MARYLAND

Lincoln ⊛

Springfield ⊛

Louisville •

Frankfort ⊛

Charleston ⊛

Richmond ⊛

Norfolk •

Topeka ⊛

Kansas City •

St. Louis •

Ohio River

KANSAS

Kansas River

Jefferson City ⊛

MISSOURI

KENTUCKY

VIRGINIA

Raleigh ⊛

Wichita •

Tennessee River

ATLANTIC OCEAN

Tulsa •

Nashville ⊛

TENNESSEE

Charlotte •

NORTH CAROLINA

OKLAHOMA

ARKANSAS

Memphis •

Columbia ⊛

Oklahoma City ⊛

Little Rock ⊛

Mississippi River

Atlanta ⊛

SOUTH CAROLINA

Charleston •

Pine Bluff •

Red River

Birmingham •

MISSISSIPPI

ALABAMA

GEORGIA

Columbus •

Savannah •

Dallas •

Shreveport •

Jackson ⊛

Montgomery ⊛

30°N

Hattiesburg •

Jacksonville •

TEXAS

Baton Rouge ⊛

LOUISIANA

FLORIDA

Tallahassee ⊛

Austin ⊛

• San Antonio

Houston •

New Orleans •

Rio Grande

Tampa •

Lake Okeechobee

Gulf   of   Mexico

N
W   E
S

Miami •

KEY

— National boundary
— State boundary
⊛ National capital
⊛ State capital
• Other city

Transverse Mercator Projection

90°W   80°W

North and South America: Political

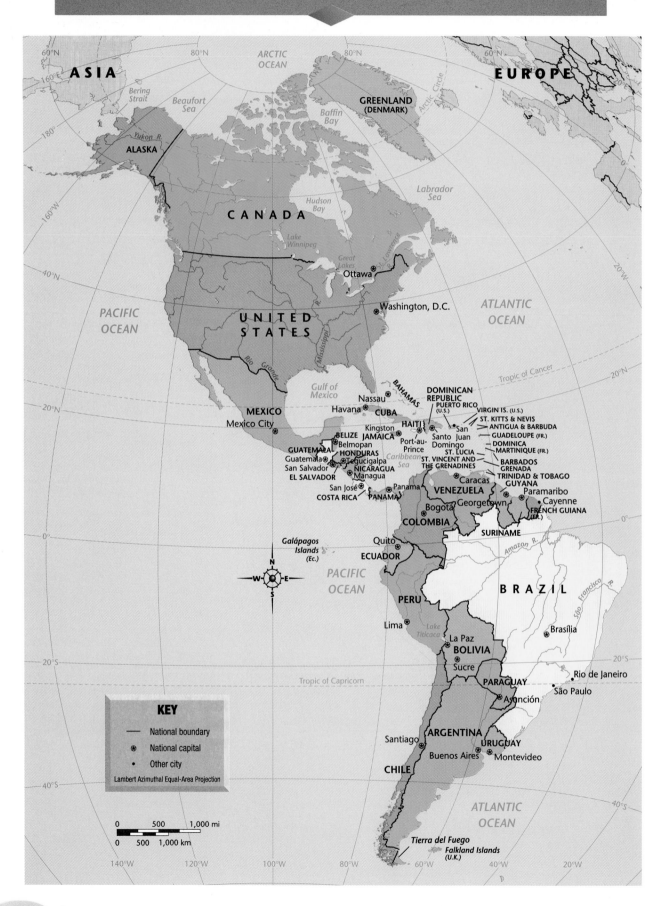

ASIA

ARCTIC OCEAN

EUROPE

160°E

60°N

80°N

80°N

60°N

20°E

Bering Strait

Beaufort Sea

GREENLAND (DENMARK)

Baffin Bay

Arctic Circle

180°

160°W

ALASKA

Yukon R.

CANADA

Labrador Sea

St. Lawrence

40°N

Hudson Bay

Lake Winnipeg

Great Lakes

20°W

Ottawa

PACIFIC OCEAN

UNITED STATES

Washington, D.C.

ATLANTIC OCEAN

Rio Grande

Mississippi R.

Tropic of Cancer

20°N

20°N

Gulf of Mexico

BAHAMAS

DOMINICAN REPUBLIC

Nassau

PUERTO RICO (U.S.)

VIRGIN IS. (U.S.)

MEXICO

Havana

CUBA

ST. KITTS & NEVIS

ANTIGUA & BARBUDA

Mexico City

Kingston

HAITI

San Juan

GUADELOUPE (FR.)

BELIZE

JAMAICA

Santo Domingo

DOMINICA

GUATEMALA

Belmopan

Port-au-Prince

ST. LUCIA

MARTINIQUE (FR.)

Guatemala

HONDURAS

Caribbean Sea

ST. VINCENT AND THE GRENADINES

BARBADOS

San Salvador

Tegucigalpa

GRENADA

EL SALVADOR

NICARAGUA

TRINIDAD & TOBAGO

Managua

Caracas

GUYANA

San José

Panama

VENEZUELA

Paramaribo

COSTA RICA

PANAMA

Georgetown

Cayenne

Bogota

FRENCH GUIANA (FR.)

COLOMBIA

SURINAME

0°

Galápagos Islands (Ec.)

Quito

Amazon R.

ECUADOR

0°

PACIFIC OCEAN

BRAZIL

São Francisco R.

PERU

Lima

Brasília

Lake Titicaca

La Paz

20°S

20°S

BOLIVIA

Rio de Janeiro

Sucre

Tropic of Capricorn

PARAGUAY

São Paulo

KEY

Asunción

— National boundary

⊛ National capital

ARGENTINA

URUGUAY

• Other city

Santiago

Montevideo

Lambert Azimuthal Equal-Area Projection

CHILE

Buenos Aires

40°S

ATLANTIC OCEAN

40°S

0   500   1,000 mi

0   500 1,000 km

Tierra del Fuego

Falkland Islands (U.K.)

140°W

120°W

100°W

80°W

60°W

40°W

20°W

North and South America: Physical

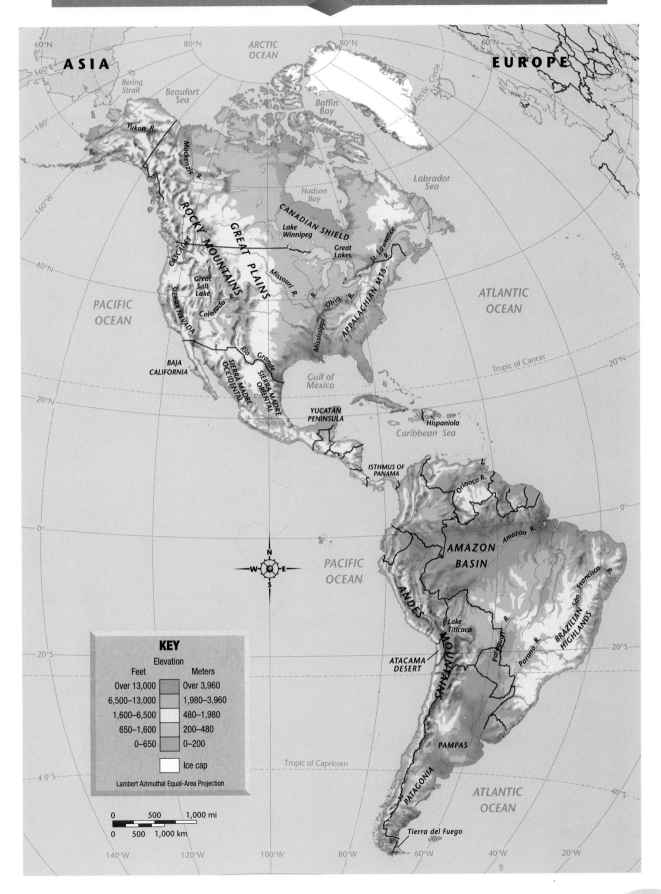

ASIA

ARCTIC OCEAN

EUROPE

Bering Strait

Beaufort Sea

Baffin Bay

Yukon R.

Mackenzie R.

Labrador Sea

Hudson Bay

ROCKY MOUNTAINS

GREAT PLAINS

CANADIAN SHIELD

Lake Winnipeg

Great Lakes

St. Lawrence R.

CASCADES

Great Salt Lake

Missouri R.

Ohio R.

APPALACHIAN MTS.

SIERRA NEVADA

Colorado R.

Mississippi R.

PACIFIC OCEAN

ATLANTIC OCEAN

BAJA CALIFORNIA

SIERRA MADRE OCCIDENTAL

SIERRA MADRE ORIENTAL

Rio Grande

Gulf of Mexico

YUCATÁN PENINSULA

Tropic of Cancer

Hispaniola

Caribbean Sea

ISTHMUS OF PANAMA

Orinoco R.

AMAZON BASIN

Amazon R.

PACIFIC OCEAN

ANDES

Lake Titicaca

São Francisco R.

ATACAMA DESERT

Paraguay R.

Paraná R.

BRAZILIAN HIGHLANDS

MOUNTAINS

PAMPAS

Tropic of Capricorn

ATLANTIC OCEAN

PATAGONIA

Tierra del Fuego

Arctic Circle

KEY

Elevation

Feet	Meters
Over 13,000	Over 3,960
6,500–13,000	1,980–3,960
1,600–6,500	480–1,980
650–1,600	200–480
0–650	0–200

Ice cap

Lambert Azimuthal Equal-Area Projection

0   500   1,000 mi

0   500   1,000 km

ARCTIC OCEAN

Reykjavik ⊛ **ICELAND**

KEY
— National boundary
⊛ National capital
• Other city

Lambert Azimuthal Equal-Area Projection

Arctic Circle

30°W 20°W 10°W 0° 10°E 20°E 30°E 40°E 50°E

FINLAND

*Faeroe Is.
(Den.)*

SWEDEN

60°N 60°N

*Shetland Is.
(U.K.)*

NORWAY
Lillehammer •

Turku • Helsinki • • St. Petersburg

**ATLANTIC
OCEAN**

Oslo ⊛ Stockholm ⊛ Tallinn ⊛ **ESTONIA** **RUSSIA**

Moscow ⊛

• Göteborg Riga ⊛ **LATVIA**

*North
Sea*

DENMARK *Baltic
Sea* **LITHUANIA**
Vilnius ⊛ **BELARUS**

IRELAND **UNITED
KINGDOM** Copenhagen ⊛ **RUSSIA** Minsk ⊛

Dublin ⊛ Gdańsk •

• Manchester Berlin ⊛ **POLAND** Kiev ⊛ 50°N

50°N Amsterdam ⊛ Warsaw ⊛
The Hague ⊛ Łódź • **UKRAINE**
London ⊛ **NETHERLANDS** **GERMANY** Katowice • Kraków •

English Channel Brussels ⊛ • Cologne **CZECH** **SLOVAKIA**
BELGIUM • Bonn Prague ⊛ **REPUBLIC** **MOLDOVA**
• Frankfurt Brno • Chişinău •
LUXEMBOURG ⊛ Luxembourg Bratislava ⊛

• Paris Munich • Vienna ⊛ Budapest ⊛ • Cluj

*Bay
of
Biscay* **FRANCE** **LIECHTENSTEIN** **AUSTRIA** **HUNGARY** **ROMANIA**
Bern ⊛ Ljubljana ⊛
SWITZERLAND **SLOVENIA** Zagreb ⊛ Bucharest ⊛ *Black
Sea*
Milan • **CROATIA** Belgrade ⊛
BOSNIA & **BULGARIA**
SAN MARINO **HERZEGOVINA** **SERBIA**
Sarajevo ⊛
PORTUGAL **ANDORRA** **MONACO** **ITALY** Podgorica • • Sophia
Corsica Rome ⊛ **MONTENEGRO** Skopje ⊛
Marseille • **VATICAN** **ALBANIA** **MACEDONIA**
Madrid ⊛ **CITY** Tiranë ⊛
Lisbon ⊛ • Barcelona Naples • *Aegean
Sea*
40°N *Sardinia* **GREECE**
SPAIN
Balearic Is. *Tyrrhenian
Sea* *Ionian
Sea* Athens ⊛

Mediterranean

*Strait of
Gibraltar* **GIBRALTAR**
(U.K.) *Sicily* *Sea* *Crete*

N
W E
S

AFRICA **MALTA**

0 250 500 mi
0 250 500 km

0° 10°E 20°E

Europe: Physical

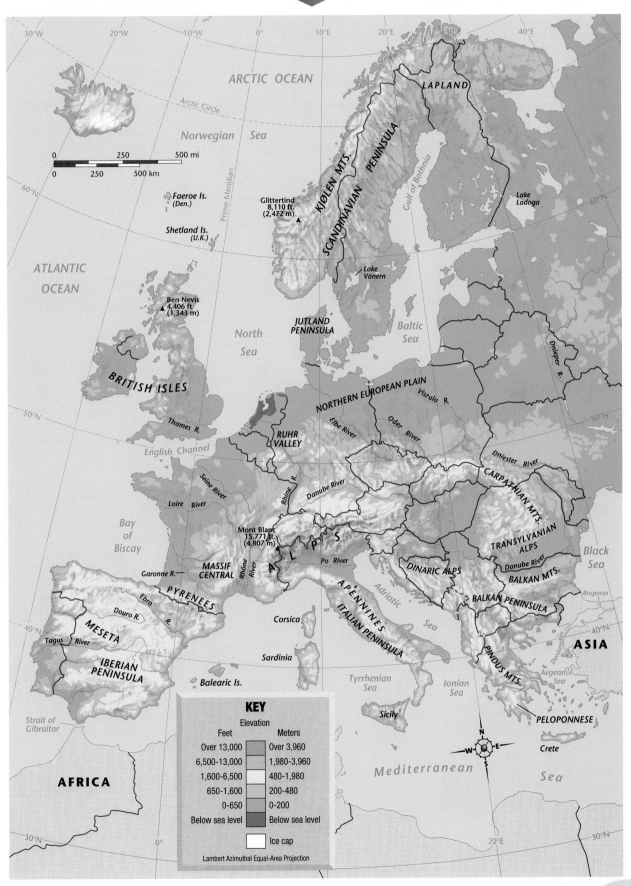

30°W   20°W   10°W   0°   10°E   20°E   30°E   40°E

ARCTIC OCEAN

LAPLAND

Arctic Circle

Norwegian Sea

Faeroe Is.
(Den.)

KIØLEN MTS.

SCANDINAVIAN PENINSULA

Gulf of Bothnia

Lake Ladoga

60°N

0   250   500 mi

0   250   500 km

Shetland Is.
(U.K.)

Glittertind
8,110 ft.
(2,472 m)

Lake Vänern

ATLANTIC OCEAN

Ben Nevis
4,406 ft
(1,343 m)

North Sea

JUTLAND PENINSULA

Baltic Sea

50°N

BRITISH ISLES

Thames R.

NORTHERN EUROPEAN PLAIN

Vistula R.

Dnieper R.

English Channel

RUHR VALLEY

Elbe River

Oder River

Dniester River

CARPATHIAN MTS.

Seine River

Rhine R.

Danube River

Loire River

Bay of Biscay

Mont Blanc
15,771 ft.
(4,807 m)

A L P S

Po River

TRANSYLVANIAN ALPS

Danube River

Garonne R.

MASSIF CENTRAL

Rhône River

A
P
E
N
N
I
N
E
S

DINARIC ALPS

BALKAN MTS.

PYRENEES

Adriatic Sea

BALKAN PENINSULA

Bosporus

Ebro R.

Douro R.

Corsica

ITALIAN PENINSULA

Black Sea

MESETA

Tagus River

40°N

Sardinia

Dardanelles

ASIA

IBERIAN PENINSULA

Balearic Is.

Tyrrhenian Sea

Ionian Sea

PINDUS MTS.

Aegean Sea

PELOPONNESE

Strait of Gibraltar

Sicily

Crete

AFRICA

Mediterranean Sea

30°N

20°E

KEY

Elevation

Feet	Meters
Over 13,000	Over 3,960
6,500-13,000	1,980-3,960
1,600-6,500	480-1,980
650-1,600	200-480
0-650	0-200
Below sea level	Below sea level
	Ice cap

Lambert Azimuthal Equal-Area Projection

Africa: Political

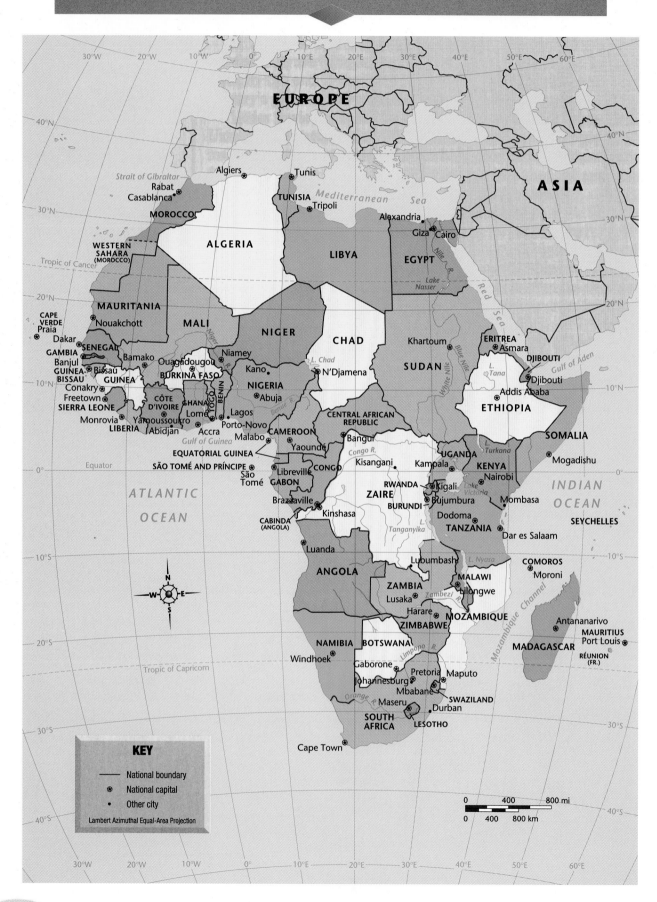

EUROPE

ASIA

Strait of Gibraltar
Rabat ⊛
Casablanca •
MOROCCO

Algiers ⊛

Tunis ⊛
TUNISIA
• Tripoli

Mediterranean Sea

Alexandria •
Giza • • Cairo

WESTERN
SAHARA
(MOROCCO)

Tropic of Cancer

ALGERIA

LIBYA

EGYPT

Lake
Nasser

MAURITANIA

Nouakchott ⊛

MALI

NIGER

CHAD

Khartoum •

ERITREA
⊛ Asmara

DJIBOUTI

Gulf of Aden

CAPE
VERDE
Praia ⊛
• Dakar
GAMBIA
Banjul •
GUINEA-
BISSAU
• Bissau

SENEGAL ⊛

Bamako ⊛
Ouagadougou ⊛

Niamey ⊛

Kano •

N'Djamena •

SUDAN

Djibouti •

Addis Ababa •

BURKINA FASO

NIGERIA

• Abuja

CENTRAL AFRICAN
REPUBLIC

ETHIOPIA

SOMALIA

GUINEA
Conakry ⊛
Freetown ⊛
SIERRA LEONE

CÔTE
D'IVOIRE
GHANA
Yamoussoukro ⊛
Abidjan •
Accra ⊛

LOMÉ
TOGO
BENIN

Lagos •
Porto-Novo ⊛
Malabo ⊛

Bangui •

UGANDA
Kisangani •
Kampala ⊛

KENYA

Mogadishu •

Monrovia ⊛
LIBERIA

CAMEROON
Yaoundé ⊛

L. Turkana

Nairobi •

Equator

EQUATORIAL GUINEA
SÃO TOMÉ AND PRÍNCIPE ⊛
São
Tomé

Libreville ⊛
GABON

CONGO

RWANDA
⊛ Kigali
Lake
Victoria

ZAIRE

Brazzaville ⊛
Kinshasa •

BURUNDI
Bujumbura ⊛

Dodoma ⊛

INDIAN
OCEAN

SEYCHELLES

ATLANTIC

OCEAN

CABINDA
(ANGOLA)

Congo R.

TANZANIA
⊛ Dar es Salaam

L.
Tanganyika

• Luanda

Lubumbashi •

L. Nyasa

COMOROS
• Moroni

ANGOLA

ZAMBIA

Lusaka ⊛

MALAWI
Lilongwe ⊛

Zambezi R.

Harare ⊛

MOZAMBIQUE

Mozambique Channel

Antananarivo •

MAURITIUS
Port Louis •

ZIMBABWE

NAMIBIA

BOTSWANA

Windhoek ⊛

Limpopo R.

Gaborone ⊛

Pretoria ⊛ • Maputo
Johannesburg •
Mbabane ⊛

MADAGASCAR

RÉUNION
(FR.)

Tropic of Capricorn

Orange R.

Maseru ⊛ • Durban

SWAZILAND

SOUTH
AFRICA

LESOTHO

Cape Town •

KEY

— National boundary

⊛ National capital

• Other city

Lambert Azimuthal Equal-Area Projection

0   400   800 mi

0   400   800 km

Africa: Physical

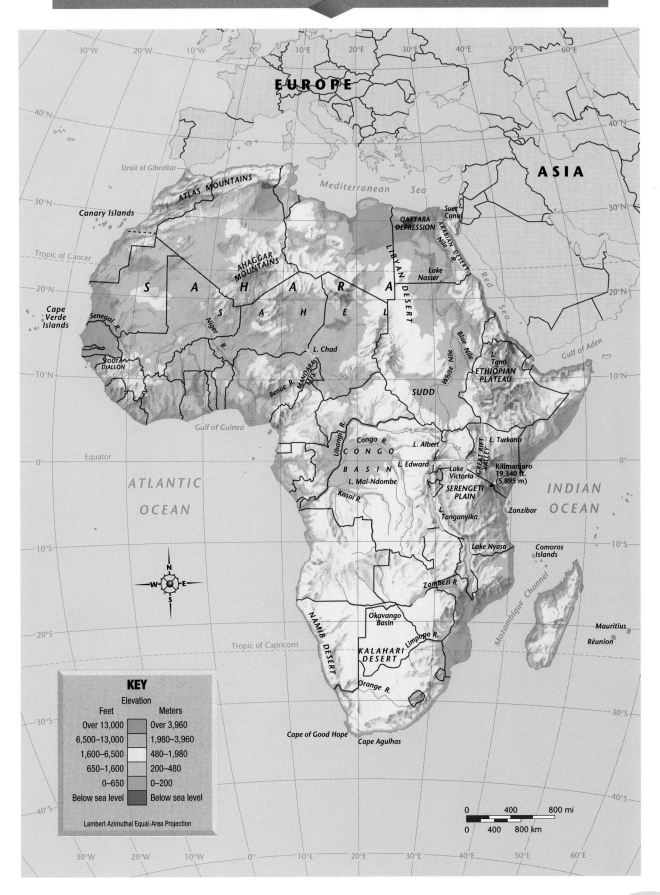

EUROPE

ASIA

Strait of Gibraltar

Mediterranean Sea

ATLAS MOUNTAINS

Canary Islands

Tropic of Cancer

AHAGGAR MOUNTAINS

QATTARA DEPRESSION

Suez Canal

ARABIAN DESERT

Nile R.

LIBYAN DESERT

Lake Nasser

S A H A R A

Cape Verde Islands

Senegal R.

Niger R.

S A H E L

Red Sea

Blue Nile

L. Tana

ETHIOPIAN PLATEAU

Gulf of Aden

FOUTA DJALLON

L. Chad

MANDARA MTS.

Benue R.

White Nile

SUDD

Gulf of Guinea

Ubangi R.

Congo R.

CONGO BASIN

L. Albert

L. Edward

L. Turkana

GREAT RIFT VALLEY

Kilimanjaro 19,340 ft. (5,895 m)

Equator

ATLANTIC OCEAN

L. Mai-Ndombe

Kasai R.

Lake Victoria

SERENGETI PLAIN

L. Tanganyika

Zanzibar

INDIAN OCEAN

Lake Nyasa

Comoros Islands

Mozambique Channel

Zambezi R.

Mauritius

Réunion

NAMIB DESERT

Okavango Basin

Limpopo R.

Tropic of Capricorn

KALAHARI DESERT

Orange R.

Cape of Good Hope

Cape Agulhas

KEY

Elevation

Feet	Meters
Over 13,000	Over 3,960
6,500–13,000	1,980–3,960
1,600–6,500	480–1,980
650–1,600	200–480
0–650	0–200
Below sea level	Below sea level

Lambert Azimuthal Equal-Area Projection

N W E S

0   400   800 mi

0   400   800 km

Asia: Political

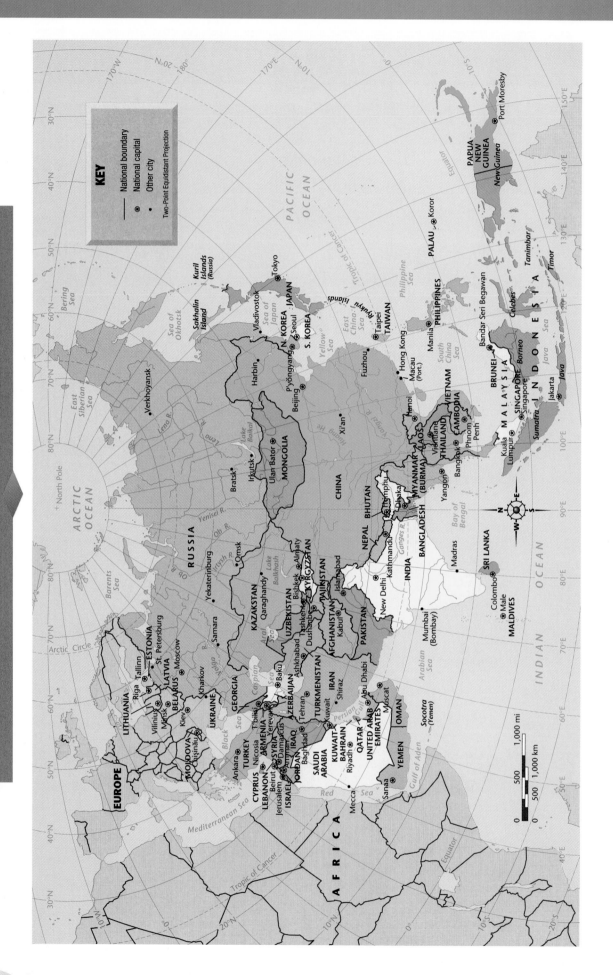

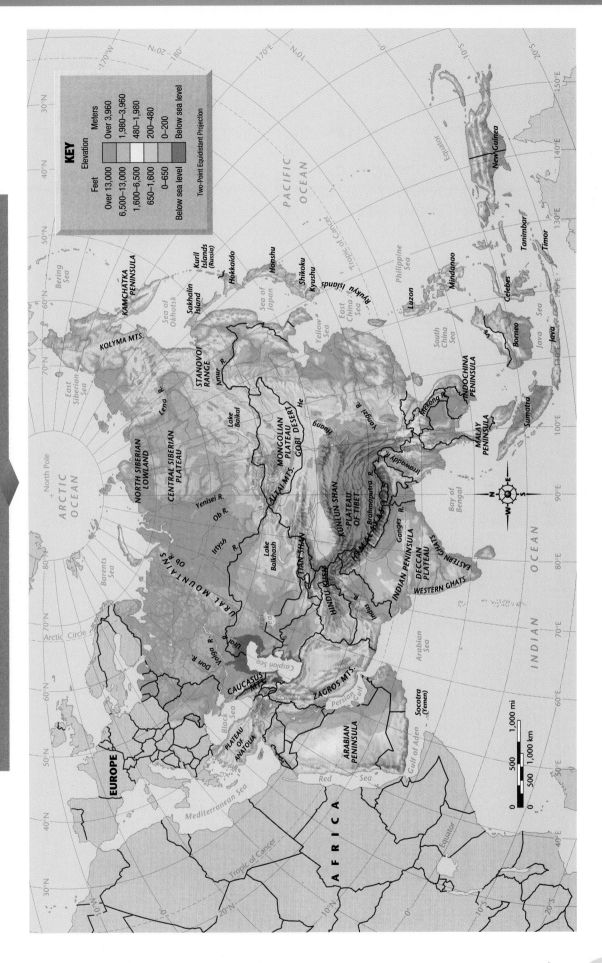

Asia: Physical

KEY

Elevation

Feet	Meters	
Over 13,000	Over 3,960	
6,500–13,000	1,980–3,960	
1,600–6,500	480–1,980	
650–1,600	200–480	
0–650	0–200	
Below sea level	Below sea level	

Two-Point Equidistant Projection

PACIFIC OCEAN

ARCTIC OCEAN

North Pole

Arctic Circle

Tropic of Cancer

Equator

Tropic of Cancer

Equator

EUROPE

AFRICA

Bering Sea

East Siberian Sea

Barents Sea

KAMCHATKA PENINSULA

KOLYMA MTS.

STANOVOI RANGE

Sea of Okhotsk

Sakhalin Island

Kuril Islands (Russia)

Hokkaido

Honshu

Shikoku

Kyushu

Sea of Japan

Ryukyu Islands

East China Sea

Yellow Sea

Luzon

Philippine Sea

Mindanao

Celebes

Borneo

Java Sea

Java

Sumatra

Tanimbar

Timor

New Guinea

South China Sea

INDOCHINA PENINSULA

MALAY PENINSULA

Bay of Bengal

NORTH SIBERIAN LOWLAND

CENTRAL SIBERIAN PLATEAU

Lena R.

Amur R.

MONGOLIAN PLATEAU

GOBI DESERT

He

Huang

Yangzi R.

Mekong R.

Irrawaddy R.

ALTAI MTS.

Yenisei R.

Ob R.

Irtysh R.

Lake Baikal

Lake Balkhash

TIAN SHAN

KUNLUN SHAN

PLATEAU OF TIBET

HIMALAYAS

Brahmaputra R.

Ganges R.

HINDU KUSH

Indus R.

INDIAN PENINSULA

DECCAN PLATEAU

EASTERN GHATS

WESTERN GHATS

URAL MOUNTAINS

Ob R.

Don R.

Volga R.

Ural R.

Caspian Sea

CAUCASUS MTS.

Black Sea

ZAGROS MTS.

Persian Gulf

PLATEAU OF ANATOLIA

ARABIAN PENINSULA

Socotra (Yemen)

Gulf of Aden

Red Sea

Mediterranean Sea

Arabian Sea

INDIAN OCEAN

1,000 mi

500   1,000 km

500

0

0

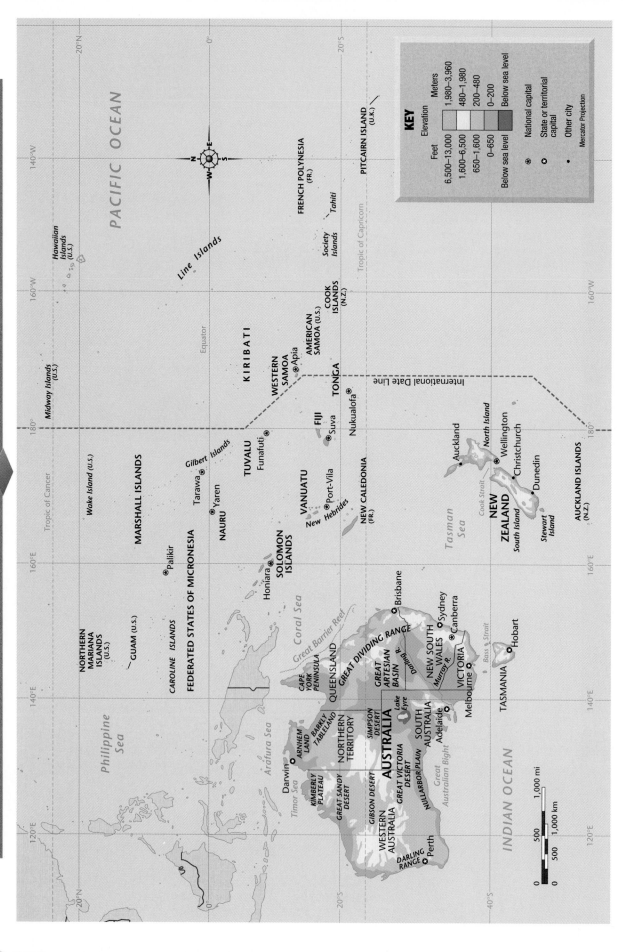

PACIFIC OCEAN

KEY

Elevation

Feet	Meters
6,500–13,000	1,980–3,960
1,600–6,500	480–1,980
650–1,600	200–480
0–650	0–200
Below sea level	Below sea level

⊕ National capital
⊛ State or territorial capital
• Other city

Mercator Projection

Hawaiian Islands (U.S.)

Line Islands

FRENCH POLYNESIA (FR.)

Society Islands ~Tahiti

PITCAIRN ISLAND (U.K.)

Tropic of Capricorn

Midway Islands (U.S.)

COOK ISLANDS (N.Z.)

AMERICAN SAMOA (U.S.)

Equator

KIRIBATI

WESTERN SAMOA ⊛ Apia

TONGA

International Date Line

Wake Island (U.S.)

Tropic of Cancer

MARSHALL ISLANDS

Gilbert Islands

Tarawa ⊛

FIJI ⊛ Suva

Nukualofa

TUVALU
Funafuti ⊛ ⊛

VANUATU
⊛ Port-Vila

New Hebrides

NEW CALEDONIA (FR.)

Auckland •

North Island

NAURU
⊛ Yaren

NEW ZEALAND
South Island

Wellington ⊛
Christchurch •
Dunedin •

AUCKLAND ISLANDS (N.Z.)

Cook Strait

Stewart Island

Tasman Sea

NORTHERN MARIANA ISLANDS (U.S.)

GUAM (U.S.)

CAROLINE ISLANDS

⊛ Palikir

FEDERATED STATES OF MICRONESIA

SOLOMON ISLANDS

Honiara ⊛

Coral Sea

Great Barrier Reef

Brisbane ⊕

Sydney •
⊛ Canberra

Hobart ⊛

Bass Strait

TASMANIA

GREAT DIVIDING RANGE

QUEENSLAND

NEW SOUTH WALES

VICTORIA

Melbourne •

Murray R.

Darling R.

GREAT ARTESIAN BASIN

CAPE YORK PENINSULA

Philippine Sea

Arafura Sea

Timor Sea

Darwin •

ARNHEM LAND

NORTHERN TERRITORY

BARKLY TABLELAND

SIMPSON DESERT

Lake Eyre

SOUTH AUSTRALIA

Adelaide ⊛

AUSTRALIA

KIMBERLY PLATEAU

GREAT SANDY DESERT

GIBSON DESERT

GREAT VICTORIA DESERT

NULLARBOR PLAIN

WESTERN AUSTRALIA

Perth ⊛

DARLING RANGE

Great Australian Bight

INDIAN OCEAN

| 0 | 500 | 1,000 mi |
| 0 | 500 | 1,000 km |

The Arctic

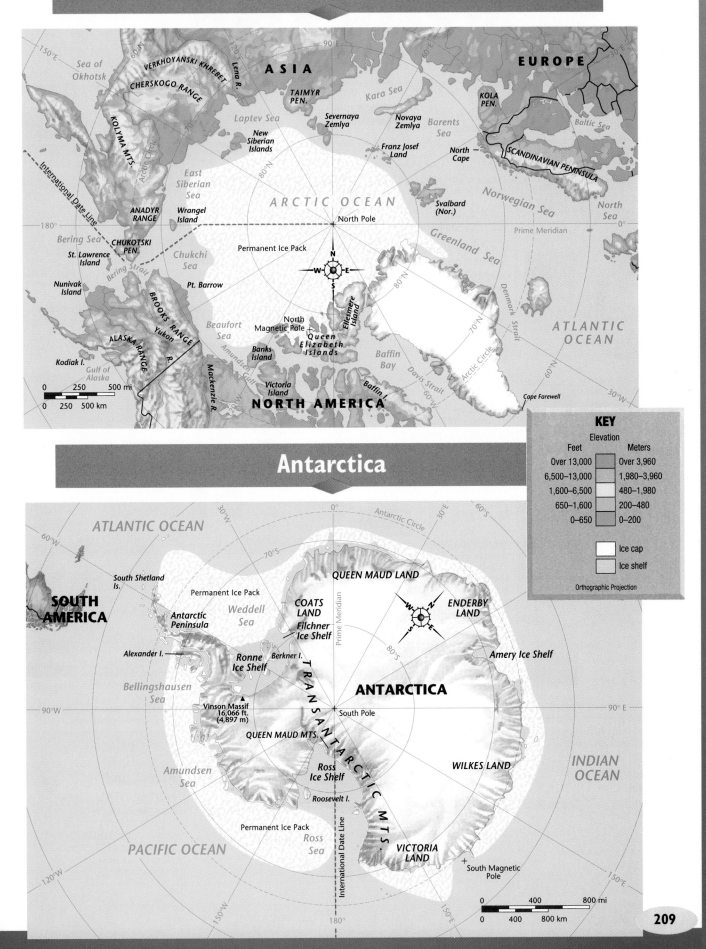

150°E
Sea of Okhotsk
VERKHOYANSKI KHREBET
CHERSKOGO RANGE
KOLYMA MTS.
60°N
Lena R.
120°E
90°E
A S I A
TAIMYR PEN.
Laptev Sea
Severnaya Zemlya
New Siberian Islands
Kara Sea
Novaya Zemlya
Franz Josef Land
Barents Sea
EUROPE
KOLA PEN.
30°E
Baltic Sea
SCANDINAVIAN PENINSULA
North Cape
International Date Line
Arctic Circle
70°N
80°N
ARCTIC OCEAN
Svalbard (Nor.)
Norwegian Sea
Prime Meridian
North Sea
0°
ANADYR RANGE
Wrangel Island
180°
North Pole
Permanent Ice Pack
Greenland Sea
Denmark Strait
Bering Sea
CHUKOTSKI PEN.
St. Lawrence Island
Chukchi Sea
N
W   E
S
80°N
ATLANTIC OCEAN
Nunivak Island
Pt. Barrow
North Magnetic Pole
Ellesmere Island
70°N
Beaufort Sea
Amundsen Gulf
Banks Island
Queen Elizabeth Islands
Baffin Bay
Davis Strait
Arctic Circle
60°N
BROOKS RANGE
Yukon R.
ALASKA RANGE
Kodiak I.
Gulf of Alaska
Victoria Island
Mackenzie R.
Baffin I.
60°N
30°W
Cape Farewell
0   250   500 mi
0   250   500 km
NORTH AMERICA

Antarctica

KEY

Elevation

Feet		Meters
Over 13,000		Over 3,960
6,500–13,000		1,980–3,960
1,600–6,500		480–1,980
650–1,600		200–480
0–650		0–200

Ice cap

Ice shelf

Orthographic Projection

ATLANTIC OCEAN
30°W
0°
Antarctic Circle
30°E
60°S
60°E
60°W
South Shetland Is.
Permanent Ice Pack
QUEEN MAUD LAND
ENDERBY LAND
SOUTH AMERICA
Antarctic Peninsula
Weddell Sea
70°S
COATS LAND
Filchner Ice Shelf
Prime Meridian
Amery Ice Shelf
Alexander I.
Ronne Ice Shelf
Berkner I.
N
W   E
S
Bellingshausen Sea
80°S
ANTARCTICA
Vinson Massif 16,066 ft. (4,897 m)
South Pole
90°W
TRANSANTARCTIC MTS.
90°E
QUEEN MAUD MTS.
Amundsen Sea
Ross Ice Shelf
WILKES LAND
INDIAN OCEAN
Roosevelt I.
120°W
Permanent Ice Pack
International Date Line
PACIFIC OCEAN
Ross Sea
VICTORIA LAND
South Magnetic Pole
150°W
180°
150°E
0   400   800 mi
0   400   800 km

209

World View

Afghanistan

CAPITAL: Kabul
POPULATION: 21,251,821
MAJOR LANGUAGES: Pashtu, Afghan Persian, Turkic, and 30 various languages
AREA: 250,010 sq mi; 647,500 sq km
LEADING EXPORTS: fruits and nuts, handwoven carpets, and wool
CONTINENT: Asia

Albania
CAPITAL: Tiranë
POPULATION: 3,413,904
MAJOR LANGUAGES: Albanian, Tosk dialect, and Greek
AREA: 11,101 sq mi; 28,750 sq km
LEADING EXPORTS: asphalt, metals and metallic ores, and electricity
CONTINENT: Europe

Algeria
CAPITAL: Algiers
POPULATION: 28,539,321
MAJOR LANGUAGES: Arabic (official), French, and Berber dialects
AREA: 919,626 sq mi; 2,381,740 sq km
LEADING EXPORTS: petroleum and natural gas
CONTINENT: Africa

Andorra
CAPITAL: Andorra La Vella
POPULATION: 65,780
MAJOR LANGUAGES: Catalan (official), French, and Castilian
AREA: 174 sq mi; 450 sq km
LEADING EXPORTS: electricity, tobacco products, and furniture
CONTINENT: Europe

Angola
CAPITAL: Luanda
POPULATION: 10,069,501
MAJOR LANGUAGES: Portuguese (official), Bantu, and various languages
AREA: 481,370 sq mi; 1,246,700 sq km
LEADING EXPORTS: oil, diamonds, and refined petroleum products
CONTINENT: Africa

Anguilla
CAPITAL: The Valley
POPULATION: 7,099
MAJOR LANGUAGE: English (official)
AREA: 35 sq mi; 91 sq km
LEADING EXPORTS: lobster and salt
LOCATION: Caribbean Sea

Antigua and Barbuda
CAPITAL: Saint John's
POPULATION: 65,176
MAJOR LANGUAGES: English (official) and various dialects
AREA: 170 sq mi; 440 sq km
LEADING EXPORTS: petroleum products and manufactures
LOCATION: Caribbean Sea

Argentina
CAPITAL: Buenos Aires
POPULATION: 34,292,742
MAJOR LANGUAGES: Spanish (official), English, Italian, German, and French
AREA: 1,068,339 sq mi; 2,766,890 sq km
LEADING EXPORTS: meat, wheat, corn, oilseed, and manufactures
CONTINENT: South America

Armenia
CAPITAL: Yerevan
POPULATION: 3,557,284
MAJOR LANGUAGES: Armenian and Russian
AREA: 11,506 sq mi; 29,800 sq km
LEADING EXPORTS: gold and jewelry, and aluminum
CONTINENT: Asia

Australia
CAPITAL: Canberra
POPULATION: 18,322,231
MAJOR LANGUAGES: English and various languages
AREA: 2,968,010 sq mi; 7,686,850 sq km
LEADING EXPORTS: coal, gold, meat, wool, and alumina
CONTINENT: Australia

Austria
CAPITAL: Vienna
POPULATION: 7,986,664
MAJOR LANGUAGE: German
AREA: 32,376 sq mi; 83,850 sq km
LEADING EXPORTS: machinery and equipment, and iron and steel
CONTINENT: Europe

Azerbaijan
CAPITAL: Baku
POPULATION: 7,789,886
MAJOR LANGUAGES: Azeri, Russian, Armenian, and various languages
AREA: 33,438 sq mi; 86,600 sq km
LEADING EXPORTS: oil and gas, chemicals, and oil field equipment
CONTINENT: Asia

Bahamas
CAPITAL: Nassau
POPULATION: 256,616
MAJOR LANGUAGES: English and Creole
AREA: 5,382 sq mi; 13,940 sq km
LEADING EXPORTS: pharmaceuticals, cement, rum, and crawfish
LOCATION: Caribbean Sea

Bahrain
CAPITAL: Manama
POPULATION: 575,925
MAJOR LANGUAGES: Arabic, English, Farsi, and Urdu
AREA: 239 sq mi; 620 sq km
LEADING EXPORTS: petroleum and petroleum products
CONTINENT: Asia

Bangladesh
CAPITAL: Dhaka
POPULATION: 128,094,948
MAJOR LANGUAGES: Bangla and English
AREA: 55,600 sq mi; 144,000 sq km
LEADING EXPORTS: garments, jute and jute goods, and leather
CONTINENT: Asia

Barbados
CAPITAL: Bridgetown
POPULATION: 256,395
MAJOR LANGUAGE: English
AREA: 166 sq mi; 430 sq km
LEADING EXPORTS: sugar and molasses, and rum
LOCATION: Caribbean Sea

Belarus
CAPITAL: Minsk
POPULATION: 10,437,418
MAJOR LANGUAGES: Byelorussian and Russian
AREA: 79,926 sq mi; 207,600 sq km
LEADING EXPORTS: machinery and transportation equipment
CONTINENT: Europe

Belgium
CAPITAL: Brussels
POPULATION: 10,081,880
MAJOR LANGUAGES: Dutch, French, and German
AREA: 11,780 sq mi; 30,510 sq km
LEADING EXPORTS: iron and steel, and transportation equipment
CONTINENT: Europe

Belize
CAPITAL: Belmopan
POPULATION: 214,061
MAJOR LANGUAGES: English (official), Spanish, Maya, and Garifuna
AREA: 8,865 sq mi; 22,960 sq km
LEADING EXPORTS: sugar, citrus fruits, bananas, and clothing
CONTINENT: North America

Benin
CAPITAL: Porto-Novo
POPULATION: 5,522,677
MAJOR LANGUAGES: Fon, Yoruba, and at least 6 various languages
AREA: 43,484 sq mi; 112,620 sq km
LEADING EXPORTS: cotton, crude oil, palm products, and cocoa
CONTINENT: Africa

Bermuda
CAPITAL: Hamilton
POPULATION: 61,629
MAJOR LANGUAGE: English
AREA: 19.3 sq mi; 50 sq km
LEADING EXPORTS: semitropical produce and light manufactures
LOCATION: Atlantic Ocean

Bhutan
CAPITAL: Thimphu
POPULATION: 1,780,638
MAJOR LANGUAGES: Dzongkha (official), Tibetan dialects, and Nepalese dialects
AREA: 18,147 sq mi; 47,000 sq km
LEADING EXPORTS: cardamon, gypsum, timber, and handicrafts
CONTINENT: Asia

Bolivia
CAPITAL: La Paz
POPULATION: 7,896,254
MAJOR LANGUAGES: Spanish, Quechua, and Aymara
AREA: 424,179 sq mi; 1,098,580 sq km
LEADING EXPORTS: metals, natural gas, soybeans, jewelry, and wood
CONTINENT: South America

Bosnia and Herzegovina

CAPITAL: Sarajevo
POPULATION: 3,201,823
MAJOR LANGUAGE: Serbo-Croatian
AREA: 19,782 sq mi; 51,233 sq km
LEADING EXPORTS: none
CONTINENT: Europe

Botswana

CAPITAL: Gaborone
POPULATION: 1,392,414
MAJOR LANGUAGES: English and Setswana
AREA: 231,812 sq mi; 600,370 sq km
LEADING EXPORTS: diamonds, copper and nickel, and meat
CONTINENT: Africa

Brazil

CAPITAL: Brasília
POPULATION: 160,737,489
MAJOR LANGUAGES: Portuguese, Spanish, English, and French
AREA: 3,286,600 sq mi; 8,511,965 sq km
LEADING EXPORTS: iron ore, soybean, bran, and orange juice
CONTINENT: South America

British Virgin Islands

CAPITAL: Road Town
POPULATION: 13,027
MAJOR LANGUAGE: English
AREA: 58 sq mi; 150 sq km
LEADING EXPORTS: rum, fresh fish, gravel, sand, and fruits
LOCATION: Caribbean Sea

Brunei

CAPITAL: Bandar Seri Begawan
POPULATION: 292,266
MAJOR LANGUAGES: Malay, English, and Chinese
AREA: 2,228 sq mi; 5,770 sq km
LEADING EXPORTS: crude oil and liquefied natural gas
LOCATION: South China Sea

Bulgaria

CAPITAL: Sofia
POPULATION: 8,775,198
MAJOR LANGUAGE: Bulgarian
AREA: 42,824 sq mi; 110,910 sq km
LEADING EXPORTS: machinery and agricultural products
CONTINENT: Europe

Burkina Faso

CAPITAL: Ouagadougou
POPULATION: 10,422,828
MAJOR LANGUAGES: French (official) and Sudanic languages
AREA: 105,873 sq mi; 274,200 sq km
LEADING EXPORTS: cotton, gold, and animal products
CONTINENT: Africa

Burundi

CAPITAL: Bujumbura
POPULATION: 6,262,429
MAJOR LANGUAGES: Kirundi, French, and Swahili
AREA: 10,746 sq mi; 27,830 sq km
LEADING EXPORTS: coffee, tea, cotton, and hides and skins
CONTINENT: Africa

Cambodia

CAPITAL: Phnom Penh
POPULATION: 10,561,373
MAJOR LANGUAGES: Khmer and French
AREA: 69,902 sq mi; 181,040 sq km
LEADING EXPORTS: timber, rubber, soybeans, and sesame
CONTINENT: Asia

Cameroon

CAPITAL: Yaounde
POPULATION: 13,521,000
MAJOR LANGUAGES: 24 various languages, English, and French
AREA: 183,574 sq mi; 475,440 sq km
LEADING EXPORTS: petroleum products and lumber
CONTINENT: Africa

Canada

CAPITAL: Ottawa
POPULATION: 28,434,545
MAJOR LANGUAGES: English and French
AREA: 3,851,940 sq mi; 9,976,140 sq km
LEADING EXPORTS: newsprint, wood pulp, timber, and crude petroleum
CONTINENT: North America

Cape Verde

CAPITAL: Praia
POPULATION: 435,983
MAJOR LANGUAGES: Portuguese and Crioulo
AREA: 1,556 sq mi; 4,030 sq km
LEADING EXPORTS: fish, bananas, and hides and skins
CONTINENT: Africa

Cayman Islands

CAPITAL: George Town
POPULATION: 33,192
MAJOR LANGUAGE: English
AREA: 100 sq mi; 260 sq km
LEADING EXPORTS: turtle products and manufactured goods
LOCATION: Caribbean Sea

Central African Republic

CAPITAL: Bangui
POPULATION: 3,209,759
MAJOR LANGUAGES: French, Sangho, Arabic, Hunsa, and Swahili
AREA: 240,542 sq mi; 622,980 sq km
LEADING EXPORTS: diamonds, timber, cotton, coffee, and tobacco
CONTINENT: Africa

Chad

CAPITAL: N'Djamena
POPULATION: 5,586,505
MAJOR LANGUAGES: French, Arabic, Sara, Songo, and over 100 various languages and dialects
AREA: 495,772 sq mi; 1,284,000 sq km
LEADING EXPORTS: cotton, cattle, textiles, and fish
CONTINENT: Africa

Chile

CAPITAL: Santiago
POPULATION: 14,161,216
MAJOR LANGUAGE: Spanish
AREA: 292,269 sq mi; 756,950 sq km
LEADING EXPORTS: copper and other metals and minerals
CONTINENT: South America

China

CAPITAL: Beijing
POPULATION: 1,203,097,268
MAJOR LANGUAGES: Mandarin, Putonghua, Yue, Wu, Minbei, Minnan, Xiang, and Gan and Hakka dialects
AREA: 3,705,533 sq mi; 9,596,960 sq km
LEADING EXPORTS: textiles, garments, footwear, and toys
CONTINENT: Asia

Colombia

CAPITAL: Bogota
POPULATION: 36,200,251
MAJOR LANGUAGE: Spanish
AREA: 439,751 sq mi; 1,138,910 sq km
LEADING EXPORTS: petroleum, coffee, coal, and bananas
CONTINENT: South America

Comoros

CAPITAL: Moroni
POPULATION: 549,338
MAJOR LANGUAGES: Arabic, French, and Comoran
AREA: 838 sq mi; 2,170 sq km
LEADING EXPORTS: vanilla, ylang-ylang, cloves, and perfume oil
LOCATION: Indian Ocean

Congo

CAPITAL: Brazzaville
POPULATION: 2,504,996
MAJOR LANGUAGES: French, Lingala, Kikongo, and other languages
AREA: 132,051 sq mi; 342,000 sq km
LEADING EXPORTS: crude oil, lumber, plywood, sugar, and cocoa
CONTINENT: Africa

Cook Islands

CAPITAL: Avarua
POPULATION: 19,343
MAJOR LANGUAGES: English and Maori
AREA: 95 sq mi; 240 sq km
LEADING EXPORTS: copra, fresh and canned fruit, and clothing
LOCATION: Pacific Ocean

Costa Rica

CAPITAL: San José
POPULATION: 3,419,114
MAJOR LANGUAGES: Spanish and English
AREA: 19,730 sq mi; 51,100 sq km
LEADING EXPORTS: coffee, bananas, textiles, and sugar
CONTINENT: Northi America

Côte d'Ivoire

CAPITAL: Yamoussoukro
POPULATION: 14,791,257
MAJOR LANGUAGES: French, Dioula, and 59 other dialects
AREA: 124,507 sq mi; 322,460 sq km
LEADING EXPORTS: cocoa, coffee, tropical woods, and petroleum
CONTINENT: Africa

Croatia

CAPITAL: Zagreb
POPULATION: 4,665,821
MAJOR LANGUAGE: Serbo-Croatian
AREA: 21,830 sq mi; 56,538 sq km
LEADING EXPORTS: machinery and transportation equipment
CONTINENT: Europe

Cuba

CAPITAL: Havana
POPULATION: 10,937,635
MAJOR LANGUAGE: Spanish
AREA: 42,805 sq mi; 110,860 sq km
LEADING EXPORTS: sugar, nickel, shellfish, and tobacco
LOCATION: Caribbean Sea

Cyprus

CAPITAL: Nicosia
POPULATION: 736,636
MAJOR LANGUAGES: Greek, Turkish, and English
AREA: 3,572 sq mi; 9,250 sq km
LEADING EXPORTS: citrus, potatoes, grapes, wines, and cement
LOCATION: Mediterranean Sea

Czech Republic

CAPITAL: Prague
POPULATION: 10,432,774
MAJOR LANGUAGES: Czech and Slovak
AREA: 30,388 sq mi; 78,703 sq km
LEADING EXPORTS: manufactured goods
CONTINENT: Europe

Denmark

CAPITAL: Copenhagen
POPULATION: 5,199,437
MAJOR LANGUAGES: Danish, Faroese, Greenlandic, and German
AREA: 16,630 sq mi; 43,070 sq km
LEADING EXPORTS: meat and meat products, and dairy products
CONTINENT: Europe

Djibouti

CAPITAL: Djibouti
POPULATION: 421,320
MAJOR LANGUAGES: French, Arabic, Somali, and Afar
AREA: 8,495 sq mi; 22,000 sq km
LEADING EXPORTS: hides and skins, and coffee (in transit)
CONTINENT: Africa

Dominica

CAPITAL: Roseau
POPULATION: 82,608
MAJOR LANGUAGES: English and French patois
AREA: 290 sq mi; 750 sq km
LEADING EXPORTS: bananas, soap, bay oil, and vegetables
LOCATION: Caribbean Sea

Dominican Republic

CAPITAL: Santo Domingo
POPULATION: 7,511,263
MAJOR LANGUAGE: Spanish
AREA: 18,815 sq mi; 48,730 sq km
LEADING EXPORTS: ferronickel, sugar, gold, coffee, and cocoa
LOCATION: Caribbean Sea

Ecuador

CAPITAL: Quito
POPULATION: 10,890,950
MAJOR LANGUAGES: Spanish, Quechua, and various languages
AREA: 109,487 sq mi; 283,560 sq km
LEADING EXPORTS: petroleum, bananas, shrimp, and cocoa
CONTINENT: South America

Egypt

CAPITAL: Cairo
POPULATION: 62,359,623
MAJOR LANGUAGES: Arabic, English, and French
AREA: 386,675 sq mi; 1,001,450 sq km
LEADING EXPORTS: crude oil and petroleum products
CONTINENT: Africa

El Salvador

CAPITAL: San Salvador
POPULATION: 5,870,481
MAJOR LANGUAGES: Spanish and Nahua
AREA: 8,124 sq mi; 21,040 sq km
LEADING EXPORTS: coffee, sugar cane, and shrimp
CONTINENT: North America

Equatorial Guinea

CAPITAL: Malabo
POPULATION: 420,293
MAJOR LANGUAGES: Spanish, Pidgin English, Fang, Bubi, and Ibo
AREA: 10,831 sq mi; 28,050 sq km
LEADING EXPORTS: coffee, timber, and cocoa beans
CONTINENT: Africa

Eritrea

CAPITAL: Asmara
POPULATION: 3,578,709
MAJOR LANGUAGES: Tigre, Kunama, Cushitic dialects, Nora Bana, and Arabic
AREA: 46,844 sq mi; 121,320 sq km
LEADING EXPORTS: salt, hides, cement, and gum arabic
CONTINENT: Africa

Estonia

CAPITAL: Tallinn
POPULATION: 1,625,399
MAJOR LANGUAGES: Estonian, Latvian, Lithuanian, and Russian
AREA: 17,414 sq mi; 45,100 sq km
LEADING EXPORTS: textiles, food products, vehicles, and metals
CONTINENT: Europe

Ethiopia

CAPITAL: Addis Ababa
POPULATION: 55,979,018
MAJOR LANGUAGES: Amharic, Tigrinya, Orominga, Guaraginga, Somali, Arabic, English, and various languages
AREA: 435,201 sq mi; 1,127,127 sq km
LEADING EXPORTS: coffee, leather products, and gold
CONTINENT: Africa

Fiji

CAPITAL: Suva
POPULATION: 772,891
MAJOR LANGUAGES: English, Fijian, and Hindustani
AREA: 7,054 sq mi; 18,270 sq km
LEADING EXPORTS: sugar, clothing, gold, processed fish, and lumber
LOCATION: Pacific Ocean

Finland

CAPITAL: Helsinki
POPULATION: 5,085,206
MAJOR LANGUAGES: Finnish, Swedish, Lapp, and Russian
AREA: 130,132 sq mi; 337,030 sq km
LEADING EXPORTS: paper and pulp, machinery, and chemicals
CONTINENT: Europe

France

CAPITAL: Paris
POPULATION: 58,109,160
MAJOR LANGUAGES: French and regional dialects and languages
AREA: 211,217 sq mi; 547,030 sq km
LEADING EXPORTS: machinery and transportation equipment
CONTINENT: Europe

Gabon

CAPITAL: Libreville
POPULATION: 1,185,749
MAJOR LANGUAGES: French, Fang, Myene, Bateke, Bapounou/Eschira, and Bandjabi
AREA: 103,351 sq mi; 267,670 sq km
LEADING EXPORTS: crude oil, timber, manganese, and uranium
CONTINENT: Africa

The Gambia

CAPITAL: Banjul
POPULATION: 989,273
MAJOR LANGUAGES: English, Mandinka, Wolof, Fula, and various languages
AREA: 4,363 sq mi; 11,300 sq km
LEADING EXPORTS: peanuts and peanut products, and fish
CONTINENT: Africa

Georgia

CAPITAL: T'bilisi
POPULATION: 5,725,972
MAJOR LANGUAGES: Armenian, Azeri, Georgian, Russian, and various languages
AREA: 26,912 sq mi; 69,700 sq km
LEADING EXPORTS: citrus fruits, tea, and wine
CONTINENT: Asia

Germany

CAPITAL: Berlin
POPULATION: 81,337,541
MAJOR LANGUAGE: German
AREA: 137,808 sq mi; 356,910 sq km
LEADING EXPORTS: machines and machine tools, and chemicals
CONTINENT: Europe

Ghana

CAPITAL: Accra
POPULATION: 17,763,138
MAJOR LANGUAGES: English, Akan, Moshi-Dagomba, Ewe, Ga, and various languages
AREA: 92,104 sq mi; 238,540 sq km
LEADING EXPORTS: cocoa, gold, timber, tuna, and bauxite
CONTINENT: Africa

Greece

CAPITAL: Athens
POPULATION: 10,647,511
MAJOR LANGUAGES: Greek, English, and French
AREA: 50,944 sq mi; 131,940 sq km
LEADING EXPORTS: manufactured goods, foodstuffs, and fuels
CONTINENT: Europe

Grenada

CAPITAL: Saint George's
POPULATION: 94,486
MAJOR LANGUAGES: English and French patois
AREA: 131 sq mi; 340 sq km
LEADING EXPORTS: bananas, cocoa, nutmeg, and fruits and vegetables
LOCATION: Caribbean Sea

Guatemala

CAPITAL: Guatemala
POPULATION: 10,998,602
MAJOR LANGUAGES: Spanish, Quiche, Cakchiquel, Kekchi, and various languages and dialects
AREA: 42,044 sq mi; 108,890 sq km
LEADING EXPORTS: coffee, sugar, bananas, cardamom, and beef
CONTINENT: North America

Guinea

CAPITAL: Conakry
POPULATION: 6,549,336
MAJOR LANGUAGES: French and various languages
AREA: 94,930 sq mi; 245,860 sq km
LEADING EXPORTS: bauxite, alumina, diamonds, gold, and coffee
CONTINENT: Africa

Guinea Bissau

CAPITAL: Bissau
POPULATION: 1,124,537
MAJOR LANGUAGES: Portuguese, Criolo, and various languages
AREA: 13,946 sq mi; 36,210 sq km
LEADING EXPORTS: cashews, fish, peanuts, and palm kernels
CONTINENT: Africa

Guyana

CAPITAL: Georgetown
POPULATION: 723,774
MAJOR LANGUAGES: English and various dialects
AREA: 83,003 sq mi; 214,970 sq km
LEADING EXPORTS: sugar, bauxite/alumina, rice, and shrimp
CONTINENT: South America

Haiti

CAPITAL: Port-au-Prince
POPULATION: 6,539,983
MAJOR LANGUAGES: French and Creole
AREA: 8,784 sq mi; 22,750 sq km
LEADING EXPORTS: light manufactures and coffee
LOCATION: Caribbean Sea

Holy See (Vatican City)

CAPITAL: Vatican City
POPULATION: 830
MAJOR LANGUAGES: Italian, Latin, and various languages
AREA: 17 sq mi; 44 sq km
LEADING EXPORTS: none
CONTINENT: Europe

Honduras

CAPITAL: Tegucigalpa
POPULATION: 5,549,743
MAJOR LANGUAGES: Spanish and various dialects
AREA: 43,280 sq mi; 112,090 sq km
LEADING EXPORTS: bananas, coffee, shrimp, lobsters, and minerals
CONTINENT: North America

Hungary

CAPITAL: Budapest
POPULATION: 10,318,838
MAJOR LANGUAGES: Hungarian and various languages
AREA: 35,920 sq mi; 93,030 sq km
LEADING EXPORTS: raw materials and semi-finished goods
CONTINENT: Europe

Iceland

CAPITAL: Reykjavik
POPULATION: 265,998
MAJOR LANGUAGE: Icelandic
AREA: 39,770 sq mi; 103,000 sq km
LEADING EXPORTS: fish and fish products, and animal products
LOCATION: Atlantic Ocean

India

CAPITAL: New Delhi
POPULATION: 936,545,814
MAJOR LANGUAGES: English, Hindi, Bengali, Telugu, Marathi, Tamil, Urdu, Gujarati, Malayam, Kannada, Oriya, Punjabi, Assamese, Kashmiri, Sindhi, Sanskrit, and Hindustani (all official)
AREA: 1,269,389 sq mi; 3,287,590 sq km
LEADING EXPORTS: clothing, and gems and jewelry
CONTINENT: Asia

Indonesia

CAPITAL: Jakarta
POPULATION: 203,583,886
MAJOR LANGUAGES: Bahasa Indonesia, English, Dutch, Javanese, and various dialects
AREA: 741,052 sq mi; 1,919,251 sq km
LEADING EXPORTS: manufactures, fuels, and foodstuffs
CONTINENT: Asia

Iran

CAPITAL: Tehran
POPULATION: 64,625,455
MAJOR LANGUAGES: Farsi (official) and Turkic languages
AREA: 634,562 sq mi; 1,643,452 sq km
LEADING EXPORTS: petroleum, carpets, fruit, nuts, and hides
CONTINENT: Asia

Iraq

CAPITAL: Baghdad
POPULATION: 20,643,769
MAJOR LANGUAGES: Arabic, Kurdish, Assyrian, and Armenian
AREA: 168,760 sq mi; 437,072 sq km
LEADING EXPORTS: crude oil and refined products, and fertilizers
CONTINENT: Asia

Ireland

CAPITAL: Dublin
POPULATION: 3,550,448
MAJOR LANGUAGES: Irish Gaelic and English
AREA: 27,136 sq mi; 70,280 sq km
LEADING EXPORTS: chemicals and data processing equipment
CONTINENT: Europe

Israel

CAPITAL: Jerusalem
POPULATION: 7,566,447
MAJOR LANGUAGES: Hebrew, Arabic, and English
AREA: 10,421 sq mi; 26,990 sq km
LEADING EXPORTS: machinery and equipment, and cut diamonds
CONTINENT: Asia

Italy

CAPITAL: Rome
POPULATION: 58,261,971
MAJOR LANGUAGES: Italian, German, French, and Slovene
AREA: 116,310 sq mi; 301,230 sq km
LEADING EXPORTS: metals, and textiles and clothing
CONTINENT: Europe

Jamaica

CAPITAL: Kingston
POPULATION: 2,574,291
MAJOR LANGUAGES: English and Creole
AREA: 4,243 sq mi; 10,990 sq km
LEADING EXPORTS: alumina, bauxite, sugar, bananas, and rum
LOCATION: Caribbean Sea

Japan

CAPITAL: Tokyo
POPULATION: 125,506,492
MAJOR LANGUAGE: Japanese
AREA: 145,888 sq mi; 377,835 sq km
LEADING EXPORTS: machinery, motor vehicles, and electronics
CONTINENT: Asia

Jordan

CAPITAL: Amman
POPULATION: 4,100,709
MAJOR LANGUAGES: Arabic and English
AREA: 34,447 sq mi; 89,213 sq km
LEADING EXPORTS: phosphates, fertilizers, and potash
CONTINENT: Asia

Kazakstan

CAPITAL: Almaty
POPULATION: 17,376,615
MAJOR LANGUAGES: Kazak and Russian
AREA: 1,049,191 sq mi; 2,717,300 sq km
LEADING EXPORTS: oil, and ferrous and nonferrous metals
CONTINENT: Asia

Kenya

CAPITAL: Nairobi
POPULATION: 28,817,227
MAJOR LANGUAGES: English, Swahili, and various languages
AREA: 224,970 sq mi; 582,650 sq km
LEADING EXPORTS: tea, coffee, and petroleum products
CONTINENT: Africa

Kiribati

CAPITAL: Tarawa
POPULATION: 79,386
MAJOR LANGUAGES: English and Gilbertese
AREA: 277 sq mi; 717 sq km
LEADING EXPORTS: copra, seaweed, and fish
LOCATION: Pacific Ocean

Korea, North

CAPITAL: P'yongyang
POPULATION: 23,486,550
MAJOR LANGUAGE: Korean
AREA: 46,542 sq mi; 120,540 sq km
LEADING EXPORTS: minerals and metallurgical products
CONTINENT: Asia

Korea, South

CAPITAL: Seoul
POPULATION: 45,553,882
MAJOR LANGUAGES: Korean and English
AREA: 38,025 sq mi; 98,480 sq km
LEADING EXPORTS: electronic and electrical equipment
CONTINENT: Asia

Kuwait

CAPITAL: Kuwait
POPULATION: 1,817,397
MAJOR LANGUAGES: Arabic and English
AREA: 6,881 sq mi; 17,820 sq km
LEADING EXPORT: oil
CONTINENT: Asia

Kyrgyzstan

CAPITAL: Bishkek
POPULATION: 4,769,877
MAJOR LANGUAGES: Kyrgyz and Russian
AREA: 76,644 sq mi; 198,500 sq km
LEADING EXPORTS: wool, chemicals, cotton, metals, and shoes
CONTINENT: Asia

Laos

CAPITAL: Vientiane
POPULATION: 4,837,237
MAJOR LANGUAGES: Lao, French, English, and various languages
AREA: 91,432 sq mi; 236,800 sq km
LEADING EXPORTS: electricity, wood products, coffee, and tin
CONTINENT: Asia

Latvia

CAPITAL: Riga
POPULATION: 2,762,899
MAJOR LANGUAGES: Lettish, Lithuanian, Russian, and various languages
AREA: 24,750 sq mi; 64,100 sq km
LEADING EXPORTS: oil products, timber, and ferrous metals
CONTINENT: Europe

Lebanon

CAPITAL: Beirut
POPULATION: 3,695,921
MAJOR LANGUAGES: Arabic, French, Armenian, and English
AREA: 4,016 sq mi; 10,400 sq km
LEADING EXPORTS: agricultural products, chemicals, and textiles
CONTINENT: Asia

Lesotho

CAPITAL: Maseru
POPULATION: 1,992,960
MAJOR LANGUAGES: Sesotho, English, Zulu, and Xhosa
AREA: 11,719 sq mi; 30,350 sq km
LEADING EXPORTS: wool, mohair, wheat, cattle, and peas
CONTINENT: Africa

Liberia

CAPITAL: Monrovia
POPULATION: 3,073,245
MAJOR LANGUAGES: English and Niger-Congo
AREA: 43,002 sq mi; 111,370 sq km
LEADING EXPORTS: iron ore, rubber, timber, and coffee
CONTINENT: Africa

Libya

CAPITAL: Tripoli
POPULATION: 5,248,401
MAJOR LANGUAGES: Arabic, Italian, and English
AREA: 679,385 sq mi; 1,759,540 sq km
LEADING EXPORTS: crude oil and refined petroleum products
CONTINENT: Africa

Liechtenstein

CAPITAL: Vaduz
POPULATION: 30,654
MAJOR LANGUAGES: German and Alemannic
AREA: 62 sq mi; 160 sq km
LEADING EXPORTS: small specialty machinery and dental products
CONTINENT: Europe

Lithuania

CAPITAL: Vilnius
POPULATION: 3,876,396
MAJOR LANGUAGES: Lithuanian, Polish, and Russian
AREA: 25,175 sq mi; 65,200 sq km
LEADING EXPORTS: electronics, petroleum products, and food
CONTINENT: Europe

Luxembourg

CAPITAL: Luxembourg
POPULATION: 404,660
MAJOR LANGUAGES: Luxembourgisch, German, French, and English
AREA: 998 sq mi; 2,586 sq km
LEADING EXPORTS: finished steel products and chemicals
CONTINENT: Europe

Macedonia

CAPITAL: Skopje
POPULATION: 2,159,503
MAJOR LANGUAGES: Macedonian, Albanian, Turkish, Serb, Gypsy, and various languages
AREA: 9,781 sq mi; 25,333 sq km
LEADING EXPORTS: manufactured goods and machinery
CONTINENT: Europe

Madagascar

CAPITAL: Antananarivo
POPULATION: 13,862,325
MAJOR LANGUAGES: French and Malagasy
AREA: 226,665 sq mi; 587,040 sq km
LEADING EXPORTS: coffee, vanilla, cloves, shellfish, and sugar
CONTINENT: Africa

Malawi

CAPITAL: Lilongwe
POPULATION: 9,808,384
MAJOR LANGUAGES: English, Chichewa, and various languages
AREA: 45,747 sq mi; 118,480 sq km
LEADING EXPORTS: tobacco, tea, sugar, coffee, and peanuts
CONTINENT: Africa

Malaysia

CAPITAL: Kuala Lumpur
POPULATION: 19,723,587
MAJOR LANGUAGES: Malay, English, Mandarin, Tamil, Chinese dialects, and various languages and dialects
AREA: 127,322 sq mi; 329,750 sq km
LEADING EXPORTS: electronic equipment
CONTINENT: Asia

Maldives

CAPITAL: Male
POPULATION: 261,310
MAJOR LANGUAGES: Divehi dialect and English
AREA: 116 sq mi; 300 sq km
LEADING EXPORTS: fish and clothing
CONTINENT: Asia

Mali

CAPITAL: Bamako
POPULATION: 9,375,132
MAJOR LANGUAGES: French, Bambara, and various languages
AREA: 478,783 sq mi; 1,240,000 sq km
LEADING EXPORTS: cotton, livestock, and gold
CONTINENT: Africa

Malta

CAPITAL: Valletta
POPULATION: 369,609
MAJOR LANGUAGES: Maltese and English
AREA: 124 sq mi; 320 sq km
LEADING EXPORTS: machinery and transportation equipment
LOCATION Mediterranean Sea

Marshall Islands

CAPITAL: Majuro
POPULATION: 56,157
MAJOR LANGUAGES: English, Marshallese dialects, and Japanese
AREA: 70 sq mi; 181.3 sq km
LEADING EXPORTS: coconut oil, fish, live animals, and trichus shells
LOCATION: Pacific Ocean

Mauritania

CAPITAL: Nouakchott
POPULATION: 2,263,202
MAJOR LANGUAGES: Hasaniya Arabic, Wolof, Pular, and Soninke
AREA: 397,969 sq mi; 1,030,700 sq km
LEADING EXPORTS: iron ore, and fish and fish products
CONTINENT: Africa

Mauritius

CAPITAL: Port Louis
POPULATION: 1,127,068
MAJOR LANGUAGES: English (official), Creole, French, Hindi, Urdu, Hakka, and Bojpoori
AREA: 718 sq mi; 1,860 sq km
LEADING EXPORTS: textiles, sugar, and light manufactures
LOCATION: Indian Ocean

Mayotte

CAPITAL: Mamoutzou
POPULATION: 97,088
MAJOR LANGUAGES: Mahorian and French
AREA: 145 sq mi; 375 sq km
LEADING EXPORTS: ylang-ylang and vanilla
CONTINENT: Africa

Mexico

CAPITAL: Mexico City
POPULATION: 93,985,848
MAJOR LANGUAGES: Spanish and Mayan dialects
AREA: 761,632 sq mi; 1,972,550 sq km
LEADING EXPORTS: crude oil, oil products, coffee, and silver
CONTINENT: North America

Micronesia

CAPITAL: Federated states of Kolonia (on the Island of Pohnpei)
*a new capital is being built about 10 km southwest in the Palikir Valley
POPULATION: 122,950
MAJOR LANGUAGES: English, Turkese, Pohnpeian, Yapese, and Kosrean
AREA: 271 sq mi; 702 sq km
LEADING EXPORTS: fish, copra, bananas, and black pepper
LOCATION: Pacific Ocean

Moldova

CAPITAL: Chisinau
POPULATION: 4,489,657
MAJOR LANGUAGES: Moldovan (official), Russian, and Gagauz dialect
AREA: 13,012 sq mi; 33,700 sq km
LEADING EXPORTS: foodstuffs, wine, and tobacco
CONTINENT: Europe

Monaco

CAPITAL: Monaco
POPULATION: 31,515
MAJOR LANGUAGES: French (official), English, Italian, and Monegasque
AREA: .73 sq mi; 1.9 sq km
LEADING EXPORTS: exports through France
CONTINENT: Europe

Mongolia

CAPITAL: Ulaanbaatar
POPULATION: 2,493,615
MAJOR LANGUAGES: Khalkha Mongol, Turkic, Russian, and Chinese
AREA: 604,270 sq mi; 1,565,000 sq km
LEADING EXPORTS: copper, livestock, animal products, and cashmere
CONTINENT: Asia

Morocco

CAPITAL: Rabat
POPULATION: 29,168,848
MAJOR LANGUAGES: Arabic (official), Berber dialects, and French
AREA: 172,420 sq mi; 446,550 sq km
LEADING EXPORTS: food and beverages
CONTINENT: Africa

Mozambique

CAPITAL: Maputo
POPULATION: 18,115,250
MAJOR LANGUAGES: Portuguese and various dialects
AREA: 309,506 sq mi; 801,590 sq km
LEADING EXPORTS: shrimp, cashews, cotton, sugar, copra, and citrus
CONTINENT: Africa

Myanmar (Burma)

CAPITAL: Rangoon
POPULATION: 45,103,809
MAJOR LANGUAGE: Burmese
AREA: 261,979 sq mi; 678,500 sq km
LEADING EXPORTS: pulses and beans, teak, rice, and hardwood
CONTINENT: Asia

Namibia

CAPITAL: Windhoek
POPULATION: 1,651,545
MAJOR LANGUAGES: English (official), Afrikaans, German, Oshivambo, Herero, Nama, and various languages
AREA: 318,707 sq mi; 825,418 sq km
LEADING EXPORTS: diamonds, copper, gold, zinc, and lead
CONTINENT: Africa

Nauru

CAPITAL: Government offices in Yaren District
POPULATION: 10,149
MAJOR LANGUAGES: Nauruan and English
AREA: 8 sq mi; 21 sq km
LEADING EXPORTS: phosphates
LOCATION: Pacific Ocean

Nepal

CAPITAL: Kathmandu
POPULATION: 21,560,869
MAJOR LANGUAGES: Nepali (official) and 20 various languages divided into numerous dialects
AREA: 54,365 sq mi; 140,800 sq km
LEADING EXPORTS: carpets, clothing, and leather goods
CONTINENT: Asia

Netherlands

CAPITAL: Amsterdam
POPULATION: 15,452,903
MAJOR LANGUAGE: Dutch
AREA: 14,414 sq mi; 37,330 sq km
LEADING EXPORTS: metal products and chemicals
CONTINENT: Europe

New Caledonia

CAPITAL: Noumea
POPULATION: 184,552
MAJOR LANGUAGES: French and 28 Melanesian-Polynesian dialects
AREA: 7,359 sq mi; 19,060 sq km
LEADING EXPORTS: nickel metal and nickel ore
LOCATION: Pacific Ocean

New Zealand

CAPITAL: Wellington
POPULATION: 3,407,277
MAJOR LANGUAGES: English and Maori
AREA: 103,741 sq mi; 268,680 sq km
LEADING EXPORTS: wool, lamb, mutton, beef, fish, and cheese
LOCATION: Pacific Ocean

Nicaragua

CAPITAL: Managua
POPULATION: 4,206,353
MAJOR LANGUAGES: Spanish (official), English, and various languages
AREA: 50,000 sq mi; 129,494 sq km
LEADING EXPORTS: meat, coffee, cotton, sugar, seafood, and gold
CONTINENT: North America

Niger

CAPITAL: Niamey
POPULATION: 9,280,208
MAJOR LANGUAGES: French (official), Hausa, and Djerma
AREA: 489,208 sq mi; 1,267,000 sq km
LEADING EXPORTS: uranium ore and livestock products
CONTINENT: Africa

Nigeria

CAPITAL: Abuja
POPULATION: 101,232,251
MAJOR LANGUAGES: English (official), Hausa, Yoruba, Ibo, and Fulani
AREA: 356,682 sq mi; 923,770 sq km
LEADING EXPORTS: oil, cocoa, and rubber
CONTINENT: Africa

Niue

CAPITAL: (Free association with New Zealand)
POPULATION: 1,837
MAJOR LANGUAGES: Polynesian and English
AREA: 100 sq mi; 260 sq km
LEADING EXPORTS: canned coconut cream, copra, and honey
LOCATION: Pacific Ocean

Norway

CAPITAL: Oslo
POPULATION: 4,330,951
MAJOR LANGUAGES: Norwegian (official), Lapp, and Finnish
AREA: 125,186 sq mi; 324,220 sq km
LEADING EXPORTS: petroleum and petroleum products
CONTINENT: Europe

Oman

CAPITAL: Muscat
POPULATION: 2,125,089
MAJOR LANGUAGES: Arabic (official), English, Baluchi, Urdu, and Indian dialects
AREA: 82,034 sq mi; 212,460 sq km
LEADING EXPORTS: petroleum, re-exports, and fish
CONTINENT: Asia

Pakistan

CAPITAL: Islamabad
POPULATION: 131,541,920
MAJOR LANGUAGES: Urdu (official), English (official), Punjabi, Sindhi, Pashtu, Urdu, Balochi, and other languages
AREA: 310,414 sq mi; 803,940 sq km
LEADING EXPORTS: cotton, textiles, clothing, rice, and leather
CONTINENT: Asia

Palau

CAPITAL: Koror
POPULATION: 16,661
MAJOR LANGUAGES: English (official), Sonsorolese, Angaur, Japanese, Tobi, and Palauan
AREA: 177 sq mi; 458 sq km
LEADING EXPORTS: trochus, tuna, copra, and handicrafts
LOCATION: Pacific Ocean

Panama

CAPITAL: Panama
POPULATION: 2,680,903
MAJOR LANGUAGES: Spanish (official) and English
AREA: 30,194 sq mi; 78,200 sq km
LEADING EXPORTS: bananas, shrimp, sugar, clothing, and coffee
CONTINENT: North America

Papua New Guinea

CAPITAL: Port Moresby
POPULATION: 4,294,750
MAJOR LANGUAGES: English, pidgin English, and Motu
AREA: 178,266 sq mi; 461,690 sq km
LEADING EXPORTS: gold, copper ore, oil, logs, and palm oil
LOCATION: Pacific Ocean

Paraguay

CAPITAL: Asuncion
POPULATION: 5,358,198
MAJOR LANGUAGES: Spanish (official) and Guarani
AREA: 157,052 sq mi; 406,750 sq km
LEADING EXPORTS: cotton, soybeans, timber, and vegetable oils
CONTINENT: South America

Peru

CAPITAL: Lima
POPULATION: 24,087,372
MAJOR LANGUAGES: Spanish (official), Quechua (official), and Aymara
AREA: 496,243 sq mi; 1,285,220 sq km
LEADING EXPORTS: copper, zinc, and fish meal
CONTINENT: South America

Philippines

CAPITAL: Manila
POPULATION: 73,265,584
MAJOR LANGUAGES: Pilipino and English (official)
AREA: 115,834 sq mi; 300,000 sq km
LEADING EXPORTS: electronics, textiles, and coconut products
CONTINENT: Asia

Poland

CAPITAL: Warsaw
POPULATION: 38,792,442
MAJOR LANGUAGE: Polish
AREA: 120,731 sq mi; 312,680 sq km
LEADING EXPORTS: intermediate goods
CONTINENT: Europe

Portugal

CAPITAL: Lisbon
POPULATION: 10,562,388
MAJOR LANGUAGE: Portuguese
AREA: 35,553 sq mi; 92,080 sq km
LEADING EXPORTS: clothing and footwear, and machinery
CONTINENT: Europe

Qatar

CAPITAL: Doha
POPULATION: 533,916
MAJOR LANGUAGES: Arabic (official) and English
AREA: 4,247 sq mi; 11,000 sq km
LEADING EXPORTS: petroleum products, steel, and fertilizers
CONTINENT: Asia

Romania

CAPITAL: Bucharest
POPULATION: 23,198,330
MAJOR LANGUAGES: Romanian, Hungarian, and German
AREA: 91,702 sq mi; 237,500 sq km
LEADING EXPORTS: metals and metal products, and mineral products
CONTINENT: Europe

Russia

CAPITAL: Moscow
POPULATION: 149,909,089
MAJOR LANGUAGES: Russian and various languages
AREA: 6,952,996 sq mi; 17,075,200 sq km
LEADING EXPORTS: petroleum and petroleum products
CONTINENT: Europe and Asia

Rwanda

CAPITAL: Kigali
POPULATION: 8,605,307
MAJOR LANGUAGES: Kinyarwanda (official), French (official), and Kiswahili
AREA: 10,170 sq mi; 26,340 sq km
LEADING EXPORTS: coffee, tea, cassiterite, and wolframite
CONTINENT: Africa

Saint Kitts and Nevis

CAPITAL: Basseterre
POPULATION: 40,992
MAJOR LANGUAGE: English
AREA: 104 sq mi; 269 sq km
LEADING EXPORTS: machinery, food, and electronics
LOCATION: Caribbean Sea

Saint Lucia

CAPITAL: Castries
POPULATION: 156,050
MAJOR LANGUAGES: English and French patois
AREA: 239 sq mi; 620 sq km
LEADING EXPORTS: bananas, clothing, cocoa, and vegetables
LOCATION: Caribbean Sea

Saint Vincent and the Grenadines

CAPITAL: Kingstown
POPULATION: 117,344
MAJOR LANGUAGES: English and French patois
AREA: 131 sq mi; 340 sq km
LEADING EXPORTS: bananas, and eddoes and dasheen (taro)
LOCATION: Caribbean Sea

San Marino

CAPITAL: San Marino
POPULATION: 24,313
MAJOR LANGUAGE: Italian
AREA: 23 sq mi; 60 sq km
LEADING EXPORTS: building stone, lime, wood, and chestnuts
CONTINENT: Europe

Sao Tome and Principe

CAPITAL: Sao Tome
POPULATION: 140,423
MAJOR LANGUAGE: Portuguese (official)
AREA: 371 sq mi; 960 sq km
LEADING EXPORTS: cocoa, copra, coffee, and palm oil
CONTINENT: Africa

Saudi Arabia

CAPITAL: Riyadh
POPULATION: 18,729,576
MAJOR LANGUAGE: Arabic
AREA: 757,011 sq mi; 1,960,582 sq km
LEADING EXPORTS: petroleum and petroleum products
CONTINENT: Asia

Senegal

CAPITAL: Dakar
POPULATION: 9,007,080
MAJOR LANGUAGES: French (official), Wolof, Pulaar, Diola, and Mandingo
AREA: 75,752 sq mi; 196,190 sq km
LEADING EXPORTS: fish, ground nuts, and petroleum products
CONTINENT: Africa

Serbia and Montenegro

CAPITAL: Belgrade
POPULATION: 11,101,833
MAJOR LANGUAGES: Serbo-Croatian and Albanian
AREA: 39,436 sq mi; 102,350 sq km
LEADING EXPORTS: none
CONTINENT: Europe

Seychelles

CAPITAL: Victoria
POPULATION: 72,709
MAJOR LANGUAGES: English (official), French (official), and Creole
AREA: 176 sq mi; 455 sq km
LEADING EXPORTS: fish, cinnamon bark, and copra
CONTINENT: Africa

Sierra Leone

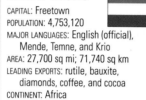

CAPITAL: Freetown
POPULATION: 4,753,120
MAJOR LANGUAGES: English (official), Mende, Temne, and Krio
AREA: 27,700 sq mi; 71,740 sq km
LEADING EXPORTS: rutile, bauxite, diamonds, coffee, and cocoa
CONTINENT: Africa

Singapore

CAPITAL: Singapore
POPULATION: 2,890,468
MAJOR LANGUAGES: Chinese, Malay, Tamil, and English
AREA: 244 sq mi; 633 sq km
LEADING EXPORTS: computer equipment
CONTINENT: Asia

Slovakia

CAPITAL: Bratislava
POPULATION: 5,432,383
MAJOR LANGUAGES: Slovak and Hungarian
AREA: 18,860 sq mi; 48,845 sq km
LEADING EXPORTS: machinery and transportation equipment
CONTINENT: Europe

Slovenia

CAPITAL: Ljubljana
POPULATION: 2,051,522
MAJOR LANGUAGES: Slovenian, Serbo-Croatian, and various languages
AREA: 7,837 sq mi; 20,296 sq km
LEADING EXPORTS: machinery and transportation equipment
CONTINENT: Europe

Solomon Islands

CAPITAL: Honiara
POPULATION: 399,206
MAJOR LANGUAGES: Melanesian pidgin and English
AREA: 10,985 sq mi; 28,450 sq km
LEADING EXPORTS: fish, timber, palm oil, cocoa, and copra
LOCATION: Pacific Ocean

Somalia

CAPITAL: Mogadishu
POPULATION: 7,347,554
MAJOR LANGUAGES: Somali (official), Arabic, Italian, and English
AREA: 246,210 sq mi; 637,660 sq km
LEADING EXPORTS: bananas, live animals, fish, and hides
CONTINENT: Africa

South Africa

CAPITAL: Pretoria (administrative), Cape Town (legislative), Bloemfontein (judicial)
POPULATION: 45,095,459
MAJOR LANGUAGES: Afrikaans, English, Ndebele, Pedi, Sotho, Swazi, Tsonga, Tswana, Venda, Xhosa, and Zulu (all official)
AREA: 471,027 sq mi; 1,219,912 sq km
LEADING EXPORTS: gold, other minerals and metals, and food
CONTINENT: Africa

Spain

CAPITAL: Madrid
POPULATION: 39,404,348
MAJOR LANGUAGES: Spanish, Catalan, Galician, and Basque
AREA: 194,892 sq mi; 504,750 sq km
LEADING EXPORTS: cars and trucks, and semifinished goods
CONTINENT: Europe

Sri Lanka

CAPITAL: Colombo
POPULATION: 18,342,660
MAJOR LANGUAGES: Sinhala (official) and Tamil
AREA: 25,333 sq mi; 65,610 sq km
LEADING EXPORTS: garments and textiles, teas, and diamonds
CONTINENT: Asia

Sudan

CAPITAL: Khartoum
POPULATION: 30,120,420
MAJOR LANGUAGES: Arabic (official), Nubian, Ta Bedawie, Nilotic, Nilo-Hamitic, and Sudanic dialects
AREA: 967,532 sq mi; 2,505,810 sq km
LEADING EXPORTS: gum arabic, livestock/meat, and cotton
CONTINENT: Africa

Suriname

CAPITAL: Paramaribo
POPULATION: 429,544
MAJOR LANGUAGES: Dutch (official), English, Sranang, Tongo, Hindustani, and Japanese
AREA: 63,041 sq mi; 163,270 sq km
LEADING EXPORTS: alumina, aluminum, and shrimp and fish
CONTINENT: South America

Swaziland

CAPITAL: Mbabane
POPULATION: 966,977
MAJOR LANGUAGES: English (official) and SiSwati (official)
AREA: 6,641 sq mi; 17,360 sq km
LEADING EXPORTS: sugar, edible concentrates, and wood pulp
CONTINENT: Africa

Sweden

CAPITAL: Stockholm
POPULATION: 8,821,759
MAJOR LANGUAGES: Swedish, Lapp, and Finnish
AREA: 173,738 sq mi; 449,964 sq km
LEADING EXPORTS: machinery, motor vehicles, and paper products
CONTINENT: Europe

Switzerland

CAPITAL: Bern
POPULATION: 7,084,984
MAJOR LANGUAGES: German, French, Italian, Romansch, and various languages
AREA: 15,943 sq mi; 41,290 sq km
LEADING EXPORTS: machinery and equipment
CONTINENT: Europe

Syria

CAPITAL: Damascus
POPULATION: 15,451,917
MAJOR LANGUAGES: Arabic (official), Kurdish, Armenian, Aramaic, Circassian, and French
AREA: 71,501 sq mi; 185,180 sq km
LEADING EXPORTS: petroleum, textiles, cotton, and fruits
CONTINENT: Asia

Taiwan

CAPITAL: Taipei
POPULATION: 21,500,583
MAJOR LANGUAGES: Mandarin Chinese (official), Taiwanese, and Hakka dialects
AREA: 13,892 sq mi; 35,980 sq km
LEADING EXPORTS: electrical machinery and electronics
CONTINENT: Asia

Tajikistan

CAPITAL: Dushanbe
POPULATION: 6,155,474
MAJOR LANGUAGES: Tajik (official) and Russian
AREA: 55,253 sq mi; 143,100 sq km
LEADING EXPORTS: cotton, aluminum, fruits, and vegetable oil
CONTINENT: Asia

Tanzania

CAPITAL: Dar Es Salaam
POPULATION: 28,701,077
MAJOR LANGUAGES: Swahili, English, and various languages
AREA: 364,914 sq mi; 945,090 sq km
LEADING EXPORTS: coffee, cotton, tobacco, tea, and cashew nuts
CONTINENT: Africa

Thailand

CAPITAL: Bangkok
POPULATION: 60,271,300
MAJOR LANGUAGES: Thai and English
AREA: 198,463 sq mi; 511,770 sq km
LEADING EXPORTS: machinery and manufactures
CONTINENT: Asia

Togo

CAPITAL: Lome
POPULATION: 4,410,370
MAJOR LANGUAGES: French, Ewe and Mina, Dagomba, and Kabye
AREA: 21,927 sq mi; 56,790 sq km
LEADING EXPORTS: phosphates, cotton, cocoa, and coffee
CONTINENT: Africa

Tonga

CAPITAL: Nukualofa
POPULATION: 105,600
MAJOR LANGUAGES: Tongan and English
AREA: 289 sq mi; 748 sq km
LEADING EXPORTS: squash, vanilla, fish, root crops, and coconut oil
LOCATION: Pacific Ocean

Trinidad and Tobago

CAPITAL: Port-of-Spain
POPULATION: 1,271,159
MAJOR LANGUAGES: English, Hindu, French, and Spanish
AREA: 1,981 sq mi; 5,130 sq km
LEADING EXPORTS: petroleum and petroleum products
LOCATION: Caribbean Sea

Tunisia

CAPITAL: Tunis
POPULATION: 8,879,845
MAJOR LANGUAGES: Arabic and French
AREA: 63,172 sq mi; 163,610 sq km
LEADING EXPORTS: hydrocarbons and agricultural products
CONTINENT: Africa

Turkey

CAPITAL: Ankara
POPULATION: 63,405,526
MAJOR LANGUAGES: Turkish, Kurdish, and Arabic
AREA: 301,394 sq mi; 780,580 sq km
LEADING EXPORTS: manufactured products, and foodstuffs
CONTINENT: Europe and Asia

Turkmenistan

CAPITAL: Ashgabat
POPULATION: 4,075,316
MAJOR LANGUAGES: Turkmen, Russian, Uzbek, and various languages
AREA: 188,463 sq mi; 488,100 sq km
LEADING EXPORTS: natural gas, cotton, and petroleum products
CONTINENT: Asia

Tuvalu

CAPITAL: Fongafale, on Funafuti atoll
POPULATION: 9,991
MAJOR LANGUAGES: Tuvaluan and English
AREA: 10 sq mi; 26 sq km
LEADING EXPORT: copra
LOCATION: Pacific Ocean

Uganda

CAPITAL: Kampala
POPULATION: 19,573,262
MAJOR LANGUAGES: English, Luganda, Swahili, Bantu languages, and Nilotic languages
AREA: 91,139 sq mi; 236,040 sq km
LEADING EXPORTS: coffee, cotton, and tea
CONTINENT: Africa

Ukraine

CAPITAL: Kiev
POPULATION: 51,867,828
MAJOR LANGUAGES: Ukranian, Russian, Romanian, Polish, and Hungarian
AREA: 233,098 sq mi; 603,700 sq km
LEADING EXPORTS: coal, electric power, and metals
CONTINENT: Europe

United Arab Emirates

CAPITAL: Abu Dhabi
POPULATION: 2,924,594
MAJOR LANGUAGES: Arabic, Persian, English, Hindi, and Urdu
AREA: 29,183 sq mi; 75,581 sq km
LEADING EXPORTS: crude oil, natural gas, re-exports, and dried fish
CONTINENT: Asia

United Kingdom

CAPITAL: London
POPULATION: 58,295,119
MAJOR LANGUAGES: English, Welsh, and Scottish Gaelic
AREA: 94,529 sq mi; 244,820 sq km
LEADING EXPORTS: manufactured goods, machinery, and fuels
CONTINENT: Europe

United States

CAPITAL: Washington, D.C.
POPULATION: 263,814,032
MAJOR LANGUAGES: English and Spanish
AREA: 3,618,908 sq mi; 9,372,610 sq km
LEADING EXPORTS: capital goods and automobiles
CONTINENT: North America

Uruguay

CAPITAL: Montevideo
POPULATION: 3,222,716
MAJOR LANGUAGES: Spanish and Brazilero
AREA: 68,041 sq mi; 176,220 sq km
LEADING EXPORTS: wool and textile manufactures
CONTINENT: South America

Uzbekistan

CAPITAL: Tashkent
POPULATION: 23,089,261
MAJOR LANGUAGES: Uzbek, Russian, Tajik, various languages
AREA: 172,748 sq mi; 447,400 sq km
LEADING EXPORTS: cotton, gold, natural gas, and minerals
CONTINENT: Asia

Vanuatu

CAPITAL: Port-Vila
POPULATION: 173,648
MAJOR LANGUAGES: English, French, pidgin, and Bislama
AREA: 5,699 sq mi; 14,760 sq km
LEADING EXPORTS: copra, beef, cocoa, timber, and coffee
LOCATION: Pacific Ocean

Venezuela

CAPITAL: Caracas
POPULATION: 21,004,773
MAJOR LANGUAGES: Spanish and various languages
AREA: 352,156 sq mi; 912,050 sq km
LEADING EXPORTS: petroleum, bauxite and aluminum, and steel
CONTINENT: South America

Vietnam

CAPITAL: Hanoi
POPULATION: 74,393,324
MAJOR LANGUAGES: Vietnamese, French, Chinese, English, Khmer, and various languages
AREA: 127,248 sq mi; 329,560 sq km
LEADING EXPORTS: petroleum, rice, and agricultural products
CONTINENT: Asia

Western Samoa

CAPITAL: Apia
POPULATION: 209,360
MAJOR LANGUAGES: Samoan and English
AREA: 1,104 sq mi; 2,860 sq km
LEADING EXPORTS: coconut oil and cream, taro, copra, and cocoa
LOCATION: Pacific Ocean

Yemen

CAPITAL: Sanaa
POPULATION: 14,728,474
MAJOR LANGUAGE: Arabic
AREA: 203,857 sq mi; 527,970 sq km
LEADING EXPORTS: crude oil, cotton, coffee, hides, and vegetables
CONTINENT: Asia

Zaire (Democratic Republic of Congo)

CAPITAL: Kinshasa
POPULATION: 44,060,636
MAJOR LANGUAGES: French, Lingala, Swahili, Kingwana, Kikongo, and Tshiluba
AREA: 905,599 sq mi; 2,345,410 sq km
LEADING EXPORTS: copper, coffee, diamonds, cobalt, and crude oil
CONTINENT: Africa

Zambia

CAPITAL: Lusaka
POPULATION: 9,445,723
MAJOR LANGUAGES: English (official) and about 70 various languages
AREA: 290,594 sq mi; 752,610 sq km
LEADING EXPORTS: copper, zinc, cobalt, lead, and tobacco
CONTINENT: Africa

Zimbabwe

CAPITAL: Harare
POPULATION: 11,139,961
MAJOR LANGUAGES: English, Shona, and Sindebele
area: 150,809 sq mi; 390,580 sq km
LEADING EXPORTS: agricultural products and manufactures
CONTINENT: Africa

Glossary of Geographic Terms

basin
a depression in the surface of the land; some basins are filled with water

bay
a part of a sea or lake that extends into the land

butte
a small raised area of land with steep sides

▲ butte

canyon
a deep, narrow valley with steep sides; often has a stream flowing through it

cataract
a large waterfall; any strong flood or rush of water

◄ cataract

delta
a triangular-shaped plain at the mouth of a river, formed when sediment is deposited by flowing water

flood plain
a broad plain on either side of a river, formed when sediment settles on the riverbanks

glacier
a huge, slow-moving mass of snow and ice

hill
an area that rises above surrounding land and has a rounded top; lower and usually less steep than a mountain

island
an area of land completely surrounded by water

isthmus
a narrow strip of land that connects two larger areas of land

mesa
a high, flat-topped landform with cliff-like sides; larger than a butte

mountain
an area that rises steeply at least 2,000 feet (300 m) above surrounding land; usually wide at the bottom and rising to a narrow peak or ridge

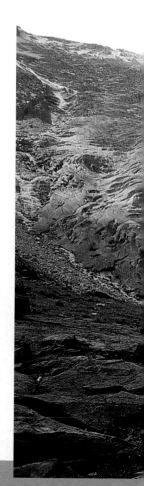

► glacier

◄ delta

mountain pass
a gap between mountains

peninsula
an area of land almost completely surrounded by water and connected to the mainland by an isthmus

plain
a large area of flat or gently rolling land

plateau
a large, flat area that rises above the surrounding land; at least one side has a steep slope

river mouth
the point where a river enters a lake or sea

strait
a narrow stretch of water that connects two larger bodies of water

tributary
a river or stream that flows into a larger river

volcano
an opening in the Earth's surface through which molten rock, ashes, and gasses from the Earth's interior escape

▶ volcano

Gazetteer

A

Aix-en-Provence (43.32°N, 5.27°E) a city in southern France, p. 104

Alpine Mountain System a range of mountains extending through south central Europe; a popular vacation and ski area, includes Mont Blanc, p. 11

Alps (46.18°N, 8.42°E) the major south-central European mountain system; the range includes Mont Blanc and the Matterhorn, p. 13

Asia (50°N, 100°E) the world's largest continent, surrounded by the Arctic Ocean, the Pacific Ocean, the Indian Ocean, and Europe, p. 10

Athens (38°N, 23.38°E) the capital city of modern Greece; the world's most powerful cultural center in the 400s B.C., p. 33

B

Barcelona (41.25°N, 2.08°E) a city and seaport in northeastern Spain, p. 16

Belgrade (44.48°N, 20.32°E) the capital city of Serbia; the capital of the former Yugoslavia, p. 150

Berlin (51.31°N, 13.28°E) the capital city of Germany; divided into East Berlin and West Berlin between 1949 and 1989, p. 74

Buckingham Palace (51.3°N, .08°W) the palace in London, England, where the British king or queen resides, p. 100

C

Caspian Sea (40°N, 52°E) a salt lake that is below sea level, located between Europe and Asia, p. 14

Central Uplands an area of mountains and plateaus in the center of southern Europe; region of pastureland and mining, p. 11

Chernobyl (51.17°N, 30.14°E) the city in northern Ukraine where a nuclear power station accident occurred in 1986, p. 158

Czech Republic (50°N, 15°E) a country in Eastern Europe, p. 84

E

Eurasia the landmass that includes the European and Asian continents, p. 10

Europe (50°N, 15°E) the world's second-smallest continent; a peninsula of the Eurasian landmass bounded by the Arctic Ocean, the Atlantic Ocean, the Mediterranean Sea, and Asia, p. 10

I

Irkutsk (52.16°N, 104°E) a city in east-central Russia, on the Central Siberian Plateau, p. 16

K

Kemerovo (55.31°N, 86.05°E) a city in south-central Russia, p. 162

Kharkov (49.33°N, 35.55°E) a province in eastern Ukraine, p. 160

Kiev (50.27°N, 30.3°E) the capital city of Ukraine, p. 154

L

Locorotondo (40.45°N, 17.20°E) a city in the "heel" of southern Italy, p. 125

London (51.3°N, .07°W) the capital city of the United Kingdom, p. 74

M

Madrid (40.26°N, 3.42°W) the capital city of Spain, p. 74

Mediterranean Sea (36.22°N, 13.25°E) the large sea that separates Europe and Africa, p. 16

Milan (45.29°N, 9.12°E) a city in northwestern Italy, p. 124

Moscow (55.45°N, 37.37°E) the capital city of modern Russia; third-largest city in the world; the home of the czars, p. 161

N

North European Plain a plain extending from the European part of Russia all the way to France, p. 11

North Sea (56.09°N, 3.16°E) an arm of the Atlantic Ocean between Great Britain and the European mainland, p. 24

Northwestern Highlands a mountainous timberland in the far north of Europe, p. 11

P

Paris (48.51°N, 2.2°E) the capital city of France, p. 74

R

Rhine River (50.34°N, 7.21°E) a river flowing from Switzerland north through Germany, then west through the Netherlands, and into the North Sea in Holland, p. 14

Rome (41.52°N, 12.37°E) the capital of modern Italy; one of the world's greatest ancient empires (753 B.C.–A.D. 476), p. 36

Ruhr (51.18°N, 8.17°E) a river along the major industrial region in western Germany, p. 26

Russia (61°N, 60°E) a country in northern Eurasia, p. 10

S

Sarajevo (43.5°N, 18.26°E) the capital city of Bosnia-Herzegovina, p. 146

Siberia (57°N, 97°E) a resource-rich region of Russia, extending east across northern Asia from the Ural Mountains to the Pacific Coast, p. 13

Silesia (50.58°N, 16.53°E) a historic region located in today's southwestern Poland, p. 27

Slovakia (48.5°N, 20°E) a country in Eastern Europe, p. 83

St. Petersburg (59.57°N, 30.2°E) the second-largest city in Russia (previous names: Petrograd, Stalingrad, Leningrad), located on the Baltic Sea; founded by Peter the Great, p. 91

U

Ural Mountains (56.28°N, 58.13°E) a mountain system in northern Eurasia forming part of the border between Europe and Asia, p. 10

V

Vatican (41.54°N, 12.22°E) an independent state situated in Rome; the seat of the Roman Catholic Church and residence of the pope, p. 121

Volga River (47.30°N, 46.20°E) the longest river in Europe, flowing from Russia through Europe to the Caspian Sea, p. 14

Glossary

A

absolute monarch a ruler who has complete power over his or her subjects, for example, Louis XIV of France, p. 43

alliance a mutual agreement between countries to protect and defend each other, p. 52

B

benefit a free service or payment, p. 115

C

ceremony a formal, set activity usually carried out by a group of people, p. 100

chernozem a rich, black soil found in Ukraine, p. 156

city-state a city that is also an independent nation; many existed in ancient Greece, p. 34

civil war a war between groups within a country, p. 62

cobblestone a round stone used with others to make streets before modern paving was invented, p. 74

Cold War a time of tension between the United States and the former Soviet Union without actual war; it lasted from about 1945 to 1991, p. 63

collective a huge government-owned farm, p. 156

colony a territory ruled by another nation, p. 43

Colosseum a stadium built in Rome about A.D. 80, p. 32

communism a theory of government in which property such as farms and factories is owned by the government for the benefit of all citizens; a political system in which the central government controls all aspects of citizens' lives, p. 61

constitutional monarchy a government in which a king or queen is the head of state but has limited powers, for example, the present government of Great Britain, p. 100

consumer goods the goods that ordinary people buy, such as food, clothing, and cars, p. 64

culture language, religious beliefs, values, customs, and other ways of life shared by a group of people, p. 77

custom usual way of doing something, p. 84

czar title of Russian emperors before the formation of the Soviet Union, p. 56

D

debate argument; discussion with people arguing opposite sides of a question, p. 110

democracy a type of government in which people rule themselves through elected representatives, p. 34

dialect a version of a language found only in a certain region, p. 83

dictator a leader who has absolute power, for example, Josef Stalin in Russia, p. 62

E

elegant graceful and beautiful, p. 91

emigrate to move away, or to leave one country to resettle in another, p. 110

empire a large collection of lands ruled by a single government, p. 35

ethnic group a group of people who share the same ancestors, culture, language, or religion, p. 83

F

fate final outcome; what happens, p. 86

feudalism a kind of society in which people worked and sometimes fought for a local lord in return for protection and the use of land, p. 38

fossil fuel fuel developed from the remains of ancient plants and animals; includes coal, oil, and natural gas, p. 26

free enterprise an economic system in which individuals can start and run their own businesses, p. 140

G

goods things and products that people can buy and sell, p. 49

H

heritage the customs and practices passed from one generation to the next, p. 88

Holocaust the execution of 6 million Jews by German Nazis during World War II, p. 129

humanism an approach to knowledge that focused on worldly rather than religious values, p. 41

hydroelectric power the power generated by water-driven turbines, p. 25

I

icon a painting of a saint or holy person used for religious purposes, p. 147

identity a sense of belonging to a certain group or place, p. 126

immigrant a person who moves from one country to another, p. 76

imperialism the control by one country of the political and economic life of another country or region, p. 50

Industrial Revolution a period in European history during the early 1800s when products once made by hand in homes began to be made by machines in factories, p. 48

intricate fancy; complicated; detailed, p. 90

investor a person who spends money on improving a business in hopes of making more money, p. 164

L

loess a type of rich, dustlike soil found on the North European Plain, p. 25

M

manor a piece of land owned by a lord in the feudal system, p. 38

manufacturing the process of turning raw materials into finished products, p. 124

Middle Ages the period in European history between ancient and modern times; approximately A.D. 500–1500, p. 34

middle class a group of people that included traders, merchants, and others who were economically between the poor and the very rich, p. 42

migration a movement from place to place, p. 82

monarch the ruler of a kingdom or empire, such as a king or queen, p. 42

multicultural influenced by many cultures, p. 77

N

national debt the amount of money a government owes, p. 118

nationalism pride in one's country; an elevation of one's own nation above others, p. 51

navigable wide enough and deep enough for ships to travel through, p. 15

P

Parliament a group of elected officials in Great Britain who help govern by deciding about taxes and other laws, p. 99

Pax Romana Roman peace; a 200-year period of peace that began when Augustus, the first emperor of Rome, took power in 27 B.C., p. 36

peninsula land area nearly surrounded by water, p. 11

permafrost soil that is permanently frozen, p. 21

plateau a large, raised area of mostly level land, p. 12

polder a new piece of land reclaimed from the sea; in the Netherlands, land created by building dikes and draining water, p. 9

policy one of the methods and plans a government uses to do its work, p. 34

population density the average number of people living in an area, p. 10

prairie an area of grassland, p. 20

propaganda the spread of ideas designed to promote a specific cause, p. 90

province a political division within a country, similar to a state in the United States, p. 149

R

rain shadow an area on the sheltered side of a mountain that receives little rainfall, p. 18

Renaissance a period of European history that included a rebirth of interest in learning and art, peaking in the 1500s, p. 41

representative a person who represents, or stands for, a group of people, usually in government, p. 99

repress to put down, keep from acting, p. 89

reserves the available supplies of something, such as oil or coal, p. 28

reunification the process of becoming unified again, p. 132

revolution a complete change in government, often achieved through violent means, p. 43

revolutionary relating to or causing the overthrow of a government or other great change, p. 60

S

Scientific Revolution a movement that took place during the 1600s and 1700s, when scientists began to base their study of the world on observable facts rather than on beliefs, p. 44

security safety; freedom from needing or wanting something important, p. 116

serf a person who lived on and farmed a lord's land in feudal times; he or she did not own land and depended on the lord for protection, p. 38

shrine a holy place, p. 142

steppe a mostly treeless plain; in Russia the steppes are grasslands of fertile soil suitable for farming, p. 21

T

taiga an enormous Russian forest, covering more than three million acres, p. 21

tariff a fee or tax that a government charges for goods entering the country, p. 79

textile a cloth product, p. 49

tradition a practice or way of doing something passed from one generation to the next, p. 99

tributary a river or stream that flows into a larger river, p. 14

tundra a treeless plain in arctic areas with permanently frozen ground; during the brief season when the topsoil thaws, grasses and mosses grow, p. 21

U

unified brought together as one; united, p. 43

United Nations an organization of countries established in 1945 that works for peace and cooperation around the world, p. 151

unique one of a kind; having no equal, p. 110

urbanization the movement of populations toward cities and the resulting city growth, p. 76

W

welfare government help to people in need, p. 117

welfare state a country in which many services are paid for by the government, p. 115

westernization the adoption of Western culture, as is taking place in Russia and many Eastern European countries, p. 55

The *italicized* page numbers refer to illustrations. The *m, c, p, t,* or *g* preceding the number refers to maps *(m)*, charts *(c)*, pictures *(p)*, tables *(t)*, or graphs *(g)*.

Index

Acknowledgments

Program Development, Design, Illustration, and Production

Proof Positive/Farrowlyne Associates, Inc.

Cover Design

Olena Serbyn and Bruce Bond

Cover Photo

Jon Chomitz

Maps

GeoSystems Global Corp.

Text

68, From *Pearl in the Egg* by Dorothy Van Woerkom. Copyright © 1980 by Dorothy Van Woerkom. Reprinted by permission of HarperCollins Publishers. 161, 166, Excerpt from "New Face of Russia a Year After Coup, Ordinary Citizens Adapt to Change," by Howard Witt, *Chicago Tribune*, August 16, 1992. Copyrighted, Chicago Tribune Company. All rights reserved. Used with permission. 172, From *Zlata's Diary* by Zlata Filipović, Translation copyright © 1994 Editions Robert Laffont/Fixot. Used by permission of Viking Penguin, a division of Penguin Books USA Inc.

Photo Research

Feldman & Associates, Inc.

Photos

1 T, © Catherine Karnow/Woodfin Camp & Associates, 1 BL, © Comstock, 1 BR © Dewitt Jones/Tony Stone Images, 4, © Mark Thayer, Boston, 7, © Vlastimir Shone/Gamma Liaison International, 8, © Julian Calder/Tony Stone Images, 9, © B. & C. Alexander/Bryan & Cherry Alexander Photography, 10, © M. Feeney/Trip Photographic, 11, © W. Jacobs/Trip Photographic, 13, © James Balog/Tony Stone Images, 14, © Robert Wallis/Sipa Press, 15, © Adam Woolfitt/Woodfin Camp & Associates, 16, © D. MacDonald/Trip Photographic, 19, My Family in Winter, by Helin Tikerpuu, age 12, Estonia. Courtesy of the International Children's Art Museum, 24, © Arnulf Husmo/Tony Stone Images, 27, © Eastcott/Momatiuk/Woodfin Camp & Associates, 29 L, R, © Wolfgang Kaehler/Wolfgang Kaehler Photography, 32, © N. Ray/Trip Photographic, 33, © Matthew Stockman/AllSport USA, 35, © SuperStock International, 36, © Scala/Art Resource, 37, © Erich Lessing/Art Resource, 38, © Marie Ueda/Tony Stone Images, 40, © The Granger Collection, 41 L, © Erich Lessing/Art Resource, 41 R, © Biblioteca Reale, Turin, Italy/SuperStock International, 42 L, R, The Granger Collection, 43, © SuperStock International, 44 L, © Explorer, Paris/SuperStock International, 44 R, © SuperStock International, 46, © Michael Newman/PhotoEdit, 48, © North Wind Picture Archives, 49, © The Granger Collection, 49 (inset), 50 BL, The Bettmann Archive/Corbis-Bettmann, 50 TR, © Stock Montage, 52, © The Granger Collection, 53, © AP/Wide World Photos, 54, © Historical Museum, Moscow, Russia/SuperStock International, 55, © Bridgeman/Art Resource, 57, © M. Jenkin/Trip Photographic, 58, © Stock Montage, 59, © SuperStock International, 60, © Novosti/Corbis-Bettmann, 61, © SuperStock International, 62, © The Granger Collection, 63, © UPI/Corbis-Bettmann, 64, © Reuters/Corbis-Bettmann, 65, © SuperStock International, 69, © Giraudon/Art Resource, 70, © Erich Lessing/Art Resource, 72, © SuperStock International, 73, © David Barnes/Stock Market, 74 T, © SuperStock International, 74 B, © Stephen Johnson/Tony Stone Images, 75, © SuperStock International, 77, © Joseph Okwesa/Trip Photographic, 78, © UPI/Corbis-Bettmann, 79, © Michael Rosenfeld/Tony Stone Images, 81, © Michael Newman/PhotoEdit, 82, © North Wind Picture Archives, 84 L, © Ibrahim/Trip Photographic, 84 R, © Alain Le Garsmeur/Tony Stone Images, 85, Prague Castle, by Darina Vassova, age 10, Czech Republic. Courtesy of the International Children's Art Museum, 87, © AP/Wide World Photos, 88, © SuperStock International, 89 L, © A. Kuznetsov/Trip Photographic, 89 R, SuperStock International, 90, © Alexandra Avakian/Woodfin Camp & Associates, 91, © Joseph Coscia, Jr., Metropolitan Museum of Art, The FORBES Magazine Collection, New York. All rights reserved/Forbes, 92 T, © J. Wiseman/Trip Photographic, 92 B, © Wolfgang Kaehler/Wolfgang Kaehler Photography, 93, © Sichuv/Sipa Press, 97, © John Drysdale/Woodfin Camp & Associates, 99 L, © AP/Wide World Photos, 99 R, © The Bettmann Archive/Corbis-Bettmann, 100, © SuperStock International, 100 (inset), © Stuart Westmorland/Tony Stone Images, 102, © John Madere/Stock Market, 103, © EKA/Eureka Slide, 104, © Chad Ehlers/Tony Stone Images, 106, © SuperStock International, 108, © Corbis-Bettmann, 109 L, © George Hunter/Tony Stone Images, 109 R, © Chad Ehlers/Tony Stone Images, 110 L, © SuperStock International, 110 R, © AP/Wide World Photos, 111, © A. M. Bazalik/Trip Photographic, 112, © Michael Newman/PhotoEdit, 114, © Joseph Nettis/Tony Stone Images, 117, © SuperStock International, 118, © Raymond Reuter/SyGMA, 119 L, © Chad Ehlers/Tony Stone Images, 119 R, © Lorentz Gullachsen/Tony Stone Images, 120, © J. Merryweather/Trip Photographic, 121, © Jean Pragen/Tony Stone Images, 123, © Mary Altier/Mary Altier Photography, 124 L, © George Steinmetz, 124 R, © The Granger Collection, 125, © SuperStock International, 126, © Archive Photos, 127, © AP/Wide World Photos, 130 L, © UPI/Corbis-Bettmann, 130 R, 131, © AP/Wide World Photos, 132 L, © SuperStock International, 132 R, © Corbis-Bettmann, 133, © Owen Franken/Corbis, 136, © Michael Newman/PhotoEdit, 137, © David Young-Wolff, 138, © Steve Vidler/Tony Stone Images, 139, © Momatiuk/Eastcott/Woodfin Camp & Associates, 141, © Reuters/Corbis-Bettman, 141 (inset), © SIPA Press, 142, © Henryk T. Kaiser/Envision, 144, © Bob & Ira Spring/Kirkendahl Spring Photography, 145, © Tony Stone Images, 146, © SuperStock International, 148 TL, © Ibrahim/Trip Photographic, 148 TR, 148 B, 149, © AP/Wide World Photos, 150 T, © Ibrahim/Trip Photographic, 150 B, © AP/Wide World Photos, 151, © Reuters/Corbis-Bettmann, 154, © AP Wide World Photos, 156, © W. Jacobs/Trip Photographic, 157, © SuperStock International, 158, © Corbis-Bettmann, 158 (inset), © Wojtek Laski/Sipa Press, 159 T, B, © UPI/Corbis-Bettmann, 160, © SuperStock International, 161, © SIPA Press, 163, © Wolfgang Kaehler/Wolfgang Kaehler Photography, 164, 164 (inset), © B. & C. Alexander/Bryan & Cherry Alexander Photography, 165, © B. Turner/Trip Photographic, 166, © SuperStock International, 167 L, © Russian State Museum, St. Petersburg, Russia/SuperStock International, 167 R, © J. Lee/Tropix Photographic Library, 170, © Kevin Schafer/Tony Stone Images, 173, © Paul Lowe/Magnum Photos, 174, © Mark Thayer, Boston, 175, © SuperStock International, 177 © Mark Thayer, Boston, 178 T, © Steve Leonard/Tony Stone Images, 178 B, © Robert Frerck/Odyssey Productions, 179 T, © Wolfgang Kaehler/Wolfgang Kaehler Photography, 179 BL, © John Elk/Tony Stone Images, 179 BR, © Will & Deni McIntyre/Tony Stone Images, 189, © G. Brad Lewis/Tony Stone Images, 191, © Nigel Press/Tony Stone Images, 218 T, © A. & L. Sinibaldi/Tony Stone Images, 218 B, © John Beatty/Tony Stone Images, 219 T, © Hans Strand/Tony Stone Images, 219 BL, © Spencer Swanger/Tom Stack & Associates, 219 BR, © Paul Chesley/Tony Stone Images.

The Pink Party

by **Maryann Macdonald**   illustrated by **Judy Stead**

Marshall Cavendish Children

Marshall Cavendish Corporation, 99 White Plains Road, Tarrytown, NY 10591
www.marshallcavendish.us/kids

Library of Congress Cataloging-in-Publication Data
Macdonald, Maryann.
The pink party / by Maryann Macdonald ; illustrated by Judy Stead. —
1st ed.   p. cm.
Originally published in 1994 in a slightly different form by Hyperion
Books for Children; illustrated by Abby Carter.

Summary: Rose and Valentina's friendship is jeopardized by a competition
over who can have the most pink things.
ISBN 978-0-7614-5814-2
[1. Pink—Fiction. 2. Friendship—Fiction.] I. Stead, Judy, ill. II.
Title.
PZ7.M1486Pi 2011
[E]—dc22
2010018173

The illustrations are rendered in digital media.
Editor: Margery Cuyler
Printed in Malaysia (T)
First edition
1 3 5 6 4 2

For Leia, who loves pink

–M.M.

To Zoe, my daughter and pink-party muse

–J.S.

Rose and Valentina were best friends.
They loved pink more than anything else in the world!

"I wish I had a magic wand," Valentina said.
"I'd make everything pink!"
"Even Fluffy?" asked Rose. "Even me?"

"Even Fluffy and you," said
Valentina. "Even your teeth."
And they both giggled.

One day, Rose got a new pink lunch box. She raced over to Valentina's house to show her.

"Is it okay if I get one, too?" Valentina asked.

Rose's heart tripped, then tumbled . . .
but she was afraid to say no.

When Rose met Valentina for school the next morning, her friend was wearing a pink backpack.

"The pink lunch boxes were sold out," said Valentina, "so I got this instead. See the heart-shaped pockets?"

Big deal, thought Rose, but she still didn't say a word.

"If you like pink so much," said Rose's dad, "let's paint your rocking chair pink."

Rose couldn't wait.

She helped her father pick out the paint, and they painted all afternoon.

"Wow!" said Valentina when she saw the shiny pink chair.
"I'm going to paint my playhouse pink."
Copycat, thought Rose, but even then she didn't say anything.

The next day, a pink envelope arrived in
Rose's mailbox, and she opened it.

You
are
invited
to
a
Pink
Party
for
Valentina's
birthday
on
Saturday
come
dressed
in
Pink!

Rose was excited! She and her mother dyed her old nightgown pink to make a princess dress.

They made a crown with pink stars all over it.

Rose's dad helped her make a magic wand for Valentina's present.

The wand was so pretty that Rose wanted to keep it for herself. But instead she wrote "V A L E N T I N A" on it in pink letters and added glitter. She couldn't wait for the party!

When Rose got to Valentina's on Saturday, Lateesha and Kim were already there. Lateesha was a pink fairy, and Kim was a pink butterfly.

"Ooooh!" they both said when they saw Rose's princess costume.

But then Valentina twirled out in a pink tutu, pink satin slippers, and a pink diamond tiara.

"OOOOooooh!" everyone said.

Valentina pranced around her pink playhouse.
All the girls followed her, all but Rose. She
couldn't keep quiet any longer.

"Show-off!" she yelled.
Then she grabbed the wand she had made for Valentina
and marched back home.

She rocked in her pink rocker on her porch and tried to feel better, even though she could hear her friends having fun next door.

She rocked and rocked until all of their friends had said good-bye.
Then she heard a voice from the other side of the hedge.

"The party's over," Valentina said.

Rose pretended she didn't hear.

"I saved you a pink cupcake and some pink lemonade," Valentina went on.

Even though she was hungry, Rose looked the other way.

"Okay, Rose," Valentina said at last, "I'm sorry I was such a show-off. I was just sooo excited about my party!"

Rose sighed. Then in a very small voice she said, "I'm sorry, too, Valentina. I'm sorry I left the party. I was just sooo jealous!"

"That's okay," said Valentina. "Can you come over now and play? Pleeease?"

"All right," said Rose. She ran inside and got the magic wand.

Valentina loved the wand.
She and Rose took turns playing with it
and all the other pink birthday presents.

At last, they squeezed onto Rose's swing and pretended they were flying.

"Even though I do have a magic wand now," said Valentina, "I've decided I don't want everything in the world to be pink."

"No," said Rose, "some things are perfect just the way they are. Like chocolate."

"Like snow," said Valentina.

"Like me and my teeth," said Rose.

Valentina giggled.
"But I still think some things might look
better in pink," she said.

So she decided to give it a try.

278 2155

JE
MAC

Macdonald, Maryann

The Pink Party

$16.99

GAYLORD